THROUGH THE LOOKING GLASS
Readings in General Anthropology

Second Edition

edited by

Lee Cronk
and
Vaughn M. Bryant

Boston Burr Ridge, IL Dubuque, IA Madison, WI New York San Francisco St. Louis
Bangkok Bogotá Caracas Lisbon London Madrid
Mexico City Milan New Delhi Seoul Singapore Sydney Taipei Toronto

McGraw-Hill Higher Education
*A Division of **The McGraw-Hill** Companies*
THROUGH THE LOOKING GLASS: READINGS IN GENERAL ANTHROPOLOGY

This book is printed on acid-free paper.

1 2 3 4 5 6 7 8 9 0 FGR/FGR 9 0 9 8 7 6 5 4 3 2 1 0 9

ISBN 0-07-228605-9

Editorial director: *Phillip A. Butcher*
Editorial assistant: *Miriam Beyer*
Marketing manager: *Leslie A. Kraham*
Project manager: *Paula M. Krauza*
Production supervisor: *Michael R. McCormick*
Freelance design coordinator: *Laurie J. Entringer*
Cover designer: *Heidi Baughman*
Credit: *Lisette Le Bon/Superstock*
Printer: *Quebecor Printing Book Group/Fairfield*

Library of Congress Cataloging – in – Publication Data

Through the looking glass: readings in general anthropology/
[edited by] Lee Cronk, Vaughn M. Bryant. – 2nd ed.
 p.   cm
ISBN 0-07-2286059 9 (softcover)
1. Anthropology.   I. Cronk Lee.   II. Bryant, Vaughn M.
GN29.T48 2000
301—dc21   99-35391

http://www.mhhe.com

TABLE OF CONTENTS

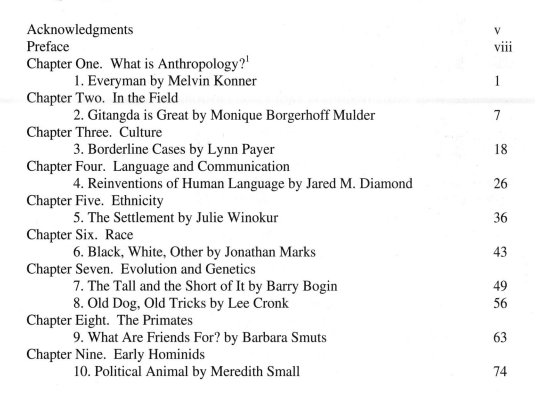

---

[1] Chapter titles are from *Anthropology, 8th Edition*, by Conrad Kottak. McGraw-Hill.

ACKNOWLEDGEMENTS

Konner, Melvin. 1988. Everyman. *The Sciences,* Nov/Dec: 6-8. Reprinted by permission of the author.

Borgerhoff Mulder, Monique. 1996. Gitangda is Great. In *I've Been Gone Far Too Long: Field Trip Fiascoes and Expedition Disasters.* Edited by Monique Borgerhoff Mulder and Wendy Logsdon. Copyright © 1996 RDR Books, 4456 Piedmont Ave., Oakland, CA 94611. Reprinted with permission from the publisher.

Payer, Lynn. 1990. Borderline Cases. *The Sciences* July/August: 38-42. Reprinted by permission of the New York Academy of Sciences.

Diamond, Jared M. 1991. Reinventions of Human Language. *Natural History* 5/91: 22-28. Reprinted by permission of the American Museum of Natural History.

Winokur, Julie. 1996/97. The Settlement. *Natural History* December/January: 38-49. Reprinted by permission of the American Museum of Natural History.

Marks, Jonathan. 1994. Black, White, Other. *Natural History* 12/94: 32-35. Reprinted by permission of the American Museum of Natural History.

Root-Bernstein, Robert, and Donald L. McEachron. 1982. Teaching Theories: The Evolution-Creation Controversy. *The American Biology Teacher* (October). Reprinted by permission of the National Association of Biology Teachers.

Cronk, Lee. 1992. Old Dog, Old Tricks. *The Sciences,* January/February: 2-4. Reprinted by permission of the New York Academy of Sciences.

Smuts, Barbara. 1987. What Are Friends For? *Natural History* 2/87: 36-44. Reprinted by permission of the American Museum of Natural History.

Small, Meredith. 1990. Political Animal. *The Sciences*, March/April: 36-42. Reprinted by permission of the New York Academy of Sciences.

Pringle, Heather. 1998. New Women of the Ice Age. *Discover* 19(4):62-69. Reprinted by permission of the publisher.

Diamond, Jared M. 1995. Why is a Cow like a Pyramid? *Natural History* 7/95: 10-12, 74-77. Reprinted by permission of the American Museum of Natural History.

Bryant, Vaughn M., Jr. 1993. In Search of the First Americans. In *1993 Yearbook of Science and the Future*, pp 8-27. Copyright © 1992 Encyclopedia Britannica, Inc. Reprinted by permission of Encylopedia Britannica, Inc.
Bryant, Vaughn M., Jr. 1995. The Paleolithic Health Club. In *1995 Yearbook of Science and the Future*, pp 114-133. Copyright © 1994 Encyclopedia Britannica, Inc. Reprinted by permission of Encylopedia Britannica, Inc.

Cronk, Lee. 1989. Strings Attached. *The Sciences,* May/June: 2-4. Reprinted by permission of the New York Academy of Sciences.

Chagnon, Napoleon. 1992. Prying Into Yanomamö Secrets. In *Yanomamö: The Last Days of Eden*, pp 23-29, 164-170. Harcourt Brace & Co. New York. Reprinted by permission of the publisher.

Roach, Mary. 1998. Why Men Kill. *Discover* 19(12):100-108. Reprinted by permission of the publisher.

Betzig, Laura. 1994. Sex in History. *Michigan Today* 26(1):1-3. Reprinted by permission of the author.

Bryant, Vaughn M., Jr. and Sylvia Grider. 1991. To Kiss. *The World and I*, December, pp 612-619. Copyright © 1991. Reprinted by permission of The Washington Times Corporation.

Goldstein, Melvyn C. 1987. When Brothers Share a Wife. *Natural History* 3/87: 39-48. Reprinted by permission of the American Museum of Natural History.

Diamond, Jared M. 1993. What Are Men Good For? *Natural History* 5/93: 24-29. Reprinted by permission of the American Museum of Natural History.

Layng, Anthony. 1989. What Keeps Women "In Their Place?" *USA Today Magazine*

(Society for the Advancement of Education), May. Reprinted by permission of the publisher.

Nash, June. 1994. Judas Transformed. *Natural History* 3/94: 46-53. Reprinted by permission of the American Museum of Natural History.

Fromartz, Samuel. 1998. Anything But Quiet. *Natural History* 3/98: 44-49. Reprinted by permission of the American Museum of Natural History.

Wilson, Samuel M. 1993. Coffee, Tea, or Opium? Natural History 11/93: 74-79. Reprinted in *The Emperor's Giraffe and Other Stories of Cultures in Contact*, written by Samuel M. Wilson and published by Westview Press of Boulder, Colorado, a member of the Perseus Books Group. Reprinted here by permission of the Perseus Books Group.

Roosevelt, Anna. 1992. Secrets of the Forest. *The Sciences*, November/December: 22-28. Reprinted by permission of the New York Academy of Sciences.

Cronk, Lee, and Beth Leech. 1993. "Where's Koisa?" *The World & I*, January, pp. 612-621. Reprinted by permission of the publisher.

Hossack, Phil. 1999. Return of the Kayak. *Canadian Geographic*, January/February, pp. 58-64. Reprinted by permission of the author.

Köhler-Rollefson, Ilse. 1995. Camels in the Land of Kings. *Natural History* 3/95: 54-61. Reprinted by permission of the American Museum of Natural History.

Klein, Alan M. 1993. Of Muscles and Men. *The Sciences,* November/December, pp. 32-37. Adapted from the book *Little Big Men: Bodybuilding Subculture and Gender Construction* by Alan M. Klein, published by the State University of New York Press. Copyright © 1993. Reprinted with permission from SUNY Press.

The first edition of this collection was edited by Bryant along with David Carlson, also of the Department of Anthropology at Texas A&M University. The effort that Dr. Carlson put into that edition has made our work on this edition that much easier, and we thank him for it. The editors would also like to thank those members of the staff of the Department of Anthropology at Texas A&M University who helped with the preparation of this volume, including Joyce Bell, Carolee Davis, Becky Jobling, Jeff Olson, Barbara Spears, and Karen Taylor, as well as the many people at McGraw-Hill, including Miriam Beyer, Nancy Blaine, and Alan McClare, who shepherded the book through the editing and production processes.

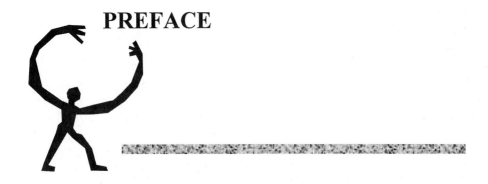

PREFACE

For more than ten years, each of us has taught a general introduction to anthropology using a variety of approaches and texts. We have gradually converged on Conrad Kottak's *Anthropology* (McGraw-Hill), supplemented by readings and monographs. This volume is an outcome of our efforts to create a collection of articles to supplement Kottak's excellent textbook. The present collection of thirty articles, mostly from popular books and magazines, includes at least one suggested reading for each of the twenty-two chapters and the Appendix in the eighth edition of Kottak's text.

Introductory students do not need any prior knowledge of anthropology to understand and hopefully, to enjoy the articles presented here. Although the presentation and sequence follows the latest edition of Kottak's *Anthropology* textbook, we believe that the readings are well-suited to any introductory course. In selecting these readings, we have emphasized readability and articles which illustrate fundamental concepts and questions in anthropology. Of the thirty articles included, all but six were originally published in the 1990s.

We would appreciate comments, criticism, and recommendations from any instructors and students who use this reader in their classes.

Lee Cronk
Vaughn M. Bryant, Jr.
Department of Anthropology
Texas A&M University
College Station, TX 77843-4352

EVERYMAN[1]

Melvin Konner

As Konner notes, anthropologists love to poke holes in simplistic assumptions about human nature. In fact, there are some basic characteristics and capacities that are common to human societies everywhere. Understanding the uniqueness of human culture requires an appreciation for both its common and variable features.

Gathered together in front of their huts, during the days of leisure after harvest-time, the Tiv, of Nigeria, had regaled Laura Bohannon with legends and folktales. It seemed only polite, then, that the anthropologist return the favor. So one day, over the customary bowls of beer, Bohannon recounted a tale whose appeal seemed so universal, it was sure to touch the hearts of the tribe's elders. But although they enjoyed the story, they were baffled by many parts. Hamlet, the young prince, objected to the idea that his mother might marry Claudius? Certainly the man was obligated to marry his brother's widow. The ghost of Hamlet's father had accused Claudius of murder? This must have been an omen sent by a witch! The prince's betrothed, Ophelia, had gone mad and drowned? What could be more conclusive proof of sorcery? And when Laertes had thrown himself on his sister's corpse in the open grave, hadn't he exposed himself as the witch? Bohannon, slightly inebriated and very confused, was forced to conclude that she had guessed wrong about the play's universal appeal.

Her experience has a familiar ring: an anthropologist encounters a way of thinking so unpredictable, it calls into question our basic assumptions about what all humans are like. There is the "semen belt" of New Guinea, a geographic stripe in which pubescent boys practice homosexuality, believing they must imbibe semen to grow, and then abandon the behavior in adulthood—thus overturning virtually every theory of how sexual orientation develops. And there are the grotesquely fat African queens and densely scarified Polynesian maidens who expose our own, Western ideal of beauty as parochial.

[1]Reprinted from *The Sciences*, Nov/Dec, 1988. Reprinted by permission of the author.

Finding exceptions to our assumptions about human nature has become the anthropologist's stock-in-trade. "Not among the people I study, they don't!" we cry when anyone mentions standards of behavior thought to apply to everyone. Indeed, some people choose anthropology as a career specifically to break down ethnocentrism, that special brand of egocentrism shared by members of a society, who feel superior to nonmembers and are unable to see clearly beyond their own, narrow cultural perspective. Those who overgeneralize—psychologists with their grand sex-role theories; plastic surgeons with their so-called classic ideal of beauty—offend us.   This is the meaning, in anthropology, of the term cultural relativism: that our very perception of reality, especially social and psychological reality, is conditioned by culture to such an extent that, without ethnological studies, we could go through life, and even through history, with blinders on. Unquestionably, anthropology's most important contribution to human knowledge so far has been to reveal the world's great cultural diversity. Ironically, though, this penchant has led to a new sort of smugness. Anthropologists have become so obsessed with the mission of overturning generalizations about human behavior that they have obscured a separate reality. Beneath the vast array of cultural variations are features of behavior that do not vary. There is, in fact, a human nature, which all of us share. And the only way to understand it fully is to find out exactly what it is made of, to know which behaviors are universal. The question is, Can anthropologists finally accept this challenge and, without sacrificing the glory of cultural relativism, identify the qualities that make us human?

An important first step toward understanding the basic similarities between cultures was taken, surprisingly, before twentieth-century anthropologists ever began their study of human diversity. In 1872, Charles Darwin wrote *The Expression of the Emotions in Man and Animals*, in which he compared the behavior of different animals as he had compared their physical traits in *The Origin of Species* thirteen years earlier—with a view toward understanding evolutionary relationships. Specifically, he compared the ways in which various mammals engage in nonverbal communication, the physical manifestations of such emotions as fear and anger. He presented vivid line drawings depicting dogs with their hackles raised, their eyes widened, their ears laid back, and the corners of their mouths drawn taut. Alongside these, he displayed realistic sketches of human faces with essentially the same fearful expressions. And to complete the picture, he provided written descriptions of primitive peoples—provided by missionaries and other travelers—whose facial expressions of fear were identical to those of the Europeans he had depicted. Darwin's conclusion: the similarities in emotional reaction displayed by different cultures, and different species, offer proof that they descended from common ancestors and thus share many traits.

Darwin's monograph inspired the science of ethology, the evolutionary study of behavior. But during the science's early years, speculations about the biological underpinnings of human behavior were widely misinterpreted as evidence that one sex, or one race, was superior to another. These misconceptions ultimately had grave political consequences, and as a result, ethologists limited themselves to studying animals, and anthropologists concentrated on the differences, not the similarities, between humans.

It was not until the 1960s that the German ethologist Irenäus Eibl-Eibesfeldt, now at the Max Planck Institute for Behavioral Physiology, in Seewiesen, West Germany, carried forward the work that Darwin had begun a century earlier. Instead of comparing drawings, Eibl-Eibesfeldt looked at films of human behavior, which he shot among diverse cultures, including the Waika of Venezuela, the Huri of New Guinea, the Balinese, the Trobriand Islanders, the Bushmen and the Himba of Namibia, as well as the Bavarians of Germany. Because his camera filmed sideways, through a mirror, so that the subjects could not tell when they were being watched, he was able to capture candid moments.

In reviewing the films, Eibl-Eibesfeldt found himself watching certain standard behaviors over and over. Toddlers in societies throughout the world engaged in hitting, kicking, biting, and spitting at one another. Adults, when embarrassed, hid their faces, and when disappointed, pouted—Indonesian, African, and European alike. And when two people met, anywhere, they usually raised and lowered their eyebrows abruptly. This gesture—called an eyebrow flash, because it takes no more than half a second—was typically accompanied with a brief, slight lift of the head and was often followed by a smile. Eyebrow flashes were used to signal parting, flirting, or agreement; if the eyebrows remained raised, disdain, or even threat.

While Eibl-Eibesfeldt was collecting his films, linguistic anthropologists were beginning to recognize certain universals in human language. They demonstrated that despite the immense variety of tongues spoken by different peoples, any infant can be placed within any culture and learn to speak the language. That is, Chinese babies are no better at learning Chinese than Brazilian babies would be, and American babies are not inherently adept at learning English. This is true because all languages are basically alike. In the sixties, Charles F. Hockett, a professor of anthropology at Cornell University, identified eight key features that characterize them. These include displacement—the way in which words can be used to describe events in the past or in the future, or in some distant location; arbitrariness—the lack of any intrinsic ties between particular words and what they represent (languages often go through major changes in vocabulary and pronunciation); and duality of patterning —the way in which the order of sounds in one word can be rearranged to produce a wholly different word (meat and team, for example). Thus, any human baby capable of learning to use the eight features is capable of learning any language.

Beyond these universals, of facial expression and language, other uniformities of human behavior have been discovered, albeit unintentionally, by the very anthropologists whose mission has been to document diversity. Some behaviors, they have found, are not manifest in everyone, but merely are tendencies that characterize a particular age group. Not all one-year-olds cry when their parents leave them with strangers, for example. But in all cultures, no matter what the child-rearing traditions, one-year-olds are much more likely to protest than are six-month-olds or four-year-olds. Other universals have been found among members of one sex or the other. Males of all ages, in every culture, exhibit more physical aggressiveness than do females (though there is great overlap in distributions: the most aggressive females are far more violent than the least aggressive males). Such patterns tell us as much about the underlying regularity of human nature as do the universals that apply to every one of us.

Anthropologists have also documented a tendency, in all human cultures, toward certain unusual, even antisocial behaviors. Some have gone to great lengths to find communities in which homicide does not occur, but this search has proved only that no such communities exist. And as Jane M. Murphy, of the Harvard School of Public Health, and others have shown, mental illnesses corresponding to schizophrenia, mania, and depression are recognized in all cultures. In some cases, one or another of these syndromes, when first manifest in an individual, may be mistaken for a culturally sanctioned hallucination, a shamanistic activity, or the like. But when the illness persists, it is ultimately recognized for what it is.

Universals of behavior often are reflected in the habits, rules, and institutions of whole societies. In his book *Social Structure,* published in 1949, the anthropologist George Peter Murdock, of the University of Pittsburgh, analyzed two hundred and fifty cultures and discovered that all have standards for determining who may have sex with whom. The most prevalent of these standards is the incest taboo. Murdock also found that one of the most important universals of culture is the nuclear family. "Either as the sole prevailing form of the family or as the basic unit from which more complex familial forms are compounded," he said, "it exists as a distinct and strongly functional group in every known society."

At the time that Murdock made this assertion, it contradicted the views of other anthropologists—for example, Ralph Linton, of Columbia University, a leader of the discipline in the thirties, who had said that the nuclear family has "an insignificant role in the lives of many societies." Linton cited the Nayar, a warrior caste in India, in which it was said to be common for newly married men to go off and live permanently among other soldiers, leaving their wives to take lovers at home. But examination of the culture revealed that this description was exaggerated and that the nuclear family is, in fact, important in Nayar society. Later, in 1954, Melford E. Spiro, now of the University of California at San Diego, cited the Israeli communal farm, the kibbutz, as an exception, because members collectively took on traditional family responsibilities. But by 1953, many kibbutzim had begun to back away from their strictly communal ideology and to allow families more responsibility for child rearing, meal preparation, and so on. Clearly, the attempt to do away with the nuclear family had failed.

This is but a brief sampling of the many similarities already observed between people in different cultures. If students of culture were to conduct a determined search, perhaps they could come up with a nearly complete accounting of the attributes all people share, no matter what their race, homeland, upbringing, or way of life. But most anthropologists are still inclined to disregard universals, arguing that the standard behaviors of mankind are only the dull foundation of the house of culture, which ends where all the interesting design features begin.

The great drawback of this way of thinking is that it prevents us from developing a science of human nature, for every science needs some framework of known principles with which to understand disparate phenomena. The science of biology could not advance until Linnaeus came up with a taxonomy that clarified and codified the relationships between various animals. Physics could not move forward until Newton delineated the basic principles of gravitation and objects in motion. Similarly, anthropologists cannot fully appreciate the significance of human diversity until they grasp the fundamentals of human nature—until they establish a human "biogram," a list of the characteristics common to all cultures.

Beyond enabling us to construct a more complete picture of what it is to be human, a full accounting of human universals would help unify anthropology and biology. After all, there is strong reason to suspect that all uniformities of human culture are biologically based. Assuming that the Waika and the Trobrianders developed their own cultures in isolation from each other, why would members of each group raise their eyebrows in greeting, in the exact same manner, unless this behavior was a reflex wired into their brains? And why would every culture in the world respect and rely on some form of the nuclear family, unless humans had some inherent propensity to do so?

When Charles Hockett identified the underlying similarities in languages, the suspicion arose that these features reflect similarities in all human brains. Displacement, arbitrariness, and duality of patterning, Hockett suggested, must be fundamental skills embedded in our neurological pathways. Anthropologists initially responded to this insight by suggesting that it was only the large size of the human brain—its great capacity and flexibility—that, in a general way, provided the thinking power to enable people in all cultures to develop language. But that was before much was known about the brain. As our understanding of neurology advances, it becomes more and more obvious that, indeed, our brains contain many highly specialized circuits, some of them designed to make possible the use of human language.

It will be quite some time before anyone will be able to discern exactly which circuits correspond to such things as the eyebrow flash, the development of fears of separation among one-year-olds, and the propensity for homicidal violence.

But, at least, by allowing that these behaviors are universal, we can assume that they have a biological substrate—that we perform them because our brains are wired for them and that the pattern for this wiring is coded in our genes. Then, by exploring the full extent of universals, we can learn the degree to which attributes of culture are inherent and thus inflexible. None of this undermines efforts to investigate the great diversity of culture; it only reveals which aspects of different cultures are truly diverse.

In this light, we can reconsider Bohannon's exchange with the Tiv. Certainly, the elders' bewilderment reflected their own, unique cultural expectations. But, beneath their confusion, one can discern a foundation of common understanding. Despite their belief that it was Claudius' duty to marry Gertrude, the Tiv were still outraged by the possibility that Claudius might have murdered his brother. They understood perfectly Hamlet's conflict between revenge for his father's death and grief at the thought of murdering his own uncle. And although they thought witchcraft had muddied the waters (much as a Western reader would assume madness had), they still responded to much of the play as we do: throughout its telling, they were riveted, and at the end, they said, as we have said, "That was a very good story."

2

Gitangda Is Great[1]

Monique Borgerhoff Mulder

The knowledge cultural anthropologists have accumulated about the world's peoples is based primarily on their fieldwork, and all successful fieldwork depends ultimately upon the people anthropologists study. As Borgerhoff Mulder can attest, efforts to gain the cooperation of a group under study can lead to some unusual adventures and some unexpected lessons about the true nature of such things as religion and rituals.

"Prepare beer 7/14/88. 7/15/88 slaughter sheep and prepare *loghamajeg*. Following Wednesday 7/16/88 set off for Fuweid, returning 7/17/88." Village Chairman, Milanda 6/27/88

The village chairman put down his pencil stub, removed sunglasses made from the bottoms of two beer bottles, and extended his hand. Our written arrangements were formalized with joint signatures. Honey beer was to be prepared on the 14th of July; a sheep to be slaughtered on the 15th, and the *loghamajeg* skin strips to be cut. On the evening of the 15th we were to arrive at his house, and at dawn on the 16th start our great pilgrimage to the Ngorongoro

Highlands with three Datoga elders. Our purpose was to pay homage to the grave of Gitangda, apical ancestor of the Daremejeg clan, spiritual leaders of the Bajuta, a subtribe of the Datoga. Gitangda had been killed in battle by the Maasai at a critical juncture in Datoga history in the middle of the last century—their eviction from the lush, rich, green Ngorongoro Highlands.

The Datoga, Tanzanian pastoralists who herd their cattle on the dry plains in the north of the country, honor their dead in a most elaborate fashion. At a man's death, his family starts to prepare a *bungeid*, the Datoga name for his funereal monument. Over a period of anything from three to eight months a pyramidal structure of stones, sticks, and

[1]Originally published in *I've Been Gone Far Too Long: Field Trip Fiascoes and Expedition Disasters*. Edited by Monique Borgerhoff Mulder and Wendy Logsdon. Copyright 1996 RDR Books, 4456 Piedmont Ave., Oakland, CA 94611. Reprinted with permission from the publisher.

earth is built over the deceased's body in a corner of his homestead. After the completion of the *bungeid* construction several hundred relatives, clan members, and neighbors come for dancing and feasting. This very ritualized celebration can last as long as a month and finishes with the eldest sons of each of the deceased's wives climbing on the *bungeid* and placing grass, honey beer, and tobacco on its cone. After these events the visitors leave and within a few days the family of the deceased abandon the old homestead. With time the eight-foot fence that protected the cattle at night from the attack of lions and leopards sinks to the ground and the flat-roofed huts fall to the ravage of termites, with the result that only a weather-beaten *bungeid* stands as a beacon to the old man and his ancestry. The *bungeid*, however, is not forgotten. For many years to come, sons and their descendants, clan members, and even Datoga of different clans and subtribes will travel to this site to pay their respects at the funeral monument of a revered ancestor.

Unknown to the visitors and indeed most Tanzanians is that one of the two most sacred Datoga *bungeidinga* (plural of *bungeid*) stands on the floor of the Ngorongoro Crater—attesting to the long history of human habitation of an area now renowned primarily for its wildlife. Ironically, traditional herdsmen are now largely prohibited from entering the crater. To learn more about the Datoga's early nineteenth-century occupation of the Ngorongoro Highlands (known to the Datoga as Fuweid),

their eviction from this sanctuary at the hands of the Maasai, and to observe the rituals involved in their honoring of an important ancestor, I decided to organize a motorized pilgrimage, starting from the eastern shore of Lake Eyasi, where I was conducting research on Datoga pastoralism and family life.

As an anthropologist who had only just begun working with the Datoga, I saw a number of potential advantages to this escapade, other than what I would of course learn about Datoga history and culture. Most important, it would gain for me some much needed street credibility. The Datoga, like most livestock herders in East Africa, are justifiably proud of their ability to thrive in an environment in which agriculturalists (of which I am an especially sorry specimen in their eyes—my father owns less than five acres which we don't farm) wilt. We are constantly digging thorns out of our feet and gasping for water at the end of a day's walk. Furthermore, since we are unable to wield a spear, we are derogatorily referred to with a Kiswahili phrase *chakula cha kuki* which means food for the spear, on which we sometimes presumably end up.

Luckily, from the start of my project in 1987, some Datoga families had been kind to me, inviting me to live in their homesteads. They nevertheless took pleasure in criticizing everything I did. My feeble attempts to make a cow, terrified at the sight of a white person, yield milk deserved such ridicule. But I found it harder to take criticism for skills of which I was more proud, such as driving across rocky river beds or taking notes in almost pitch-dark huts, particularly since no Datoga in the community knew how to do either of these things. I had already learned to live with my apparent ineptitude (anthropologists do well to wear thick skin), but I increasingly sensed a need to upgrade my image. By visiting a sacred site deep in the country of the forsworn enemy neighboring tribe, the Maasai, with a group of respected Datoga elders, albeit in the relative safety and comfort of a Land Rover, I might gain just a little respect, especially if we did everything right.

In respect for Tanzanian Democratic Socialism I left the choice of our guides to Simon, a Datoga who as *Mwenye Kiti* ("him having the chair" is the literal translation of the Kiswahili term) has nominal control over some scattered ten cell units; these are all that is left of the Tanzanian government's attempts to develop socialist awareness at the northern end of the Lake Eyasi basin. Simon had presented himself to me the year before as a leader, albeit with one of the natural weaknesses that accompany leadership in these remote parts: a fondness for beer. This year, on hearing of my interest in visiting Gitangda's *bungeid*, Simon studiously developed an itinerary. On this (see the epigraph to this story) I shook his hand.

On the afternoon of the 15th, Momoya, Daniela, and I headed up the lakeside towards Simon's home, as instructed. Momoya had been a friend

and ally since the day I arrived at Lake Eyasi in 1987; at seventeen years of age (in 1988), he was one of the very few Datoga young men who had some years of primary education (before the school teacher was murdered) and he speaks good Kiswahili, the national language of Tanzania. Daniela was new to the area; that summer she was initiating a research project on the role of women in Datoga society.

Passing the party office in Milanda we were a little surprised to see a group of six Maasai elders under a tree, drinking bottled Safari beer—a rarity in the Eyasi backwaters. Maasai warriors lurked in the bushes beyond. I looked more carefully and spotted Simon amongst the elders, jubilant. He caught sight of the Land Rover and came to welcome us excitedly. He explained that last month some Datoga had killed a number of Maasai at the top of the escarpment near Endulin, and intertribal relations had become even more tense than usual. He had therefore called a meeting of elders. It was clear that, at least today, the ice had melted. A crate of twenty-five bottles, mostly empties, lay in the shade of the tree. Simon and each of the Maasai elders were delivering elaborate rhetoric on the sanctity of *umoja* (the national slogan denoting unity), usually at the same time, and frequently drifting out of Kiswahili back into their mother tongues, Kimaasai and Kidatoga. The designated clerk for the meeting, a man from a different ethnic group altogether, scribbled frantically, looking seriously confused.

I was hungry and tired, having just come back from a week of exhausting demographic survey work at the south end of the lake. I did not relish the prospect of joining in the revelry. Indeed, knowing my fuse would be short, I decided to stay in the car and wait until Simon had finished his meeting. Daniela and Momoya did likewise. Beers (by now hot) were brought for us. Daniela was regaled with offers of marriage by a toothless septuagenarian Maasai who insisted he was called "Land Rover" (which, due to the common interchange of "r" and "l" in this language, sounded more like "randy lover"). Toward evening the interethnic summit was drawn to a close and we accompanied Simon to the house of the old man who was to lead us to Gitangda's *bungeid* next day. Empties of course had to be returned, so I decanted the last of several Safari lagers into my large water bottle.

Forty minutes later we were at Hirba's home, an idyllic spot at the northern end of the lake, encircled with duomo palms through which the evening breeze gently rustled. The picturesque elder who, in my mind's eye, was to star on the cover of some glossy magazine such as *Natural History* as a representative of the remarkably beautiful Datoga people, strolled out of his house in a pink hat and a very inauthentic garish *shuka* (cloth wrap). His side-kick, Girgis, an uncle half Hirba's age, looked decidedly surly and sported a floral shirt beneath his more traditional black

shuka. Simon, staggering unmistakably as he coasted from the Land Rover door, was rebuked by Hirba: Why had he brought us so late? It was now dusk and too dark to slaughter the sheep. The itinerary was already violated; we would not be able to leave at dawn the next day, as custom dictates for pilgrimages to a *bungeid*. Simon uttered some weak excuse pertaining to the urgency of his meeting with the Maasai, and the matter was dropped. More importantly, the beer was brewing and had to be tested, so we each took a sample, served in a long ivory-colored ox horn. Datoga beer is essentially mead; we found it mixes nicely with Safari lager. At some stage much later in the evening, Daniela, Momoya, and I left, agreeing to return at dawn the next morning to slaughter the sheep so we could still make an early getaway to Fuweid.

At 4:30 A.M. on the dot Momoya woke me, responding to his magical and unfailing internal alarm clock. I proposed that we should leave Daniela to sleep. She had just done two, two-day focal studies, which entailed staying in a woman's company and recording all her work and social activities. To collect these data Daniela moved into her subject's household and slept in her hut, so long as the woman was willing; most found it great fun. Because this was an exceptionally dry July and the women had much work to do drawing water from distant springs and seepages, they would often get up to grind maize and do housework in the small hours of the night, dozing off again before dawn. Daniela had consequently stayed up most of the last four nights recording activities and was exhausted. In addition, she would not be very interested in watching a sheep be suffocated to death, the traditional form of slaughter among the Datoga. I therefore suggested to Momoya that we pick her up when we returned from the north end of the lake, on our way to Ngorongoro. This however was not acceptable. Some ritual had to be performed at the slaughter, and Daniela would not be eligible to pay her respects to Gitangda if she failed to show up for the slaughter.

We crashed through the bush into Hirba's place soon after dawn and were taken into a hut where a sheep was slowly being suffocated to death. As blood began to spout from its nose, the skinning began. Numerous triangular strips were cut from the chest and then slit with a knife; they were then placed as rings over the right-hand middle finger of each of us pilgrims. I got a reasonably fluffy bit on which the blood had already congealed; Daniela's was long and still very bloody. Finally with a gourd of soured milk, a large pot of honey beer, a saucepan of meat, and some tobacco we left.

Within ten minutes of leaving Hirba's, Simon asked me to stop. All three elders climbed out of the back with their pots and paraphernalia and headed into the bush. Momoya explained something about another *bungeid*. Daniela and I were horrified; how many *bungeidinga* are there between here and Ngorongoro? It turned out we were

stopping for the grave of Hirba and Simon's father, a great-great-great-grandson of Gitangda; this was reasonable, so we relaxed, and enjoyed watching the golden early morning sunlight creep along the rift valley wall. After half an hour or so the men returned, in fine spirits, and we started off on the perilously eroded tracks that skirt the west and southern sides of Oldeani Mountain, finally reaching the main road up into the Ngorongoro Highlands. Signing in at the Conservation Area gate was awkward: my *loghmed* was much less attractive than it had been in the morning. I had had to top up the rear differential oil, and an oily scrap of rather fatty, fresh goat skin left its mark on the Free Permit Entry book.

We wound our way up into the cold, clouded forest of the crater rim, completed some painless formalities at the Ngorongoro Headquarters (our rather unorthodox visit had been cleared in advance with the authorities), and followed the rim road around to the wide deep slopes stretching northwards to the Serengeti plains. Here you feel like you are on top of the world, as you gaze across the endless savannah that melts into the sky. We stopped at the junction with a steep road leading down into the crater. Hirba, Simon, and Girgis peered down one thousand feet below in anticipation and excitement: Our pilgrimage had now begun in earnest.

We reached the crater floor and headed towards the Lerai Forest, for it was on the fringes of the forest that the *bungeid* was supposed to stand. Hirba had been here before some forty years ago with his father and a group of singing women. Driving toward Lerai, we stopped several times for Hirba to *piga ramani* (fix a map in his head), which entailed his getting bearings from the numerous cattle paths that zigzag down the crater wall. Before reaching the forest he directed me up to Fig Tree campsite where a magnificent old tree shades a lush meadow. Since the Kenya/Tanzania border reopened to tourists in 1984 this has become a very busy spot with permanently pitched tents, toilets, and showers. Hirba clambered out of the back of the Land Rover, looking exceptionally confused by these new amenities, talked a lot more about piga ramani and disappeared, with his cronies and their spears, into the long grass.

It was hot and I was tired from the six-hour drive; I was also rather disappointed at Hirba's lack of conviction as to where exactly the *bungeid* stood. From everything Momoya and I had heard earlier, it was on the other side of the forest. I felt that we were wasting time at this particular spot, and went to sit in the shade for a long drink of water from my bottle. It was yesterday's beer but it didn't seem to matter. Forty-five minutes later there was a squeal of brakes as a park warden's pickup spun on two wheels into Fig Tree campsite with three very frightened Datoga crouched in the back. I was bombarded with accusations: "my tourists" were on foot and not in a vehicle, and were therefore flaunting a principal Conser-

vation Authority regulation that is intended to ensure the safety of tourists. For my lack of responsibility I was to forfeit my Land Rover and be immediately driven up to the chief park warden's office on the rim. Our pilgrimage was off.

It was of course true that Hirba and company had been footing it across the bush, but I was at a loss to know how to plead our case. Datoga live in the remotest of bush country, killing elephants, lions, and buffalo with only a spear. These were no blue-rinsed American dowagers venturing out to pat a lion, and they hardly seemed at great personal risk, given their ancestors had survived in this very crater for centuries. Inevitably, of course, I played abjectly apologetic: what a senseless, irresponsible, cruel *mzungu* (white person) I was, sending my servants out at such personal danger to look for a private campsite for me (this was, of course, what the warden thought I was up to); how kind of the warden to retrieve my men, etc. After a good deal of this the warden left, convinced that Europeans were even more stupid than he had previously imagined. We had a good laugh, particularly over Hirba and his crews' smart pretense of failing to understand even a word of Kiswahili, the national language of Tanzania.

After the warden's departure, Hirba, rather shaken by the events of the last hour, confided privately that he was having some problems with his bearings. The shape of the rim and the lines of the cattle paths suggested to him that the *bungeid* was nearby, but he, Simon, and Girgis had searched the area high and low before they were picked up by the warden, and they could not find it. I drank some more "water" and came to a quick decision; it was already 5 P.M. Rather than search on the three other sides to the forest, we should go straight to the rangers' forest post and ask if any of the rangers knew where the Datoga *bungeid* was. This was dreadfully humiliating to all concerned, but it seemed the only feasible option if we were to get settled at our shrine before dark.

At the Lerai cabin, adjacent to the ranger station, there were some strange goings-on. First, there was a white woman preparing an enormous fruit salad out of passion fruit, papaw, pineapples, and mangos, apparently for nobody--at least there was no one around. The sight of this enormously cheered Daniela, who had been sunk in gloom and exhaustion since 4:30 A.M.; we hadn't eaten anything fresh for a long time; it was nice just to look at the cut fruit. Next, gathered in the shade behind the cabin we spotted about seven young men. Momoya must, I think, have thought they were off-duty rangers because, pointing towards the forest, he asked if any of them knew where Gitangda's *kaburi* was; *kaburi* is a pretty reasonable translation of *bungeid* into Kiswahili (it means grave). At this question, the young men swung into a frantic excited cross-examination of Momoya: "Who? Where is he? Does he live here? Is he still alive? Can we go and see him?" Momoya backed off

nervously. I subsequently found out that this was a group of West African students with only a smattering of Kiswahili. They must have been anticipating quite a spectacle, perhaps the remains of a body recently gored by a rhino.

At the ranger station itself we found a very helpful man, who knew exactly what we were looking for and offered to guide us. He happened to be Maasai. He climbed into the Land Rover, casting withering looks on the four Datoga unable to find their own sacred site. The elders kept their eyes fixed on their spears and the gourds of honey beer. The ranger, a very educated man, explained to me in English that the Datoga would occasionally come down to the *bungeid* in the crater to sing and make offerings, so he knew the site well.

He directed us straight back along the track to Fig Tree campsite, where Hirba had first alighted. Here we left the car and followed our Maasai guide to the showers, from the showers to the toilets, from around the back of the toilets into the deep grass where people went when they didn't quite make it to the toilets in time, from the deep grass to the rubbish pits, and then finally, from around the back of the campsite dump, picking our way over Kimbo cooking-oil cans, we reached a small heap of stones–Gitangda's *bungeid*, with its own empty tin of Blue Band margarine rampant. Suddenly there was a flurry of activity. Hirba had all of a sudden got his *ramani* straight and knew exactly where everything was.

In his words, "the toilets and showers disappeared back into the future." He and the other two elders raced to the car and came back with their equipment. Leather sandals were kicked off, beer was gulped and then spat over the stones, same for the milk; tobacco and meat were placed between the stones, and *loghamajeg* skin strips were attached to the rough face of the small monument. By the time Daniela had collected her camera from the Land Rover it was all over, and anyhow the light was bad and the rubbish heap was most unsightly.

Then there was a wild scamper, gourds and sandals swinging, across the campsite to the huge fig onto which more *loghamajeg* were pinned and the same victuals offered. This horrified the Americans enjoying their sundowners in the comforting shelter of the great tree; it amazed the safari company cooks who were preparing the tourists' beef bourguignon on a fire set in the roots of the sacred tree. Little did any of them know they were camped at the shrine of Magusachand, father of brave Magena who subsequently saved the Datoga from the continued ravages of the Maasai after the death of Gitangda. Daniela and I struggled unsuccessfully to get pictures of these rituals in the dying light under the vast dark fig canopy, between taking off our own shoes and spitting beer and milk in the requisite spots. The elders, at least, were content with their work and settled down to the gourds of honey beer. I drove our Maasai guide back to his post and returned to Fig Tree campsite to face the interethnic music.

The tourists' tents were already pitched and their food was being cooked as they tranquilly gazed on the Ngorongoro Crater, "a spectacle of a lifetime" in the golden evening light. We rather upset the tone of things. Up went my old army tent, and outside it sat four Datoga wrapped in their dirty blankets, with two equally dirty Englishwomen, all drinking large quantities of honey beer out of ox horns and getting progressively more raucous. At some stage during the evening—about when the safari group, largely comprised of elderly ladies, were about to be served their dinner—the elders demanded their food. Under the invaluable instruction of Momoya, we chopped up the sheep (not a young one) with an ax, and prepared the fire and *ugali* (a staple maize porridge). Momoya exhibited his limitless skills in cross-cultural dialogue by getting onions and salt with which to increase the palatability of our efforts from the Mbulu cooks of the safari company. When the food was ready we brought water for the men to wash their hands and served our meal. After much yarn-telling deep into the night about who Gitangda, Magusachand, and Magena were, what they did and how they died, the men retired into my tent and Daniela and I snuggled up with the toolbox and mutton bones in the back of the Land Rover.

The next morning it was exceptionally cold and the old men, taking their cue from the safari campers, demanded early morning tea, and subsequently more ugali and meat. Daniela and I did the honors again and then, as we were clearing up this feast, the old men nipped off back to Gitangda's *bungeid* to make their parting offerings of beer, etc., each taking home a small handful of soil from the grave as a souvenir. Somehow between scrubbing the pans and taking down the tent, we again managed to miss valuable anthropological data and photo footage. Simon also took the Blue Band can (it would be useful at home, he said), and the other two raided the rubbish pit and came back with bottles, cans, and half a pot of *pili-pili* sauce (a wonderful hot relish that turns any meal into a feast). This was a bonanza—never had Gitangda so much to offer!

The back of the car was by now a stinking pit of slopped honey beer and sour milk, dirty calabashes and rubbish, but everyone was happy. We had apparently done everything just right. There was certainly no mention ever again of the help we received from the Maasai ranger. After all, had we not reached the spot, consumed sufficient quantities of beer and soured milk, made the appropriate offerings to Gitangda and Magena, decorated the graves with *loghamajeg*, and recounted heroic tales of our ancestors into the night? Was this not what a successful pilgrimage required? There was much serious discussion on this question, and unanimously it was agreed that we had succeeded on every count. It seemed that, with the Datoga at least, conducting rituals is a lot less demanding than one might suspect from reading anthropo-

logical texts, where ceremonies are laid out as a list of prescriptions, not the (let's be honest now) bungled amalgam of memory-dredging, improvisation, and chance that I was witnessing. I was learning a lot about what ritual really entails, with its intriguing blend of solemnity and fun.

As our discussion drew to a close, it emerged there was another requirement of pilgrims, and this was to return home immediately when the business was successfully completed, to ease the fears of the loved ones left behind; Maasailand after all is not a safe place for a Datoga. On this particular occasion, however, Simon proposed that a little "game drive" would not constitute a serious infringement. A quick loop around the Gorrigor Lake, which the Datoga knew to be the core home range of a large pride of lions, was agreed upon by all. Daniela was thrilled. She had never been in the Ngorongoro Crater before, and until now it looked like all she might see of this jewel, aptly dubbed "the eighth wonder of the world," would be its rubbish dump and toilets.

Momoya too was delighted. He has a limitless ability to adapt to all cultural contexts. We could hang out happily together, whether as free guests entertaining tourists at safari lodges, on month-long stints in the bush with the Datoga, paying courtesy calls on party officials in Arusha, or at the postseminar dinner parties of Serengeti Wildlife Institute scientists. Momoya is apparently at home everywhere, initiating conversation and asking stimulating and provocative questions of everyone he comes across, so long of course as the conversation stays in Kiswahili. His infinite social skills never failed to amaze me.

But he follows one rule that helps a lot: a variant of "When in Rome...." And he had followed it that morning. Knowing that white people love to have showers at every opportunity, he reckoned that as a camper at Fig Tree campsite he should take advantage of the facilities, and accordingly headed off to the little shower hut in front of Gitangda's *bungeid*. This is indeed what the American and European visitors to the Crater do, but in the heat of the day, not at 6:00 A.M. when the Crater is shrouded in freezing fog and bitter chill. There is of course no hot water. Without a towel he had dried himself with the thin cotton shuka that he subsequently wore and three hours later, despite the tea and mutton, he still looked blue in the face. The idea of a game drive, while the sun gradually rose in the sky, pierced through the early morning mist, and warmed the metal flanks of the Land Rover, strongly appealed to Momoya.

We didn't have to go very far before everyone was satisfied. The first scan through binoculars over Gorrigor Lake revealed a dramatic sight; a lion and lioness consuming a hippo carcass in the reeds. Daniela and I sat up front with the Datoga in the back. We could approach quite closely and our passengers turned frantic with excitement. A Datoga man can earn up to fifty cows and a reputation for life from spearing a lion, if he has witnesses. But lions, like all wild animals, are of course protected in the Ngorongoro Conservation Area. The threat of ever-tightening knuckles on the spears did not, however, unnerve me; I had lain all four spears safely under the spare tire, in anticipation of just such an encounter. We, and finally the lions, left safely, with no Conservation Authority regulation violated.

More delighted than ever, we decided to call our game drive to a close and headed for the "up" road, slowly climbing the tortuous crater wall and watching Magusachand's tree get smaller and smaller beneath us. Back at Hirba's the following evening (we had to delay our return to replace a broken spring leaf in the local town), our arrival stimulated considerable sprinting through the bush. The neighboring women who were supposed to welcome us pilgrims with singing and dancing had given up and gone home when we failed to arrive the previous night. However the car's engine, which could be heard for miles over the Eyasi Basin, drew them again to their posts. It was a pretty sight, arriving at sunset on the side of the lake, to see the track to Hirba's gate lined with women in their beaded leather finery, singing songs about the bravery of Gitangda and Magena in their battles with the Maasai. We relaxed in the cool evening air and were served more honey beer which we drank with the men of the local community.

To some extent we were heroes ourselves, having done everything as custom dictates. The game drive, the Maasai ranger, the drunkenness the night before we left, these things were all forgotten. Momoya had lost his loghmed; he probably left it in the shower (this he whispered to me as we reached the crater rim—I refused to go back down for it), but luckily no one had noticed, for it is a serious violation of custom not to wear a loghmed for three days following the pilgrimage; he was now drinking beer with his left hand. In everyones' eyes, and even our own, we

would bring a measure of peace and prosperity to the Datoga of Eyasi, on behalf of Gitangda and Magena.

Finally the singing was over, and we were left to drink deep into the night. The women from neighboring households went home—one with a Blue Band can, another with a half-full jar of *pili-pili*.

Gitangda is great, or so the legend goes. Certainly the woman with the pili-pili believed it.

3

Borderline Cases[1]

Lynn Payer

The power of culture to shape human behavior in radically different ways is easy to see when we look at the great variety of human societies around the world. When we look at areas in which scientific evidence is supposed to hold sway, however, we expect a certain uniformity. Lynn Payer argues that this is not necessarily the case. Even in the rigorous, scientific field of Western medicine, there are remarkable cultural differences among practitioners from different countries regarding such issues as the diagnosis and treatment of disease.

Marie R., a young woman from Madagascar, was perplexed. Hyperventilating and acutely anxious, tired and afflicted with muscle spasms, she visited a French physician who told her she suffered from spasmophilia, a uniquely French disease thought to be caused by magnesium deficiency. The physician prescribed magnesium and acupuncture and advised her that, because of the danger associated with the disease, she should return home to the care of her parents.

Yet when Marie R. ultimately moved to the United States, American physicians diagnosed her symptoms quite differently. As she soon learned, spasmophilia, a diagnosis that increased sevenfold in France between 1970 and 1980, is not recognized as a disease by American physicians. Instead Marie R. was told she suffered from an anxiety disorder; only after taking tranquilizers and undergoing psychotherapy did her condition improve. Now she seems cured, though she still wonders what she has been cured *of*.

Western medicine has traditionally been viewed as an international science, with clear norms applied consistently throughout western Europe and North America. But as Marie R.'s experience illustrates, the disparity among the diagnostic traditions of England, France, the United States and West Germany belies the supposed universal-

[1]This article is reprinted by permission of *The Sciences* and is from the July/August 1990 issue. Individual subscriptions are $28 per year. Write to: *The Sciences*, 2 East 63rd Street, New York, NY 10021.

ity of the profession. In 1967 a study by the World Health Organization found that physicians from several countries diagnosed different causes of death even when presented with identical information from the same death certificates. Diagnoses of psychiatric patients vary significantly as well: until a few years ago a patient labeled schizophrenic in the U.S. would likely have been called manic-depressive or neurotic in England and delusional psychotic in France.

Medical treatments can vary as widely as the diagnoses themselves. Myriad homeopathic remedies that might be dismissed by most U.S. physicians as outside the realm of scientific medicine are actively prescribed in France and West Germany. Visits to the many spas in those countries are paid for by national health insurance plans; similar coverage by insurance agencies in the U.S. would be unthinkable. Even for specific classes of prescription drugs there are disparities of consumption. West Germans, for instance, consume roughly six times as much cardiac glycoside, or heart stimulant, per capita as do the French and the English, yet only about half as much antibiotic.

In one recent study an attempt was made to understand why certain coronary procedures, such as angiography—a computer-aided method of observing the heart—and bypass surgery, are done about six times as frequently in the U.S. as they are in England. Physicians from each country were asked to examine the case histories of a group of patients and then determine which patients would benefit from treatment. Once cost considerations were set aside, the English physicians were still two to three times as likely as their American counterparts to regard the procedures as inappropriate for certain patients. This result suggests that a major reason for the frequent use of the procedures here has less to do with cost than with the basic climate of medical opinion.

The diversity of diagnoses and treatments takes on added importance with the approach of 1992, the year in which the nations of the European economic community plan to dissolve all barriers to trade. Deciding which prescription drugs to allow for sale universally has proved particularly vexing. Intravenous nutrition solutions marketed in West Germany must contain a minimum level of nitrogen, to promote proper muscle development; in England, however, the same level is considered toxic to the kidneys. French regulators, following their country's historic preoccupation with the liver, tend to insist with vigor that new drugs be proved nontoxic to that organ.

Ultimately the fundamental differences In the practice of medicine from country to country reflect divergent cultural outlooks on the world. Successful European economic unification will require a concerted attempt to understand the differences. At the same time, we Americans, whose medicine originated in Europe, might gain insight into our own traditions by asking the same question: Where does science end and culture begin?

West German medicine is perhaps best characterized by its preoccupation with the heart. When examining a patient's electrocardiogram, for example, a West German physician is more likely than an American internist to find something wrong. In one study physicians following West German criteria found that 40 percent of patients had abnormal EKGs; in contrast, according to American criteria, only 5 percent had abnormal EKGs. In West Germany, patients who complain of fatigue are often diagnosed with *Herzinsuffizienz,* a label meaning roughly weak heart, but it has no true English equivalent; indeed, the condition would not be considered a disease in England, France or the United States. Herzinsuffizienz is currently the single most common ailment treated by West German general practitioners and one-major reason cardiac glycosides are prescribed so frequently in that country.

In fact, for older patients, taking heart medicine is something of a status symbol—in much the same way that not taking medicine is a source of pride among the elderly in the U.S. Some West German physicians suggest that such excessive concern for the heart is a vestige of the romanticism espoused by the many great German literary figures who grappled with ailments of the heart. "It is the source of all things," wrote Johann Wolfgang von Goethe in *The Sorrows of Young Werther,* "all strength, all bliss, all misery." Even in modern-day West Germany, the heart is viewed as more than a mere mechanical device:

it is a complex repository of the emotions. Perhaps this cultural entanglement helps explain why, when the country's first artificial heart was implanted, the recipient was not told for two days - allegedly so as not to disturb him.

The obsession with the heart—and the consequent widespread prescription of cardiac glycosides — makes the restrained use of antibiotics by West German physicians all the more striking. They decline to prescribe antibiotics not only for colds but also for ailments as severe as bronchitis. A list of the five drug groups most commonly prescribed for patients with bronchitis does not include a single class of antibiotics. Even if bacteria are discovered in inflamed tissue, antibiotics are not prescribed until the bacteria are judged to be causing the infection. As one West German specialist explained, "If a patient needs an antibiotic, he generally needs to be in the hospital."

At least a partial explanation for this tendency can be found in the work of the nineteenth-century medical scientist Rudolph Virchow, best known for his proposal that new cells arise only from the division of existing cells. Virchow was reluctant to accept the view of Louis Pasteur that germs cause disease, emphasizing instead the protective role of good circulation. In Virchow's view numerous diseases, ranging from dyspepsia to muscle spasms, could be attributed to insufficient blood flow to the tissues. In general, his legacy remains strong: if one is ill, it is a reflection of internal imbalances, not external invaders.

In French medicine the intellectual tradition has often been described as rationalist, dominated by the methodology of its greatest philosopher, René Descartes. With a single phrase, *cogito ergo sum,* Descartes managed logically to conjure forth the entire universe from the confines of his room. His endeavor is looked on with pride in France: every French schoolchild is exhorted to "think like Descartes."

Abroad, however, Cartesian thinking is not viewed so favorably, as it often manifests itself as elegant theory backed by scanty evidence. When investigators at the Pasteur Institute in Paris introduced a flu vaccine that had the supposed ability to anticipate future mutations of the flu virus, they did so without conducting any clinical trials. More recently, French medical workers held a press conference to announce their use of cyclosporin to treat AIDS - even though their findings were based on a mere week's use of the drug by just six patients. American journalists and investigators might have been less puzzled by the announcement had they understood that, in France, the evidence or outcome is not nearly as important as the intellectual sophistication of the approach.

Disease in France, as in West Germany, is typically regarded as a failure of the internal defenses rather than as an invasion from without. For the French, however, the internal entity of supreme importance is not the heart or the circulation but the *terrain*—roughly translated as constitution, or, more modernly, a kind of nonspecific immunity. Consequently, much of French medicine is an attempt to shore up the *terrain* with tonics, vitamins, drugs and spa treatments. One out of 200 medical visits in France results in the prescription of a three-week cure at one of the country's specialized spas. Even Pasteur, the father of modern microbiology, considered the *terrain* vital: "How many times does the constitution of the injured, his weakening, his morale . . . set up a barrier to the invasion of the infinitely tiny organisms that is insufficient."

The focus on the *terrain* explains in part why the French seem less concerned about germs than do Americans. They tolerate higher levels of bacteria in foods such as foie gras and do not think twice about kissing someone with a minor infection: such encounters are viewed as a kind of natural immunization. Attention to the *terrain* also accounts for the diagnostic popularity of spasmophilia, which now rivals problems with hearing in diagnostic frequency. One is labeled a spasmophile not necessarily because of specific symptoms but because one is judged to have some innate tendency toward those symptoms.

Although French medicine often attempts to treat the *terrain* as a whole, the liver is often singled out as the source of all ills. Just as West Germans tend to fixate on herzinsuffizienz, many

French blame a "fragile liver" for their ailments, whether headache, cough, impotence, acne or dandruff. Ever since French hepatologists held a press conference fourteen years ago to absolve the liver of its responsibility for most diseases, the *crise de foie* has largely gone out of style as a diagnosis—though one still hears of the influence of bile ducts.

Unlike their French and West German counterparts, physicians in England tend to focus on the external causes of disease and not at all on improving circulation or shoring up the *terrain*. Prescriptions for tonics, vitamins, spa treatments and the like are almost absent, and antibiotics play a proportionally greater role. The English list of the twenty most frequent prescriptions includes three classes of antibiotics; in West Germany, in contrast, the top-twenty list includes none.

English physicians are also known for their parsimony, and for that reason they are called (by the French) "the accountants of the medical world." They do less of virtually everything: They prescribe about half as many drugs as their French and West German counterparts; and, compared with U.S. physicians, they perform surgery half as often, take only half as many X rays and with each X ray use only half as much film. They recommend a daily allowance of vitamin C that is half the amount recommended elsewhere. Overall in England, one has to be sicker to be defined ill, let alone to receive treatment.

Even when blood pressure or cholesterol readings are taken, the thresholds for disease are higher. Whereas some physicians in the U.S. believe that a diastolic pressure higher than ninety should be treated, an English physician is unlikely to suggest treatment unless the reading is more than a hundred. And whereas some U.S. physicians prescribe drugs to reduce cholesterol when the level is as low as 225 milligrams per decaliter, in England similar treatment would not be considered unless the blood cholesterol level was higher than 300.

To a great extent, such parsimony is a result of the economics of English medicine. French, U.S. and West German physicians are paid on a fee-for-service basis and thus stand to gain financially by prescribing certain treatments or referring the patient to a specialist. English physicians, on the other hand, are paid either a flat salary or on a per-patient basis, an arrangement that discourages overtreatment. In fact, the ideal patient in England is the one who only rarely sees a physician—and thus reduces the physician's workload without reducing his salary.

But that arrangement only partly accounts for English parsimony. Following the empirical tradition of such philosophers as Francis Bacon, David Hume and John Locke, English medical investigators have always emphasized the careful gathering of data from randomized and controlled clinical trials. They are more likely than their colleagues elsewhere to include a placebo in a clinical trial, for example. When the U.S. trial for the Hypertension Detection and Follow-up Program was devised, American physicians were so certain mild hypertension should be treated, they considered it unethical not to treat some patients. A study of mild hypertension conducted by the Medical Research Council in England, however, included a placebo group, and the final results painted a less favorable picture of the treatment than did the American trial.

Almost across the board, the English tend to be more cautious before pronouncing a treatment effective. Most recently experts in England examined data regarding the use of the drug AZT by people testing positive for HIV (the virus associated with AIDS). These experts concluded that the clinical trials were too brief to justify administration of the drug, at least for the time being. Americans, faced with the same data, now call for treatment.

American medicine can be summed up in one word: aggressive. That tradition dates back at least to Benjamin Rush, an eighteenth-century physician and a signer of the Declaration of Independence. In Rush's view one of the main obstacles to the development of medicine was the "undue reliance upon the powers of nature in curing disease," a view he blamed on Hippocrates. Rush believed that the body held about twenty-five pints of blood—roughly double the actual quantity—and urged his disciples to bleed patients until four-fifths of the blood had been removed.

In essence, not much has changed. Surgery is more common and more extensive in the U.S. than it is elsewhere: the number of hysterectomies and of cesarean sections for every 100,000 women in the population is at least two times as high as are such rates in most European countries. The ratio of the rates for cardiac bypasses is even higher. Indeed, American physicians like the word *aggressive* so much that they apply it even to what amounts to a policy of retrenchment. In 1984, when blood pressure experts backed off an earlier recommendation for aggressive drug treatment of mild hypertension, they urged that nondrug therapies such as diet, exercise and behavior modification be "pursued aggressively."

To do something, anything, is regarded as imperative, even if studies have yet to show conclusively that a specific remedy will help the patient. As a result, Americans are quick to jump on the bandwagon, particularly with regard to new diagnostic tests and surgical techniques. (Novel drugs reach the market more slowly, since they must first be approved by the Food and Drug Administration.) Naturally, an aggressive course of action can sometimes save lives. But in many instances the cure is worse than the disease. Until recently, American cardiologists prescribed antiarrhythmia drugs to patients who exhibited certain signs of arrhythmia after suffering heart attacks. They were afraid that not to do so might be considered unethical and would leave them vulnerable to malpractice suits. But when the treatment was finally studied, patients who received two of the three drugs administered were dying at a higher rate than patients who received no treatment at all. Likewise, the electronic monitoring of fetal heart rates has never been shown to produce healthier babies; in fact, some critics charge that incorrect diagnosis of fetal distress, made more likely by the monitors, often leads to unnecessary cesarean sections.

Even when the benefits of a treatment are shown to exceed the risks within a particular group of patients, American physicians are more likely to extrapolate the favorable results to groups for which the benefit-to-risk ratio has not been defined. American physicians now administer AZT to people who are HIV-positive. But some physicians have taken the treatment a step further and are giving the drug to women who have been raped by assailants whose HIV status is unknown—to patients, in other words, whose risk of infection may be low. Whether the pressure for treatment originates with the patient or with the physician, the unspoken reasoning is the same: it is better to do something than it is to do nothing.

Unlike the French and the West Germans, Americans do not have a particular organ upon which they focus their ills—perhaps because they prefer to view themselves as naturally healthy. In reading the obituary column, for instance, one notices that no one ever dies of "natural" causes; death is always as-

cribed to some external force. Disease, likewise, is always caused by a foreign invader of some sort. As one French physician put it, "The only things Americans fear are germs and Communists." The germ mentality helps explain why antibiotic use in the U.S. is so high: one study found that American physicians prescribe about twice as much antibiotic as do Scottish physicians, and Americans regularly give antibiotics for ailments such as a child's earache for which Europeans would deem such treatment inappropriate. The obsession with germs also accounts for our puritanical attitudes toward cleanliness: our daily washing rituals, the great lengths to which we go to avoid people with minor infections, and our attempts to quarantine people with diseases known to be nontransmissible by casual contact alone.

Nor do Americans exhibit much patience for the continental notion of balance. Substances such as salt, fat and cholesterol are often viewed by U.S. physicians as unmitigated evils, even though they are essential to good health. Several studies, including a recent one by the National Heart, Blood and Lung Institute in Bethesda, Maryland, have shown that if death rates in men are plotted against cholesterol levels, the lowest death rates are associated with levels of 180; cholesterol levels higher or lower are associated with higher death rates. Low cholesterol levels have been linked to increased rates of cancer and even suicide - yet Americans tend to be proud when their levels are low.

The array of viable medical traditions certainly suggests that medicine is not the international science many think it is. Indeed, it may never be. Medical research can indicate the likely consequences of a given course of action, but any decision about whether those consequences are desirable must first pass through the filter of cultural values. Such a circumstance is not necessarily bad. Many of the participants at a recent symposium in Stuttgart, West Germany, felt strongly that the diverse medical cultures of Europe should not be allowed to merge into a single one. Most medical professionals, however, ignore the role cultural values play in their decisions, with unfortunate consequences.

One result is that the medical literature is confusing. The lead paper in a 1988 issue of *The Lancet,* for example, superficially appeared to satisfy international standards of medical science. Its authors were German and Austrian; the journal was English; and the paper itself, which addressed the treatment of chronic heart failure, made reference to the functional classification of this disorder by the New York Heart Association. But on a closer look an American cardiologist found that many of the patients referred to in the paper would not, according to U.S. standards, be classified as having heart failure at all. Fewer than half of the patients' chest X rays showed enlargement of the heart, an almost universal finding in people with heart failure as diagnosed in the U.S. It would take a careful reader—or one attuned to German diagnostic traditions—to ferret out such misleading results.

The diverse ways different countries practice medicine present a kind of natural experiment. Yet because few people are aware of the experiment, no one is collecting the rich data the experiment could supply. What is the effect, for example, of the widespread prescription of magnesium for spasmophilia in France and for heart disease in West Germany? Likewise, soon after the hypertension drug Selacryn was introduced to U.S. markets, two dozen people died of liver complications attributed to the drug. Yet Selacryn had already been used for several years in France. Had similar cases gone unnoticed there and been attributed to the fragility of the French liver? Lacking an awareness of their differing values, medical experts of different nations may be missing out on an opportunity to advance their common science.

Finally, recognizing American biases may help us head off medical mistakes made when our own instincts lead us astray. As English medicine frequently illustrates, it is *not* always better to do something than it is to do nothing. And as the continental outlook reveals, a more balanced view of the relation between the individual and the disease might make us less fearful of our surroundings. If we put our own values in perspective, future decisions might be made less according to tradition and more according to what can benefit us most as physicians and patients.

4

REINVENTIONS OF HUMAN LANGUAGE[1]

Jared M. Diamond

How was language invented? Jared Diamond explores this question by looking at pidgins and creoles, simplified mixtures of two languages. Although these simple languages may sound like baby-talk to our ears, they are vastly more complex than the call systems used by non-human primates.

Try to understand this advertisement for a department store, in a language related to English:

Kam insait long stua bilong mipela—stua bilong salim olgeta samting—mipela i-ken helpim yu long kisim wanem samting yu laikim bikpela na liklik long gutpela prais.

If some of the words look strangely familiar but don't quite make sense, read the ad aloud to yourself, concentrate on the sounds, and ignore the strange spelling. As the next step, here is the same ad rewritten with English spelling:

Come inside long store belong me-fellow—store belong sellim altogether something—me-fellow can helpim you long catchim what-name

something you likim, big-fellow na liklik, long good-fellow price.

A few explanations should help you make sense of the remaining strangenesses. All the words in this text are derived from English, except for the word *liklik* for "little." The strange language has only two pure prepositions: *bilong,* meaning "of" or "in order to," and *long,* meaning almost any other English preposition. The English consonant *f* becomes *p,* as in *pela* for "fellow." The suffix *-pela* is added to monosyllabic adjectives (hence *bikpela* for "big") and also makes the singular pronoun "me" into the plural "we" (hence *mipela*). *Na* means "and." Thus, the ad means:

Come into our store—a store for selling everything—we can help you get what-

[1]Reprinted with permission from *Natural History* 5/91. Copyright © 1991 American Museum of Natural History.

ever you want, big and small, at a good price.

The language of the ad is Neo-Melanesian, alias New Guinea pidgin English, which serves in Papua New Guinea (PNG) as the language not only of much conversation but also of many schools and newspapers, and much parliamentary discussion. It developed as a lingua franca for communication between New Guineans and English-speaking colonists, and among New Guineans themselves, since PNG boasts about 700 native languages within an area similar to California's. When I arrived in PNG and first heard Neo-Melanesian, I was scornful of it. It sounded like long-winded, grammarless baby talk. On talking English according to my own notion of baby talk, I was jolted to discover that New Guineans weren't understanding me. My assumption that Neo-Melanesian words meant the same as their English cognates led to spectacular disasters, notably when I tried to apologize to a woman in her husband's presence for accidentally jostling her, only to find that Neo-Melanesian *pushim* doesn't mean "push" but instead means "have sexual intercourse with."

Neo-Melanesian proved to be as strict as English in its grammatical rules and as capable of expressing complex ideas. Its supple vocabulary is based on a modest number of core words whose meaning varies with context and becomes extended metaphorically. As an illustration, consider the derivation of *banis bilong susu* as the

Neo-Melanesian words for "bra." *Banis,* meaning "fence," comes from that English word as spoken by New Guineans who have difficulty pronouncing our consonant S and our double consonants like *nc. Susu,* taken over from Malay as the word for "milk," is extended to mean "breast" as well. That sense, in turn, provides the expressions for "nipple" (*ai* [eye] *bilong susu*), "prepubertal girl" *(i no gat susu bilong em),* "adolescent girl" *(susu i sanap* [stand up]), and "aging woman" *(susu i pundaun pinis* [fall down finish]). Combining these two roots, *banis bilong susu* denotes a bra as the fence to keep the breasts in, just as *banis pik* denotes pigpen as the fence to keep pigs in.

At first, I ignorantly assumed that Neo-Melanesian was a delightful aberration among the world's languages. It had obviously arisen in the 170 years since English ships started visiting New Guinea, but I supposed that it had somehow developed from baby talk that colonists spoke to natives they believed incapable of learning English. Only when I began working in Indonesia and learned the language did I sense that Neo-Melanesian origins exemplified a much broader phenomenon. On the surface, Indonesian is incomprehensible to an English speaker and totally unrelated to Neo-Melanesian because its vocabulary is largely Malay. Still, Indonesian reminded me of Neo-Melanesian in its word use and in the grammatical items that it possessed or lacked.

As it turns out, dozens of other languages resemble Neo-Melanesian and Indonesian in structure. Known as pidgins and creoles (I'll explain the difference later), they have arisen independently around the globe, with vocabularies variously derived largely from English, French, Dutch, Spanish, Portuguese, Malay, or Arabic. Their interest stems from the insights they may offer us into human language origins, the most challenging mystery in understanding how our species rose from animal status to become uniquely human. Linguist Derek Bickerton's articles and his stimulating recent book, *Language and Species* (University of Chicago Press, 1990), have much to say on this subject and are the basis for my discussion here.

Language is what lets us communicate with one another far more precisely than can any animals. It lets us lay joint plans, teach one another, and learn from what others experienced elsewhere or in the past. With it, we can mentally store precise representations of the world and hence encode and process information far more efficiently than can any animals. Without language we could never have conceived and built Chartres Cathedral—or the gas chambers of Auschwitz. These are the reasons for speculating that our species' Great Leap Forward within the last hundred thousand years—that stage in human history when innovation and art at last emerged, and when modern *Homo sapiens* replaced Neanderthals in Europe—was made possible by the emergence of spoken language.

Between human language and the vocalizations of any animal lies a seemingly unbridgeable gulf. As has been clear since the time of Darwin, the mystery of human language origins is an *evolutionary* problem: how was this unbridgeable gulf nevertheless bridged? If we accept that we evolved from animals lacking human speech, then our language—along with the human pelvis, tools, and art—must have evolved and become perfected with time. There must once have been intermediate language-like stages linking monkeys' grunts to Shakespeare's sonnets. However, the origins of language prove harder to trace than the origins of the human pelvis, tools, and art. All those latter things may persist as fossils that we can recover and date, but the spoken word vanishes in an instant.

Fortunately, two exploding bodies of knowledge are starting to build bridges across the seemingly unbridgeable gulf, starting from each of its opposite shores. Sophisticated new studies of wild animal vocalizations, especially those of our primate relatives, such as vervet monkeys, constitute the bridgehead on the gulf's animal shore. The bridgehead on the human shore has been harder to place, since all existing human languages seem infinitely advanced over animal sounds. That's what lends such interest to Bickerton's argument that pidgins and creoles exemplify two primitive stages on the human side of the causeway.

One difference between human language and vervet vocalizations is that we possess grammar—the variations in word order, prefixes, suffixes, and changes in word roots (like they/them/their) that modulate the sense of the roots. A second difference is that vervet vocalizations, if they constitute words at all, stand only for things with referents that one can point to or act out, such as "eagle" or "watch out for eagle." While our language also has words with referents (nouns, verbs, and adjectives), up to half of the words in typical human speech are purely grammatical items, with no referents. These words include prepositions, conjunctions, articles, and auxiliary verbs (such as can, may, do, and should). It's much harder to understand how grammatical terms could evolve than it is for items with referents. Given someone who understands no English, you can point to your nose to explain the noun "nose." How, though, do you explain the meaning of by, because, the, and did to someone who knows no English? How could apes have stumbled on such grammatical terms?

Still another difference between human and vervet vocalizations is that ours possess a hierarchical structure, such that a modest number of items at each level create a larger number of items at the next level up. Our languages use many different syllables, all based on the same set of only a few dozen sounds. We assemble those syllables into thousands of words. Those words aren't merely strung together haphazardly but are organized into phrases, such as prepositional phrases. Those phrases in turn interlock to form a potentially infinite number of sentences. In contrast, vervet calls cannot be resolved into modular elements and lack even a single stage of hierarchical organization.

As children, we master all this complex structure of human language without ever learning the explicit rules that produce it. The earliest written languages of 5,000 years ago were as complex as those of today, so that human language must have achieved its modern complexity long before that. Surviving hunter-gatherers and other technologically primitive peoples speak languages as complex as the rest of us do. Little wonder that most linguists never discuss how human language might have evolved from animal precursors.

One approach to bridging this gulf is to ask whether some people, deprived of the opportunity to hear any of our fully evolved modern languages, ever spontaneously invented a primitive language. Certainly, solitary children reared in social isolation, like the famous wolf-boy of Aveyron, remain virtually speechless and don't invent or discover a language. However, a variant of the wolf-boy tragedy has occurred dozens of times in the modern world. In this variant, whole populations of children heard adults around them speaking a grossly simplified and variable form of language, somewhat similar to what children themselves usually speak around the age of two. The children proceeded unconsciously to evolve their own new language, far advanced over vervet communication but simpler than normal human languages.

These new languages were the ones commonly known as creoles. They appeared especially in plantation, fort, and trading post situations, where populations speaking different languages came into contact and needed to communicate, but where social circumstances impeded the usual solution of each group learning the other's language. Many cases throughout the tropical Americas and Australia, and on tropical islands of the Caribbean and the Pacific and Indian oceans, involved the importing by European colonists of workers who came from afar and spoke many different tongues. Other European colonists set up forts or trading posts in already densely populated areas of China, Indonesia, or Africa.

Strong social barriers between the dominant colonists and the imported workers or local populations made the former unwilling, the latter unable, to learn the other's language. Even if those social barriers had not existed, the workers would have had few opportunities to learn the colonists' tongue, because workers so greatly outnumbered colonists. Conversely, the colonists would also have found it difficult to learn "the" workers' tongue, because so many different languages were often represented.

Out of the temporary linguistic chaos that followed the founding of plantations and forts, simplified but stabilized new languages emerged. Consider the evolution of Neo-Melanesian as an example. After English ships began to visit Melanesian islands just east of New Guinea about 1820, the English took islanders to work on the sugar plantations of Queensland and Samoa, where workers of many language groups were thrown together. From this babel somehow sprang the Neo-Melanesian

language, whose vocabulary is 80 percent English, 15 percent Tolai (the Melanesian group that furnished many of the workers), and the rest Malay and other languages. Linguists distinguish two stages in the emergence of the new languages: initially, the crude languages termed pidgins, then later, the more complex ones referred to as creoles. Pidgins arise as a second language for colonists and workers who speak differing native (first) languages and need to communicate with each other. Each group (colonists or workers) retains its native language for use within its own group; each group uses the pidgin to communicate with the other group. In addition, workers on a polyglot plantation may use pidgin to communicate with other groups of workers. Compared with vervet vocalizations, even the crudest pidgins are enormously advanced in their hierarchical organization of phonemes into syllables, syllables into words, and words into word strings. Compared with normal languages, however, pidgins are greatly impoverished in their sounds, vocabulary, and syntax. A pidgin's sounds are generally only those common to the two or more native languages thrown together. Words of early-stage pidgins consist largely of nouns, verbs, and adjectives, with few or no articles, auxiliary verbs, conjunctions, prepositions, or pronouns. As for grammar, early-stage pidgins typically consist of short strings of words with little phrase construction, no regularity in word order, no subordinate clauses, and no inflectional word endings. Along with that impoverishment, variability of speech within and between individuals is a hallmark of early stage pidgins, which approximate an anarchic linguistic free-for-all.

Pidgins that are used only casually by adults who otherwise retain their own separate native languages persist at this rudimentary level. For example, a pidgin known as Russonorsk grew up to facilitate barter between Russian and Norwegian fishermen who encountered each other in the Arctic. That lingua franca persisted throughout the nineteenth century but never developed further, as it was used only to transact simple business during brief visits. When speaking with their compatriots, each group of fishermen spoke either Russian or Norwegian. In New Guinea, on the other hand, the pidgin gradually became more regular and complex over many generations because it was used intensively on a daily basis; nevertheless, most children of New Guinea workers continued to learn their parents' native languages as their first language until after World War II.

Pidgins evolve rapidly into creoles whenever a generation of the groups contributing to a pidgin begins to adopt the pidgin itself as its native language. That generation then finds itself using pidgin for all social purposes, not just for discussing plantation tasks or bartering. Compared with pidgins, creoles have a larger vocabulary, a much more complex grammar, and consistency within and between individuals. Creoles can express virtually any thought expressible in a normal language, whereas trying to say anything

even slightly complex is a desperate struggle in pidgin. Somehow, without any equivalent of the Académie Française to lay down explicit rules, a pidgin expands and stabilizes to become a uniform and fuller language.

Creolization is a natural experiment in language evolution that has unfolded independently many times over much of the world. The laborers have ranged from Africans through Portuguese and Chinese to New Guineans; the dominant colonists, from the English to Spaniards to other Africans and Portuguese; and the century, from at least the seventeenth to the twentieth. The linguistic outcomes of all these independent natural experiments share many striking similarities, both in what they lack and in what they possess. On the negative side, creoles are simpler than normal languages in mostly lacking such seemingly standard grammatical items as conjugations of verbs for tense and person, declensions of nouns for case and number, most prepositions, and the passive voice of verbs. On the positive side, creoles are advanced over pidgins in many respects, including consistent word order, conjunctions, relative clauses, and auxiliary verbs to express verb moods and aspects and anterior tense. Most creoles agree in placing a sentence's subject, verb, and object in that particular order, and also agree in the order of auxiliaries preceding the main verb and in the meanings of those auxiliaries alone and in combination.

The factors responsible for this remarkable convergence are still controversial among linguists. It's as if you drew a dozen cards fifty times from well-shuffled decks and almost always ended up with no hearts or diamonds, but with one queen, a jack, and two aces. Derek Bickerton derived his interpretation from his studies of creolization in Hawaii, where sugar planters imported workers from China, the Philippines, Japan, Korea, Portugal, and Puerto Rico in the late nineteenth century. Out of that linguistic chaos, and following Hawaii's annexation by the United States in 1898, a pidgin based on English developed into a full-fledged creole. The immigrant workers themselves retained their original native language. They also learned pidgin that they heard, but they did not improve on it, despite its gross deficiencies as a medium of communication. That, however, posed a big problem for the immigrants' Hawaii-born children. Even if the kids were lucky enough to hear a normal language at home because both mother and father were from the same ethnic group, that normal language was useless for communicating with kids and adults from other ethnic groups. Many children were less fortunate and heard nothing but pidgin at home, when mother and father came from different ethnic groups. Nor did the children have adequate opportunities to learn English because of the social barriers isolating them and their worker parents from the English-speaking plantation owners. Presented with an inconsistent and impoverished model of human language in the form of pidgin, Hawaiian laborers' children spontaneously "expanded"

pidgin into a consistent and complex creole within a generation.

In the mid-1970s, Bickerton was still able to trace the history of this creolization by interviewing working-class people born in Hawaii between 1900 and 1920. Like all of us, those children soaked up language skills in their early years but then became fixed in their ways, so that in their old age their speech continued to reflect the language spoken around them in their youth. (My children, too, will soon be wondering why their father persists in saying "icebox" rather than "refrigerator," decades after the iceboxes of my parents' own childhood disappeared.) Hence, the old adults of various ages, whom Bickerton interviewed in the 1970s, gave him virtually frozen snapshots of various stages in Hawaii's pidgin-to-creole transition, depending on the subjects' birth year. In that way, Bickerton was able to conclude that creolization had begun by 1900, was complete by 1920, and was accomplished by children in the process of their acquiring the ability to speak. In effect, the Hawaiian children lived out a modified version of the wolf-boy story. Unlike the wolf-boy, the Hawaiian children did hear adults speaking and were able to learn words. Unlike most children, however, the Hawaiian children heard little grammatical speech, and much of what they did hear was inconsistent and rudimentary. Instead, they created their own grammar. That they did indeed create it, rather than somehow borrowing grammar from the language of Chinese laborers or English plantation owners, is clear from the many features of Hawaiian creole that differ from English or from the workers' languages. The same is true for Neo-Melanesian: its vocabulary is largely English, but its grammar has many features that English lacks.

I don't want to exaggerate the grammatical similarities among creoles by implying that they're all essentially the same. Creoles do vary depending on the social history surrounding creolization. But many similarities remain, particularly among those creoles quickly arising from early-stage pidgins. How did each creole's children come so quickly to agree on a grammar, and why did the children of different creoles tend to reinvent the same grammatical features again and again?

It wasn't because they did it in the easiest or sole way possible to devise a language. For instance, creoles use prepositions (short words preceding nouns), as do English and some other languages, but there are other languages that dispense with prepositions in favor of postpositions following nouns, or else noun case endings.

Again, creoles happen to resemble English in placing subject, verb, and object in that order, but borrowing from English can't be the explanation, because creoles derived from languages with a different word order still use the subject-verb-object order.

These similarities among creoles seem instead likely to stem from a genetic blueprint that the human brain possesses for learning language during childhood. Such a blueprint has been widely assumed ever since the linguist Noam Chomsky argued that in the absence of any hard-wired instructions, the structure of human language is far too complex for a child to learn within just a few years. For example, at age two my twin sons were just beginning to use single words. As I write this paragraph a bare twenty months later, still several months short of their fourth birthday, they have already mastered most rules of basic English grammar that people who immigrate to English-speaking countries as adults often fail to master after decades. Even before the age of two, my children could make sense of the initially incomprehensible babble of adult sound coming at them, recognize groupings of syllables into words, and realize which groupings constituted underlying words despite variations of pronunciation within and between adult speakers.

Such difficulties convinced Chomsky that children learning their first language would face an impossible task unless much of language's structure were already preprogrammed into them. Hence, Chomsky reasoned that we are born with a "universal grammar" already wired into our brains to give us a spectrum of grammatical models encompassing the range of grammars in actual languages. This prewired universal grammar would be like a set of switches, each with various alternative positions. The switch positions would then become fixed to match the grammar of the local language that the growing child hears.

However, Bickerton goes further than Chomsky and concludes that we are preprogrammed not just to a universal grammar with adjustable switches but to a particular set of switch settings: the settings that surface again and again in creole grammars. The preprogrammed settings can be overridden if they conflict with what a child hears in its local language. But when a child hears no local switch settings because it grows up amid the structureless anarchy of a pidgin language, the creole settings can persist.

If Bickerton is correct and we really are preprogrammed at birth with creole settings that can be overridden by later experience, then one would expect children to learn creolelike features of their local language earlier and more easily than features conflicting with creole grammar. This reasoning might explain English-speaking children's notorious difficulty in learning how to express negatives: they insist on creolelike double negatives, such as "Nobody don't have this." The same reasoning could explain the difficulties that English-speaking children have with word order in questions.

To pursue the latter example, English happens to be among the languages that use the creole word order of subject, verb, and object for statements: for instance, "I want juice." Many languages, including creoles, preserve this word order in questions, which are merely distinguished by altered tone of voice ("You want juice?"). However, the English language does not treat questions in this way. Instead, our questions deviate from creole word order by inverting the subject and verb ("Where are you?" not "Where you are?") or by placing the subject between an auxiliary verb (such as "do") and the main verb ("Do you want juice?"). My wife and I have been barraging my sons from early infancy onward with grammatically correct English questions, as well as statements. My sons quickly picked up the correct order for statements, but both of them still use the incorrect creolelike order for questions, despite the hundreds of correct counterexamples that my wife and I model for them every day. Today's samples from Max and Joshua include, "Where it is?" "What that letter is?" "What the handle can do?" and "What you did with it?" It's as if they're not ready to accept the evidence of their ears, because they're still convinced that their preprogrammed creolelike rules are correct.

Now let's use these studies to assemble a coherent, if speculative, picture of how our ancestors progressed from grunts to Shakespeare's sonnets. A well-studied early stage is represented by vervet monkeys, with at least ten different calls that are used for communication and have external referents. The single words of young toddlers, like "juice" as uttered by my son Max, constitute a next stage beyond animal grunts. But Max made a decisive advance on vervets by assembling his "juice" word from the smaller units of vowels and consonants, thereby scaling the lowest level of modular linguistic organization. A few dozen such phonetic units can be reshuffled to produce a very large number of words, such as the 142,000 words in my English desk dictionary. That principle of modular organization lets us recognize far more distinctions than vervets can. For example, they name only six types of animals, whereas we name nearly two million.

A further step toward Shakespeare is exemplified by two-year-old children, who in all human societies proceed spontaneously from a one-word to a two-word stage and then to a multiword one. But those multiword utterances are still mere word strings with little grammar, and their words are still nouns, verbs, and adjectives with concrete referents. As Bickerton points out, those word strings are like the pidgins that human adults spontaneously reinvent when necessary. They also resemble the strings of symbols produced by captive apes whom we have instructed in the use of those symbols.

From pidgins to creoles, or from the word strings of two-year-olds to the complete sentences of four-year-olds, is another giant step. In that step were added words lacking external referents and serving purely grammatical functions; elements of grammar such as word order, prefixes and suffixes, and word root variation; and more levels of hierarchical organization to produce phrases and sentences. Perhaps that step

is what triggered the Great Leap Forward in human innovation and art within the last hundred thousand years. Nevertheless, creole languages reinvented in modern times still give us clues to how these advances arose, through the creoles' circumlocutions to express prepositions and other grammatical elements.

If you compare a Shakespearean sonnet with the Neo-Melanesian ad that introduced this piece, you might conclude that a huge gap still remains. But I'd argue that with an ad like "Kam insait long stua bilong mipela," we have come 99.9 percent of the way from vervet calls to Shakespeare. Creoles already constitute expressive complex languages. For example, Indonesian, which arose as a creole to become the language of conversation and government for the world's fifth most populous country, is also a vehicle for serious literature.

Thus, animal communication and human language once seemed to be separated by an unbridgeable gulf. Now, we have identified not only parts of bridges starting from both shores but also islands and bridge segments spaced across the gulf. We are beginning to understand in broad outline how the unique and important attribute that distinguishes us from animals arose from animal precursors.

5

THE SETTLEMENT[1]

Julie Winokur

Ethnic identity is often an important factor in how people define who they are as individuals and groups. One common basis for ethnic identification is religion. The members of the Jewish West Bank settlement of Bat Ayin are a case in point. For them, the very act of living where they do is an expression of their ethnicity as well as of their piety. As Julie Winokur describes, the members of Bat Ayin see themselves as distinct not only from their Arab neighbors but also from other Israelis, and they follow a wide range of strict rules in order to maintain their separate identity.

At four o'clock in the morning, the winds of the Judean desert rattle the windows of Zvi Anosh's trailer. He rises from bed, walks to the sink, and fills a small, two-handled plastic bucket. He washes each hand with three quick splashes, recites a blessing, and then replaces the bucket in the sink. His morning ablutions done, Zvi gets dressed in the dark and sits in the living room studying the Torah for an hour, while his wife and five children sleep. When the roosters of the settlement begin to crow, he straps a gun around his waist, climbs into his dust-coated Renault wagon, and heads for the synagogue down the road.

Bat Ayin, a settlement of sixty religious families, is a place where Jewish traditionalism coexists with modern-day strife. Perched on a picturesque hilltop half an hour south of Jerusalem, the town's tranquil atmosphere belies its position on the front line of a war - both ideological and actual - for the West Bank. Claimed by both Arabs and Jews as their rightful possession, this is one of the most hotly disputed parcels of land in the world. Conquered by Israel in 1967 during the Six-Day War, the West Bank was never officially annexed. Along with the Gaza Strip, it was branded an "occupied territory," a term despised by its mostly Palestinian inhabitants. But for settlers like Zvi, the region goes by the name Judea and Samaria, the ancient land of the Bible and sanctified domain of the Jews.

---

[1]Reprinted with permission from *Natural History* (December, 1996/January, 1997). Copyright © the American Museum of Natural History (1996/1997).

Bat Ayin lies in an area heavily populated by Jewish settlers, but it is also within sight of the nearest Arab village. While Zvi davens at the synagogue, muezzins can be heard in the distance summoning Muslims to prayer. Denying Palestinian claims to the land, the religious Jews who choose to live here see their presence as part of a spiritual imperative - as God's will. And whatever actions they have to take to fulfill that imperative are justifiable in their eyes.

Mindful of the image of settlers as gun-toting religious fanatics, Zvi and his wife, Ofra, are reluctant at first to open their lives to me. They're not interested in public scrutiny and finally decide to embrace me not as a journalist but as a sign from God of the inevitable return of the Jews of the Diaspora. As time passes, I find it increasingly hard to reconcile their warmth and hospitality with their inflexible claims to the West Bank and their intolerant attitude toward Arabs.

This is a community of Jews that defies simple classification. While some of Israel's ultra-Orthodox oppose all West Bank expansion, believing that Israel's very existence postpones the arrival of the Messiah, Bat Ayin's residents do not repudiate the state. Most adults have served in the Israeli army and are now part of the reserves. Perhaps more important, most are *baale tchuva*, secular Jews who discovered religion later in life. Zvi and Ofra, native Israelis, believe their Western education taught them to hate their Jewishness and to deny their ancestry. After years of soul searching, experimenting with everything from sensitivity training to astrology, they finally found solace in the body of Jewish writings known as the Torah. Now they are Hasidim, or "pious ones," following the strict practices of a mystical branch of Jewish orthodoxy that evolved in eastern Europe in the eighteenth century. Unlike the traditional rabbis they broke with, Hasidic spiritual leaders stressed an emotional connection to God, in which faith is measured not by learning alone but by piety.

While the word *Hasidim* may conjure up images of men with long sideburns, wearing black coats and wide-brimmed hats, most of the men of Bat Ayin, in their lumberjack shirts and blue jeans, are more reminiscent of the early pioneers of Zionism than of the Orthodox Jews of Eastern European *shtetls*. The women, in bright, flowing skirts and Indian-print head scarves, also have a robust, earthy quality.

On my first night in Bat Ayin, Zvi and I drive to a neighbor's house. An eerie stillness seems to announce our vulnerability, but Zvi is unfazed. Calm and serious, he points to a yellow security gate and says the army insisted on putting it there. The gate secures nothing because, as he explains, the people of Bat Ayin refuse to have a fence constructed around the settlement.

Perhaps the most notable thing about Bat Ayin is the absence of fear. Confrontations between Jews and Arabs in the West Bank have sometimes proved deadly, yet life in Bat Ayin appears to be peaceful and uneventful. As in any small town, children race to catch school buses in the morning, and parents commute to jobs that range from dentist to television producer to tour guide. Although several women work outside the home, most devote themselves to child rearing. At night, while the men are at the synagogue, children play freely in the streets or sit at home studying their dog-eared textbooks. Free of crime, drugs, and poverty, Bat Ayin could inspire envy in many Americans. Neighbors watch out for one another's children, front doors are never locked, and even teenagers dress modestly. It is easy for a visitor to forget that outside is a war zone. The children's school buses are made with reinforced steel and bullet-proof windows, and parents commute to Jerusalem along a hastily constructed bypass road that slices through Arab vineyards to avoid cities recently placed under Palestinian control.

Sitting around the dining table in the dim light of Israel Horovitz's trailer, Horovitz and Zvi Anosh look like characters out of Moses' time, their long, graying beards resting on their chests, their weathered faces severe and committed. Horovitz has just returned from the Galilee region, where he collected grapevines for planting. Planting vineyards, he explains, means repatriating Jews on the land. This, he says, is a more meaningful political statement than Shimon Peres's vision of a New Middle East. Horovitz is one of the more outspoken members of the community, but to call any resident of Bat Ayin radical would be redundant. The

people with whom I spoke were neither surprised nor saddened by Prime Minister Yitzak Rabin's assassination the previous year. They viewed him and his Labor Party successor, Peres, as antireligious because they were responsible for the Oslo accords, which placed the Gaza Strip and portions of the West Bank under Palestinian control. In the last election, Bat Ayin was one of only three settlements out of more than 140 that cast a majority vote for Israel's most extreme party, Moledet. (This party, although it is not religious, advocates transfer of Palestinian populations out of Israel as the only solution to the Arab-Israeli conflict.)

"This is the land of the Jewish people. Everybody agrees," says Horovitz unflinchingly. He blesses his cup of tea and takes a cautious sip. Like the rest of Bat Ayin, he rejects the Oslo accords as a detour from messianic Judaism. "There are two systems in Israel," Zvi pipes up. "Some say let's be like all the nations. Others, like us, say let's reconnect to our real roots in the Torah. Torah is the only way to tell right from wrong, good from bad. It is a whole system of life."

Unlike some Protestant sects that preach a salvation achieved through faith alone, Judaism teaches that spirituality must be attained through specific actions. A strict code of conduct, known as Halacha, consists of 613 mitzvoth, or commandments. In Bat Ayin, close attention is paid to Halacha. Zvi and Ofra purify their hands before every meal. They never eat shellfish, never mix dairy and meat; do not drive, cook, or work on the Sabbath; and sleep in separate beds during her menstrual cycle. Men never touch women in public, even to shake hands; married women cover their heads to insure modesty; prayers are said three times a day; and every cup of tea, every afternoon snack, every plate of spaghetti is acknowledged with the appropriate Hebrew blessing, both before and after eating.

"This world is detailed," explains Zvi. "That's why Jewish law is so detailed." A tall, lanky man, his hair is cropped short and his long sideburns, called *payot*, are tucked behind his ears. On his head is a black *kippa* and under his clothes he wears a *tallit katan*, which he takes off only to bathe. The *tzitzit* (fringes) on the *tallit katan* are a sign of his covenant with God. "There is meaning, which we learn," he says."Some of it makes sense, some of it doesn't. But to keep being Jews, we have to obey." He fingers the *tzitzit* and explains that they are tied in such a way as to denote the 613 mitzvoth.

The Anoshes, along with six other families, founded Bat Ayin in 1989. "We didn't want the standard material life where we would work so we could rest and rest so we could work," says Ofra, as she sits on the couch nursing her three-month-old son, her long, rose-colored skirt layered fold upon fold in her lap. The settlement's ground rules, based on antisecularism and a kind of 1970s back-to-the-earth counterculturalism, have been exclusionary from the outset: no Arab workers, no German products, no television, no recreational drugs, no pesticides.

Today Bat Ayin has sixty families and more than 200 children. Fifteen more families are on the waiting list, and a new yeshiva, or religious school, has opened for young single women. Despite its growth, however, the settlement is a half-made world, with most people living in a random array of trailers. Scraps of debris and children's toys litter the ground, and laundry blows relentlessly in the wind. Nevertheless, the more established families, like the Anoshes, have started to build permanent homes. These are scattered along the periphery of the settlement.

The most striking differences between Bat Ayin and other West Bank settlements are the uniqueness of each house and the relatively large amount of land allotted to each family. Towns like nearby Efrat have grown to resemble outposts of suburbia, replete with tract housing, swimming pools, supermarkets, and shopping centers. These settlements have been forced to open up to secular Jews as a stipulation for continued government support and have therefore become divided between religious Zionists and suburbanites who are seeking a more satisfying quality of life, but who are not ideologically committed to expansion.

Bat Ayin lacks such conflict because it is strictly religious. In fact, the people of the settlement are so convinced of their right to Judea and Samaria that they continued to expand despite the Peres government's freeze on all building in the West Bank. Police and army personnel were sometimes sent on wild goose chases while trailers were moved stealthily along the roads. "They forced us to act like thieves," says Zvi, disturbed by the Peres government's lack of support.

This style of homesteading may recall the early Zionists, who often put down stakes under cover of night to skirt British Mandate laws. But many people in Bat Ayin resent such comparisons. "We don't live the Zionist dream, we live the Torah," Ofra is quick to point out. She pulls a load of laundry from the washing machine and hangs it out to dry. "Zionism did a lot of damage. The Zionists created an image of Israelis as strong, beautiful, invincible. They put people, not God, at the center. Pride, a quality admired by Zionists, is the opposite of the Jewish way of life. You have to work, to struggle, to be modest, because all your beauty and talent comes from God."

The religious nationalist movement, to which Bat Ayin owes its existence, was born out of the Six-Day War in 1967. That surprising victory, in which Israel won on all fronts against Egypt, Syria, and Jordan, added a whole new dimension to the conflict in the Middle East. Israel took control of the Golan Heights, the West Bank (including East Jerusalem), and the Gaza Strip. Jews reclaimed their holiest sites, including the Western Wall of the Second Temple in Jerusalem and the Cave of the Patriarchs in Hebron, where Abraham is said to be buried. Many religious Israelis took this apparent miracle as a sign from God that the Age of the Messiah had arrived, that an ancient prophecy was being fulfilled.

"Scholars used to say that messianic tension rises when people are tortured or persecuted," says Aviezer Ravitzky, head of the Department of Jewish Thought at Hebrew University in Jerusalem. "We face the exact opposite today. Messianism is coming from a place of success, not weakness. The march forward in 1967 was perceived as a biblical victory."

Messianists believe that when all the Jews of the Diaspora return to Eretz (Greater) Israel, the way will be paved for the ultimate spiritual redemption, the End of Days. "They believe that a return to the Torah and pure ethics will lead to universal peace and to the building of the Third Temple," says Ravitzky. "It's a radical attitude. If you adopt the messianic approach, you certainly must have all of the land of Israel. There is no compromise."

"The Western-educated, liberal point of view is that spirituality is about tolerance, understanding, patience," says Ofra as she sorts through handfuls of rice. The Torah forbids Jews to eat bugs, which are considered unclean, so she inspects the rice grain by grain, looking for black spots. "Tolerance is a social concept." She pulls a plate of pasta out of the microwave and gives it to her youngest daughter, then sets a dish in the sink reserved for dairy foods. "Harmony is with God, not with other people, and you have to do everything possible to get closer to God." When I ask her how inspecting individual grains of rice could possibly bring her closer to God, she picks up a butter knife and suspends it from its handle. As the knife swings, pendulumlike, she notes how little the base moves and yet how wide an arc the tip traces. "Something that seems small on earth, like keeping Shabbat, has a large impact on a spiritual level," she says.

Shabbat, the Sabbath, which begins Friday at sundown, is the day of rest--a time for reflection, prayer, giving thanks, and communing with God and family. The week comes to a complete halt, and a new set of rules goes into effect. The meaning of some widely practiced mitzvoth, such as not driving or cooking, is self-evident; others, like not carrying boxes or spreading toothpaste, have a more obscure rationale. The categories of forbidden work on Shabbat are said to reflect the thirty-nine activities that were necessary to build the tabernacle that was a precursor to the Second Temple. These include shoveling, writing, and lifting; any act that employs these is strictly forbidden.

The synagogue is the geographical and spiritual center of Bat Ayin, its jagged limestone bricks plucked from the surrounding hills. When Shabbat begins, Zvi joins the other men of Bat Ayin as they filter into the synagogue through one door, while the women enter through another into a room that is shielded by a curtain. The congregation ranges from traditionalists with ultralong sideburns and black hats to more bohemian characters in colorful *kippot* and blue jeans. In honor of Shabbat, Zvi and Ofra are dressed head to toe in white.

During services, most of the women stay at home with small chil-

dren; but outside the synagogue, herds of other kids jump rope or race around on bicycles. As the service gets under way, prayer breaks into song, and within minutes, the men are on their feet swaying. The energy rises as they sing, "Come my beloved to greet the bride, the Sabbath presence, let us come." They lock arms and dance in a circle, moving hypnotically, lost in reverie. "The One and Only God made us hear, Hashem is One and His Name is One." Later Zvi walks home and, by the light of the Sabbath candles, places his hands on each of his five children's heads and solemnly blesses them.

Hasidism often involves allegiance to certain charismatic rabbis called rebbes, but the residents of Bat Ayin do not share a spiritual leader. Yoel Ben-Avraham, who converted to Judaism in his native Canada, enjoys Bat Ayin's eclectic Hasidism. Back home, he explains, the Jewish community was divided into various camps: religious nationalists, secularists, or followers of particular rebbes. "Here," he says, "I'm just one of the guys." Ben-Avraham's on-line computer training company is one of the few businesses to operate out of Bat Ayin. He sits in his office in the "industrial park" of the settlement, which amounts to one prefabricated, hangar-like building. A large man, he is wearing a T-shirt with the name of his company, LearnSkills, stretched across his belly.

Ben-Avraham insists that unlike his Hasidic neighborhood in Canada, which he says was oppressively xenophobic, Bat Ayin is not imbued with hatred. He explains that the community has a "special understanding" with the local Arabs that amounts to a "don't bother us, we won't bother you" arrangement. "Our fence is a psychological fence. The Arabs think we are the *mishigoyim*, the crazy people. When someone occasionally makes a mistake and comes to steal, he regrets it." Asked to elaborate, he declines.

The Arabs in the nearby villages say they know what he means. "Someone just goes near their land and they start shooting," says Ahmad Mifala, a teacher in the Palestinian village of Safa. "It is not a true peace if we live close but separate," he says. "They're not like other Jews because they don't let us do business with them," says Mahmoud Shobaki, the town imam. "Bat Ayin's Jews don't give us a chance to communicate," Shobaki adds. "They have the power to come here. We can't go there. They must come here and start talking."

Yaki Morag, a wild-eyed man with a nervous edge, is currently in charge of security for Bat Ayin. In every Palestinian shepherd, he sees a potential thief. Morag drives around town in a black Suzuki Samurai jeep equipped with a loudspeaker and a two-way radio; a semiautomatic gun is strapped around his waist. Morag describes the periodic emergency drills in Bat Ayin in which three soldiers from the nearby army base pretend to be terrorists. Bat Ayin has been supplied with guns by the army, which also provides for target practice.

Unlike other parts of the West Bank, Gush Etzion, where Bat Ayin is located, has a relatively secure future because of its proximity to Jerusalem and the extensive degree of settlement. Even left-wing politicians view this region as an extension of Israel that would not be turned over to the Palestinian Authority as part of the peace process.

Zvi and Ofra's new home, which is ready just before Passover, is a sign of the presumed permanence of Bat Ayin. Made of pink Jerusalem stone, with huge picture windows and panoramic views, the new house is practically twice the size of the Anoshes' old trailer. The family seems dwarfed and strangely out of sorts as they unpack their belongings. When I say the place feels palatial, Ofra shrugs, slightly embarrassed.

In a few hours, the Passover Seder will begin, and in homes throughout Bat Ayin, people will tell the story of how their ancestors fled Egypt and the bonds of slavery. The bitter herbs, the unleavened bread, and the salt water are laden with symbolism, and the service is exactly the same as it has been for centuries.

Zvi explains, "When you have a mission, you do the word of God and then try to understand. When I first became religious, I disagreed with many things, but I obeyed until I learned. I'm always trying to understand why, and if I don't understand, I ask again and again until I'm satisfied. That's what we've been doing for five thousand years.

"All these books," he says, gesturing toward the shelves, "they're full of answers."

6

BLACK, WHITE, OTHER[1]

Jonathan Marks

For many people, the concept of race is an important way of identifying oneself and others, and we are often asked to do this for the census and on other official forms. In this article, biological anthropologist Jonathan Marks explains why anthropologists find the concept of race to be unscientific. Although it may be important culturally to put people in categories based on such physical characteristics as skin and hair color, there is no way to sort people out that will hold up to biological scrutiny. The concept of race is fundamentally a cultural construct, not a biological one.

While reading the Sunday edition of the *New York Times* one morning last February, my   attention was drawn by an editorial inconsistency. The article I was reading was written by attorney Lani Guinier. (Guinier, you may remember, had been President Clinton's nominee to head the civil rights division at the Department of Justice in 1993. Her name was hastily withdrawn amid a blast of criticism over her views on political representation of minorities.) What had distracted me from the main point of the story was a photo caption that described Guinier as being "half-black." In the text of the article, Guinier had described herself simply as "black."

How can a person be black and half-black at the same time? In algebraic terms, this would seem to describe a situation where x = ½ x, to which the only solution is $x = 0$.

The inconsistency in the *Times* was trivial, but revealing. It encapsulated a longstanding problem in our use of racial categories—namely, a confusion between biological and cultural heredity. When Guinier is described as "half-black," that is a statement of biological ancestry, for one of her two parents is black. And when Guinier describes herself as black, she is using a cultural category, according to which one can either be black or white, but not both.

Race— as the term is commonly used—is inherited, although not in a strictly biological fashion. It is passed down according to a system of folk heredity, an all-or-nothing system that is different from the quantifiable heredity of biology. But the incompatibility of the two notions of race is sometimes starkly evident—as when the state decides that racial differences are so important that interracial marriages must be regulated or outlawed entirely. Miscegenation laws in this country (which stayed on the books in many states through the 1960s) obliged the legal system to define who belonged in what category. The resulting formula stated that anyone with one-eighth or more black ancestry was a "negro." (A similar formula, defining Jews, was promulgated by the Germans in the Nuremberg Laws of the 1930s.)

Applying such formulas led to the biological absurdity that having one black great-grandparent was sufficient to define a person as black, but having seven white great-grandparents was insufficient to define a person as white. Here, race and biology are demonstrably at odds. And the problem is not semantic but conceptual, for race is presented as a category of nature.

Human beings come in a wide variety of sizes, shapes, colors, and forms—or, because we are visually oriented primates, it certainly seems that way. We also come in larger packages called populations; and we are said to belong to even larger and more confusing units, which have long been known as races. The history of the study of human variation is to a large extent the pursuit of those human races—the attempt to identify the small number of fundamentally distinct kinds of people on earth.

This scientific goal stretches back two centuries, to Linnaeus, the father of biological systematics, who radically established *Homo sapiens* as one species within a group of animals he called Primates. Linnaeus's system of naming groups within groups logically implied further breakdown. He consequently sought to establish a number of subspecies within *Homo sapiens.* He identified five: four geographical species (from Europe, Asia, Africa, and America) and one grab-bag subspecies called *monstrosus.* This category was dropped by subsequent researchers (as was Linnaeus's use of criteria such as personality and dress to define his subspecies).

While Linnaeus was not the first to divide humans on the basis of the continents on which they lived, he had given the division a scientific stamp. But in attempting to determine the proper number of subspecies, the heirs of Linnaeus always seemed to find different answers, depending upon the criteria they applied. By the mid-twentieth century, scores of anthropologists—led by Harvard's Earnest Hooton—had expended enormous energy on the problem. But these scholars could not convince one another about the precise nature of the fundamental divisions of our species.

Part of the problem—as with the *Times's* identification of Lani Guinier—

was that we humans have two constantly intersecting ways of thinking about the divisions among us. On the one hand, we like to think of "race"—as Linnaeus did—as an objective, biological category. In this sense, being a member of a race is supposed to be the equivalent of being a member of a species or of a phylum except that race, on the analogy of subspecies, is an even narrower (and presumably more exclusive and precise) biological category.

The other kind of category into which we humans allocate ourselves— when we say "Serb" or "Hutu" or "Jew" or "Chicano" or "Republican" or "Red Sox fan"—is cultural. The label refers to little or nothing in the natural attributes of its members. These members may not live in the same region and may not even know many others like themselves. What they share is neither strictly nature nor strictly community. The groupings are constructions of human social history.

Membership in these unbiological groupings may mean the difference between life and death, for they are the categories that allow us to be identified (and accepted or vilified) socially. While membership in (or allegiance to) these categories may be assigned or adopted from birth, the differentia that mark members from nonmembers are symbolic and abstract; they serve to distinguish people who cannot be readily distinguished by nature. So important are these symbolic distinctions that some of the strongest animosities are often expressed between very similar-looking peoples. Obvious examples are Bosnian Serbs and Muslims, Irish and English, Huron and Iroquois.

Obvious natural variation is rarely so important as cultural difference. One simply does not hear of a slaughter of the short people at the hands of the tall, the glabrous at the hands of the hairy, the red-haired at the hands of the brown-haired. When we do encounter genocidal violence between different looking peoples, the two groups are invariably socially or culturally distinct as well. Indeed, the tragic frequency of hatred and genocidal violence between biologically indistinguishable peoples implies that biological differences such as skin color are not motivations but, rather, excuses. They allow nature to be invoked to reinforce group identities and antagonisms that would exist without these physical distinctions. But are there any truly "racial" biological distinctions to be found in our species?

Obviously, if you compare two people from different parts of the world (or whose ancestors came from different parts of the world), they will differ physically, but one cannot therefore define three or four or five basically different kinds of people, as a biological notion of race would imply. The anatomical properties that distinguish people—such as pigmentation, eye form, body build—are not clumped in discrete groups, but distributed along geographical gradients, as are nearly all the genetically determined variants detectable in the human gene pool.

These gradients are produced by three forces. Natural selection adapts populations to local circumstances (like climate) and thereby differentiates them from other populations. Genetic drift (random fluctuations in a gene pool) also differentiates populations from one another, but in non-adaptive ways. And gene flow (via intermarriage and other child-producing unions) acts to homogenize neighboring populations.

In practice, the operations of these forces are difficult to discern. A few features, such as body build and the graduated distribution of the sickle cell anemia gene in populations from western Africa, southern Asia, and the Mediterranean can be plausibly related to the effects of selection. Others, such as the graduated distribution of a small deletion in the mitochondrial DNA of some East Asian, Oceanic, and Native American peoples, or the degree of flatness of the face, seem unlikely to be the result of selection and are probably the results of random biohistorical factors. The cause of the distribution of most features, from nose breadth to blood group, is simply unclear.

The overall result of these forces is evident, however. As Johann Friedrich Blumenbach noted in 1775, "you see that all do so run into one another, and that one variety of mankind does so sensibly pass into the other, that you cannot mark out the limits between them." (Posturing as an heir to Linnaeus, he nonetheless attempted to do so.) But from humanity's gradations in appearance, no defined groupings resembling races readily emerge. The racial categories with which we have become so familiar are the result of our imposing arbitrary cultural boundaries in order to partition gradual biological variation.

Unlike graduated biological distinctions, culturally constructed categories are ultra sharp. One can be French or German, but not both; Tutsi or Hutu, but not both; Jew or Catholic, but not both; Bosnian Muslim or Serb, but not both; black or white, but not both. Traditionally, people of "mixed race" have been obliged to choose one and thereby identify themselves unambiguously to census takers and administrative bookkeepers —a practice that is now being widely called into question.

A scientific definition of race would require considerable homogeneity within each group, and reasonably discrete differences between groups, but three kinds of data militate against this view: First, the groups traditionally described as races are not at all homogeneous. Africans and Europeans, for instance, are each a collection of biologically diverse populations. Anthropologists of the 1920s widely recognized *three* European races: Nordic, Alpine, and Mediterranean. This implied that races could exist within races. American anthropologist Carleton Coon identified ten European races in 1939. With such protean use, the term race came to have little value in describing actual biological entities within *Homo sapiens*. The scholars were not only grappling with a broad north-south gradient in human appearance across Europe, they were trying to bring the data into line with their belief in profound and fundamental constitutional differences between groups of people.

But there simply isn't one European race to contrast with an African race, nor three, nor ten: the question (as scientists long posed it) fails to recognize the actual patterning of diversity in the human species. Fieldwork revealed, and genetics later quantified, the existence of far more biological diversity within any group than between groups. Fatter and thinner people exist everywhere, as do people with type 0 and type A blood. What generally varies from one population to the next is the *proportion* of people in these groups expressing the trait or gene. Hair color varies strikingly among Europeans and native Australians, but little among other peoples. To focus on discovering differences between presumptive races, when the vast majority of detectable variants do not help differentiate them, was thus to define a very narrow—if not largely illusory—problem in human biology. (The fact that Africans are biologically more diverse than Europeans, but have rarely been split into so many races, attests to the cultural basis of these categorizations.)

Second, differences between human groups are only evident when contrasting geographical extremes. Noting these extremes, biologists of an earlier era sought to identify representatives of "pure," primordial races—pre-

sumably located in Norway, Senegal, and Thailand. At no time, however, was our species composed of a few populations within which everyone looked pretty much the same. Ever since some of our ancestors left Africa to spread out through the Old World, we humans have always lived in the "in-between" places. And human populations have also always been in genetic contact with one another. Indeed, for tens of thousands of years, humans have had trade networks; and where goods flow, so do genes. Consequently, we have no basis for considering *extreme* human forms the most pure, or most representative, of some ancient primordial populations. Instead, they represent populations adapted to the most disparate environments.

And third, between each presumptive "major" race are unclassifiable populations and people. Some populations of India, for example, are darkly pigmented (or "black"), have European-like ("Caucasoid") facial features, but inhabit the continent of Asia (which should make them "Asian"). Americans might tend to ignore these "exceptions" to the racial categories, since immigrants to the United States from West Africa, Southeast Asia, and northwest Europe far outnumber those from India. The very existence of unclassifiable peoples undermines the idea that there are just three human biological groups in the Old World. Yet acknowledging the biological distinctiveness of such groups leads to a rapid proliferation of categories.   What about Australians? Polynesians? The Ainu of Japan?

Categorizing people is important to any society. It is, at some basic psychological level, probably necessary to have group identity about who and what you are, in contrast to who and what you are not. The concept of race, however, specifically involves the recruitment of biology to validate those categories of self-identity.

Mice don't have to worry about that the way humans do. Consequently, classifying them into subspecies entails less of a responsibility for a scientist than classifying humans into subspecies does. And by the 1960s, most anthropologists realized they could not defend any classification of *Homo sapiens* into biological subspecies or races that could be considered reasonably objective. They therefore stopped doing it, and stopped identifying the endeavor as a central goal of the field. It was a biologically intractable problem—the old square-peg-in-a-round-hole enterprise; and people's lives, or welfares, could well depend on the ostensibly scientific pronouncement. Reflecting on the social history of the twentieth century, that was a burden anthropologists would no longer bear.

This conceptual divorce in anthropology—of cultural from biological phenomena—was one of the most fundamental scientific revolutions of our time. And since it affected assumptions so rooted in our everyday experience, and resulted in conclusions so counterintuitive—like the idea that the earth goes around the sun, and not vice-versa—it has been widely underappreciated.

Kurt Vonnegut, in *Slaughterhouse Five,* describes what he remembered being taught about human variation: "At that time, they were teaching that there was absolutely no difference between anybody. They may be teaching that still." Of course there are biological differences between people, and between populations. The question is: How are those differences patterned? And the answer seems to be: Not racially. Populations are the only readily identifiable units of humans, and even they are fairly fluid, biologically similar to populations nearby, and biologically different from populations far away.

In other words, the message of contemporary anthropology is: You may group humans into a small number of races if you want to, but you are denied biology as a support for it.

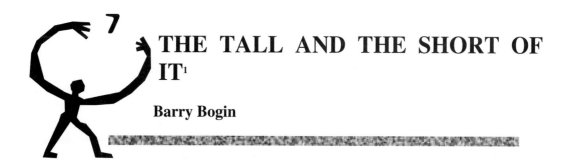

THE TALL AND THE SHORT OF IT[1]

Barry Bogin

A common misunderstanding of genetics is the idea that if you have a gene for a particular characteristic, be it your eye color or a heritable disease, then you are simply stuck with it. In fact, the way that genetic traits are expressed – an organism's phenotype – is always a product of an interaction between an organism's genes and its environment. Many characteristics are subject to a great deal of environmental influence, particularly when an organism is growing and developing. As biological anthropologist Barry Bogin explains, this concept of developmental plasticity is crucial to understanding such basic issues as stature, and it also may shed light on some diseases.

Baffled by your future prospects? As a biological anthropologist, I have just one word of advice for you: plasticity. Plasticity refers to the ability of many organisms, including humans, to alter themselves – their behavior or even their biology – in response to changes in the environment. We tend to think that our bodies get locked into their final form by our genes, but in fact we alter our bodies as the conditions surrounding us shift, particularly as we grow during childhood. Plasticity is as much a product of evolution's fine-tuning as any particular gene, and it makes just as much evolutionary good sense. Rather than being able to adapt to a single environment, we can, thanks to plasticity, change our bodies to cope with a wide range of environments. Combined with the genes we inherit from our parents, plasticity accounts for what we are and what we can become.

Anthropologists began to think about human plasticity around the turn of the century, but the concept was first clearly defined in 1969 by Gabriel Lasker, a biological anthropologist at Wayne State University in Detroit. At that time scientists tended to consider only those adaptations that were built into the genetic makeup of a person and passed on automatically to the next generation. A classic example of this is the

---

[1]Reprinted from *The Sciences*, Nov/Dec, 1988. Reprinted by permission of the author.

ability of adults in some human societies to drink milk. As children, we all produce an enzyme called lactase, which we need to break down the sugar lactose in our mother's milk. In many of us, however, the lactase gene slows down dramatically as we approach adolescence – probably as the result of another gene that regulates its activity. When that regulating gene turns down the production of lactase, we can no longer digest milk.

Lactose intolerance – which causes intestinal gas and diarrhea – affects between 70 and 90 percent of African Americans, Native Americans, Asians, and people who come from around the Mediterranean. But others, such as people of central and western European descent and the Fulani of West Africa, typically have no problem drinking milk as adults. That's because they are descended from societies with long histories of raising goats and cattle. Among these people there was a clear benefit to being able to drink milk, so natural selection gradually changed the regulation of their lactase gene, keeping it functioning throughout life.

That kind of adaptation takes many centuries to become established, but Lasker pointed out that there are two other kinds of adaptation in humans that need far less time to kick in. If people have to face a cold winter with little or no heat, for example, their metabolic rates rise over the course of a few weeks and they produce more body heat. When summer returns, the rates sink again.

Lasker's other mode of adaptation concerned the irreversible, lifelong modification of people as they develop – that is, their plasticity. Because we humans take so many years to grow to adulthood, and because we live in so many different environments, from forests to cities and from deserts to the Arctic, we are among the world's most variable species in our physical form and behavior. Indeed, we are one of the most plastic of all species.

One of the most obvious manifestations of human malleability is our great range of height, and it is a subject I've made a special study of for the last 25 years. Consider these statistics: in 1850 Americans were the tallest people in the world, with American men averaging 5'6". Almost 150 years later, American men now average 5'8", but we have fallen in the standings and are now only the third tallest people in the world. In first place are the Dutch. Back in 1850 they averaged only 5'4" – the shortest men in Europe – but today they are a towering 5'10". (In these two groups, and just about everywhere else, women average about five inches less than men at all times.)

So what happened? Did all the short Dutch sail over to the United States? Did the Dutch back in Europe get an infusion of "tall genes"? Neither. In both America and the Netherlands life got better, but more so for the Dutch, and height increased as a result. We know this is true thanks in part to studies on how height is determined. It's the product of plasticity in our childhood and in our mother's childhood as well. If a girl is undernourished and suffers poor health, the growth of her body, including her reproductive system, is usually reduced. With a shortage of raw materials, she can't build more cells to construct a bigger body; at the same time, she has to invest what materials she can get into repairing already existing cells and tissues from the damage caused by disease. Her shorter stature as an adult is the result of a compromise her body makes while growing up.

Such a woman can pass on her short stature to her child, but genes have nothing to do with it for either of them. If she becomes pregnant, her small reproductive system probably won't be able to supply a normal level of nutrients and oxygen to her fetus. This harsh environment reprograms the fetus to grow more slowly than it would if the woman was healthier, so she is more likely to give birth to a smaller baby. Low-birthweight babies (weighing less than 5.5 pounds) tend to continue their prenatal program of slow growth through childhood. By the time they are teenagers, they are usually significantly shorter than people of normal birth weight. Some particularly striking evidence of this reprogramming comes from studies on monozygotic twins, which develop from a single fertilized egg cell and are therefore identical genetically. But in certain cases, monozygotic twins end up being nourished by unequal portions of the placenta. The twin with the smaller fraction of the placenta is often born with low birth weight, while the other one is normal.

Follow-up studies show that this difference between the twins can last throughout their lives.

As such research suggests, we can use the average height of any group of people as a barometer of the health of their society. After the turn of the century both the United States and the Netherlands began to protect the health of their citizens by purifying drinking water, installing sewer systems, regulating the safety of food, and, most important, providing better health care and diets to children. The children responded to their changed environment by growing taller. But the differences in Dutch and American societies determined their differing heights today. The Dutch decided to provide public health benefits to all the public, including the poor. In the United States, meanwhile, improved health is enjoyed most by those who can afford it. The poor often lack adequate housing, sanitation, and health care. The difference in our two societies can be seen at birth: in 1990 only 4 percent of Dutch babies were born at low birth weight, compared with 7 percent in the United States. For white Americans the rate was 5.7 percent, and for black Americans the rate was a whopping 13.3 percent. The disparity between rich and poor in the United States carries through to adulthood: poor Americans are shorter than the better-off by about one inch. Thus, despite great affluence in the United States, our average height has fallen to third place.

People are often surprised when I tell them the Dutch are the tallest people in the world. Aren't they shrimps compared with the famously tall Tutsi (or "Watusi," as you probably first encountered them) of Central Africa? Actually, the supposed great height of the Tutsi is one of the most durable myths from the age of European exploration. Careful investigation reveals that today's Tutsi men average 5'7" and that they have maintained that average for more than 100 years. That means that back in the 1800s, when puny European men first met the Tutsi, the Europeans suffered strained necks from looking up all the time. The two-to-three-inch difference in average height back then could easily have turned into fantastic stories of African giants by European adventurers and writers.

The Tutsi could be as tall or taller than the Dutch if equally good health care and diets were available in Rwanda and Burundi, where the Tutsi live. But poverty rules the lives of most African people, punctuated by warfare, which makes the conditions for growth during childhood even worse. And indeed, it turns out that the Tutsi and other Africans who migrate to Western Europe or North America at young ages end up taller than Africans remaining in Africa.

At the other end of the height spectrum, Pygmies tell a similar story. The shortest people in the world are the Mbuti, the Efe, and other Pygmy peoples of Central Africa. Their average stature is about 4'9" for adult men and 4'6" for women. Part of the reason Pygmies are short is indeed genetic: some evidently lack the genes for pro-

ducing the growth-promoting hormones that course through other people's bodies, while others are genetically incapable of using these hormones to trigger the cascade of reactions that lead to growth. But another important reason for their small size is environmental. Pygmies living as hunter-gatherers in the forests of Central African countries appear to be undernourished, which further limits their growth. Pygmies who live on farms and ranches outside the forest are better fed than their hunter-gatherer relatives and are taller as well. Both genes and nutrition thus account for the size of Pygmies.

Peoples in other parts of the world have also been labeled pygmies, such as some groups in Southeast Asia and the Maya of Guatemala. Well-meaning explorers and scientists have often claimed that they are genetically short, but here we encounter another myth of height. A group of extremely short people in New Guinea, for example, turned out to eat a diet deficient in iodine and other essential nutrients. When they were supplied with cheap mineral and vitamin supplements, their supposedly genetic short stature vanished in their children, who grew to a more normal height.

Another way for these so-called pygmies to stop being pygmies is to immigrate to the United States. In my own research, I study the growth of two groups of Mayan children. One group lives in their homeland of Guatemala, and the other is a group of refugees living in the United States. The Maya in Guatemala live in the village of San

Pedro, which has no safe source of drinking water. Most of the water is contaminated with fertilizers and pesticides used on nearby agricultural fields. Until recently, when a deep well was dug, the townspeople depended on an unreliable supply of water from rain-swollen streams. Most homes still lack running water and have only pit toilets. The parents of the Mayan children work mostly at clothing factories and are paid only a few dollars a day.

I began working with the schoolchildren in this village in 1979, and my research shows that most of them eat only 80 percent of the food they need. Other research shows that almost 30 percent of the girls and 20 percent of the boys are deficient in iodine, that most of the children suffer from intestinal parasites, and that many have persistent ear and eye infections. As a consequence, their health is poor and their height reflects is: they average about three inches shorter than better-fed Guatemalan children.

The Mayan refugees I work with in the United States live in Los Angeles and in the rural agricultural community of Indiantown in Central Florida. Although the adults work mostly in minimum-wage jobs, the children in these communities are generally better off than their counterparts in Guatemala. Most Maya arrived in the 1980s as refugees escaping a civil war as well as a political system that threatened them and their children. In the United States they found security and started new lives, and before long their children began growing faster and big-

ger. My data show that the average increase in height among the first generation of these immigrants was 2.2 inches, which means that these so-called pygmies have undergone one of the largest single-generation increases in height ever recorded. When people such as my own grandparents migrated from the poverty of rural life in Eastern Europe to the cites of the United States just after World War I, the increase in height of the next generation was only about one inch.

One reason for the rapid increase in stature is that in the United States the Maya have access to treated drinking water and to a reliable supply of food. Especially critical are school breakfast and lunch programs for children from low-income families, as well as public assistance programs such as the federal Women, Infants, and Children (WIC) program and food stamps. That these programs improve health and growth is no secret. What is surprising is how fast they work. Mayan mothers in the United States tell me that even their babies are bigger and healthier than the babies they raised in Guatemala., and hospital statistics bear them out. These women must be enjoying a level of health so improved from that of their lives in Guatemala that their babies are growing faster in the womb. Of course, plasticity means that such changes are dependent on external conditions, and unfortunately the rising height – and health – of the Maya is in danger from political forces that are attempting to cut funding for food stamps and the WIC program. If that funding is cut, the negative impact on the lives of poor Americans, including the Mayan refugees, will be as dramatic as were the former positive effects.

Height is only the most obvious example of plasticity's power; there are others to be found everywhere you look. The Andes-dwelling Quechua people of Peru are well-adapted to their high-altitude homes. Their large, barrel-shaped chests house big lungs that inspire huge amounts of air with each breath, and they manage to survive on the lower pressure of oxygen they breathe with an unusually high level of red blood cells. Yet these secrets of mountain living are not hereditary. Instead the bodies of young Quechua adapt as they grow in their particular environment, just as those of European children do when they live at high altitudes.

Plasticity may also have a hand in determining our risks for developing a number of diseases. For example, scientists have long been searching for a cause for Parkinson's disease. Because Parkinson's tends to run in families, it is natural to think there is a genetic cause. But while a genetic mutation linked to some types of Parkinson's disease was reported in mid-1997, the gene accounts for only a fraction of people with the disease. Many more people with Parkinson's do not have the gene, and not all people with the mutated gene develop the disease.

Ralph Garruto, a medical researcher and biological anthropologist at the National Institutes of Health, is investigating the role of the environment and human plasticity not only in Parkinson's but in Lou Gehrig's disease as well. Garruto and his team traveled to the islands of Guam and New Guinea, where rates of both diseases are 50 to 100 times higher than in the United States. Among the native Chamorro people of Guam these diseases kill one person out of every five over the age of 25. The scientists found that both diseases are linked to a shortage of calcium in the diet. This shortage sets off a cascade of events that result in the digestive system's absorbing too much of the aluminum present in the diet. The aluminum wreaks havoc on various parts of the body, including the brain, where it destroys neurons and eventually causes paralysis and death.

The most amazing discovery made by Garruto's team is that up to 70 percent of the people they studied in Guam had some brain damage, but only 20 percent progresses all the way to Parkinson's or Lou Gehrig's disease. Genes and plasticity seem to be working hand in hand to produce these lower-than-expected rates of disease. There is a certain amount of genetic variation in the ability that all people have in coping with calcium shortages – some can function better than others. But thanks to plasticity, it's also possible for people's bodies to gradually develop ways to protect themselves against aluminum poisoning. Some people develop biochemical barriers to the aluminum they eat, while others develop ways to prevent the aluminum from reaching the brain.

An appreciation of plasticity may temper some of our fears about these diseases and even offer some hope. For if Parkinson's and Lou Gehrig's diseases can be prevented among the Chamorro by plasticity, then maybe medical researchers can figure out a way to produce the same sort of plastic changes in you and me. Maybe Lou Gehrig's disease and Parkinson's disease – as well as many others, including some cancers – aren't our genetic doom but a product of our development, just like variations in human height. And maybe their danger will in time prove as illusory as the notion that the Tutsi are giants, or the Maya pygmies – or Americans still the tallest of the tall.

8

OLD DOG, OLD TRICKS[1]

Lee Cronk

Evolution occurs to organisms in specific environments. When organisms are removed from the environments in which they evolved, or when those environments change rapidly, the organism may not be able to cope, and some behaviors that were once reliably adaptive may suddenly be maladaptive. As Cronk reports, a growing number of researchers are applying this insight to human beings in an effort to understand the evolutionary roots of some of the physical, psychological, and social problems of modern society.

"HELP WANTED: Healthy males wanted as semen donors. Help infertile couples." The advertisement runs in the classified section of *The Battalion*, the student newspaper at Texas A&M University. "Confidentiality ensured. Ages 18 to 35, excellent compensation." But in spite of the blandishments, donors are scarce. Meanwhile, on highways in the surrounding Texas countryside, armadillos routinely kill themselves by springing into the air in front of oncoming cars, in misguided attempts to foil their perceived attackers.

What could two such disparate phenomena possibly have in common? Each of them sheds light on the environment in which a species evolved. In each case some aspect of the original environment has changed, and an old behavior that might once have been adaptive is no longer so. The problem for the armadillos is cars: for most of armadillo evolution there were none, and the armadillo's habit of springing into the air when it is threatened worked well enough to confuse snakes and other predators. Leap two feet high in front of a Buick, though, and you're buzzard bait.

The Texas A&M undergraduates also are disadvantaged—somewhat less drastically, to be sure—by their evolutionary heritage. In a Darwinian sense, an adaptive behavior is one that increases the individual organism's chance of passing on its genes. The adaptive response to the sperm bank's advertisement (which represents a chance to reproduce, free of any cost beyond a few minutes' effort) would be to visit the bank as often as possible.

[1]This article is reprinted by permission of *The Sciences* and is from the January/February 1992 issue. Individual subscriptions are $28 per year. Write to: *The Sciences*, 2 East 63rd Street, New York, NY 10021.

But throughout most of human evolution, reproductive opportunities have involved human females, not test tubes. Focusing on females was adaptive in the past, but here, in the novel environment of a sperm bank, it is a diversion and a handicap. For the few men who do make deposits, the incentive is usually financial, not sexual; an acceptable donor can make more than $100 a week for just a few minutes' work.

The English psychologist John Bowlby, in his treatise *Attachment and Loss*, was the first to point out the importance of understanding the environment in which an adaptation arose—what he called the environment of evolutionary adaptedness. Behavioral and physical adaptations that seem to make no sense in an organism's current environment can be traced to the legacy of an earlier, different environment in which those traits were favored. Human beings, now the major source of environmental change on earth, have altered the environments of many other animals besides the armadillo, and the results have been incongruous and often poignant.

Rabbits dart back and forth in the paths of oncoming cars, attempting to confuse what they perceive as predators intensely bearing down on them at great speed. Toads are undone by their feeding behavior. They snap reflexively at almost any small, moving object—behavior that serves them well in their normal surroundings, where such an object is likely to be a tasty insect. But when cane toads were introduced on the Hawaiian islands in 1932, their environment included a novel element: trees that produce strychnine and deposit the poison in their flowers for protection against insects. As the blossoms fall from the trees and blow along the ground, toads searching for food sometimes snatch them up, with predictable results. In Korea toads faced another novel environment when they were captured by bored American GIs, who amused themselves by rolling shotgun pellets past the toads. The animals would fill up with lead like little amphibious beanbags until they were unable even to hop.

In addition to changing the environments of other species, we humans are building a strange and in many ways novel environment for ourselves. The ability to do so sets us apart from other species. Fortunately, so does the ability to respond flexibly to new conditions of our own making. Any animal is likely to be confused between a new stimulus and a familiar one. Rabbits and armadillos react to moving cars as if they were predators; toads react to blossoms and shotgun pellets as if they were insects. Most people react to sperm banks as if they had nothing to do with reproduction; after all, sperm donation certainly lay outside the behavioral repertoire of our ancestors. But people also have fewer simple behavioral programs, and our intelligence makes it possible for us to shape our behavior to new circumstances. The sperm bank near Texas A&M may not be as popular as the local ice-cream parlor, but the bank still attracts enough donors to stay in business.

Yet there are limits to our flexibility. In some features of our physiology or psychology we seem to be rather like the armadillo and the toad: we carry on in ways that were once adaptive but have become a handicap in our new, artificial environment. Many of those legacies remain obscure. But by conceptually reconstructing the environment of our own evolutionary upbringing and comparing it with our present surroundings, we may be able to locate the roots of certain contemporary medical, behavioral and social problems. We may even find clues about how best to deal with them.

To begin we need a picture of our ancestors' world. That phrase usually conjures images of the African savanna or the caves of Ice Age Europe—in other words, the physical environments in which the human species evolved. Changes in the physical environment surely lie at the root of some of the current difficulties. Certain diseases of advanced age, for example—high blood pressure, heart disease, some cancers - seem to emerge from the clash between a Stone Age physiology and one aspect of the new physical environment: diet. Salt was once scarce, and early humans evolved both a taste for it and some mechanisms for conserving it. Those adaptations no longer serve now that salt is plentiful. By the same token, the human body became adapted, over tens of thousands of years, to a diet low in fat and high in fiber, and the recent departure from that pattern is blamed for many health problems.

But emphasizing the physical aspects of our species' past may be a mistake. Investigators are beginning to explore the possibility that the social environment may have been a source of selective pressure at least as strong as the physical environment during the evolution of humans and other primates. The psychologist Nicholas Humphrey of Kings College at the University of Cambridge draws an analogy between human evolution and the story of Robinson Crusoe. Crusoe certainly faced physical challenges when he was alone on the island—getting enough to eat and drink, avoiding danger and so on—but, as Humphrey puts it, "it was the arrival of man Friday [that] really made things difficult for Crusoe. If Monday, Tuesday, Wednesday and Thursday had turned up as well then Crusoe would have had every need to keep his wits about him."

Indeed, the anthropologist Sue Taylor Parker of Sonoma State University in Rohnert Park, California, has argued that one defining human characteristic, the capacity for abstract reasoning, evolved in response to the demands of the social world, as well as to the demands of toolmaking and tool use. The traditional human societies in our time all impose on their members an exceedingly complicated social environment, no matter how simple their technology. The Australian aborigines, for example, never developed the bow and arrow, but their social systems are well known among anthropologists for their intricacy. The Tiwi of northern Australia maintain an elaborate system of political bargaining, favors and intrigue, all centered on the rights of men to bestow women on one another. Other aboriginal groups regulate marriage and kinship according to systems of Byzantine complexity. Such social systems, assuming they existed earlier in human evolution, would have strongly favored an ability to generalize rules from experience and apply the rules in new situations.

If the social environment of our ancestors played a major role in shaping human physiology and behavior, current social, economic and political arrangements might be a good hunting ground for conditions that strain our evolutionary heritage. One main difference between the present environment and that of our ancestors is in the nature of work. Traditional societies have simple divisions of labor, based only on age and sex, and consequently their members are generalists. In foraging societies men usually do most of the hunting for meat and women do most of the gathering of plant foods. All grown men take part in such activities as toolmaking, stalking and butchering, and the women likewise share a broad range of activities. Many herding societies go even further in sharing tasks: all members—men, women and children—tend the livestock.

Modern societies, in contrast, subdivide labor in infinite and subtle ways. Some people specialize in deboning chickens or soldering circuit boards; others spend their days taking telephone orders or running office copiers. An office, a hospital or a construction site is a hive of finely divided responsibilities. Although such division of labor has brought enormous increases in productivity and wealth, it has led also to specific physical problems.

Through most of evolution everyone performed a wide range of physical activities. Today specialization has gone so far that some jobs have been reduced to a single pattern of motion, repeated over and over again, day after day. The result, for some workers, is a cumulative trauma disorder. Carpal tunnel syndrome is one of the most common of those ailments: the tissues of the wrist and hand become inflamed and press on the nerves that run through the carpal tunnel, causing pain, numbness and weakness. Butchers, meat packers and assembly line workers have long been subject to carpal tunnel syndrome, but as computer keyboards have proliferated, the ailment has spread to white-collar workers as well. Indeed, carpal tunnel syndrome has now become so common among the new groups that it is sometimes called computeritis or journalist's disease. According to Linda H. Morse, medical director of the Repetitive Motion Institute in San Jose, California, the growth of cumulative trauma disorders is a sign that "the electronic revolution has outstripped our human muscular and skeletal evolution."

Economic changes have not only led to physical activities unanticipated by evolution; they have also disrupted traditional patterns of childbearing and child rearing. Again specialization is to blame, at least in part. Many jobs now require long periods of schooling and apprenticeship. Women are finding increased opportunities in such specialized fields, and as a result they are delaying childbearing, often into their thirties. In response to career pressures, many limit the size of their families and return to work quickly after giving birth. Breast-feeding is also curtailed, since it is rarely accommodated in the workplace. In all, fewer than 10 percent of married American women between the ages of eighteen and thirty-four expect to have more than three babies, and fewer than 20 percent of American women nurse their babies for six months or more.

A strikingly different pattern prevailed for most of human evolution, and it is still evident in traditional societies. There, women usually become pregnant not long after they begin to ovulate, between the ages of fifteen and nineteen. They continue to bear children until menopause, nursing each one for as long as three years. Although both the rights of women and population control make such a pattern unacceptable in modern industrial societies, it may be what human physiology is best equipped for. Consider that tens of thousands of years has settled the body into the strategy of early and abundant childbirth. Only in the past few decades has that pattern changed.

There is increasing evidence that the change may not sit well with our Stone Age reproductive physiology. For example, the change in reproductive behavior may be contributing to the high incidence of breast cancer in industrial society. An epidemiological study by Peter M. Layde and others at the Centers for Disease Control in Atlanta found that getting pregnant early in life, having several children and breast-feeding them for long periods—in other words, following the reproductive regimen of early humans —all reduced the risk of breast cancer. In some cases the reductions were dramatic. Women who had breast-fed for a total of more than twenty-five months were 33 percent less likely to develop breast cancer than were women who had children but had never breast-fed. And women

who had had only one child had more than twice the cancer risk of women with seven or more children.

People have carried a Stone Age physiology into an age of fast food and commuter marriages, but they may also be carrying some aspects of Stone Age psychology—traits evolved over tens of thousands of years of foraging. Are there any signs of an emotional legacy from the past? No one knows how much human behavior comes from the genes and how much is learned; any argument that people are hobbled by a Stone Age psychology is necessarily speculative. But it may prove useful to look at certain modern social problems from the perspective of the early human environment, where aspects of the psyche may have been forged.

Just as the division of labor has fragmented the economy, so it has atomized social life. We move from city to city; we work with colleagues and bosses rather than with kinfolk; we often gain recognition and rewards for our own efforts rather than through family influence. The clans, lineages and extended-family networks that structured life for our ancestors (and for the members of traditional societies today) have disintegrated, and in the West most people now live in nuclear families. The loss of such kin networks may be another factor that has led parents to have fewer children, later in life: many people can no longer call on relatives to share the work of child rearing.

It may also have had disturbing psychological effects. The feelings of alienation so often ascribed to modern urban life may reflect the evolutionary novelty of that environment, in which families and small, often short-lived webs of friendship take the place of widespread kin networks. David P. Barash, a professor of psychology and zoology at the University of Washington in Seattle, has argued that social pathologies such as drug use and crimes against strangers may reflect this uneasy fit between aspects of our psyche, evolved long ago, and the strange social world we now inhabit.

Although traditional societies have drugs, the drugs rarely become the center of a person's life. And crime is less of a problem, because it is difficult to accomplish anonymously. Crimes of passion and impulse concerning adultery, unpaid debts and unreturned favors predominate, whereas premeditated robberies and burglaries barely exist. "A small-town resident doesn't rob the corner grocer; everyone knows nice old Mr. McPherson," Barash writes in his 1986 book *The Hare and the Tortoise*. "But if McPherson is a nameless, familyless, disembodied, and anonymous spirit in a big city, he can be attacked with relative ease."

Even if the novel human environment is perilous to creatures that evolved to meet the demands of the Pleistocene, what can be done about it? After all, the adaptive advantages of the artificial environment far outweigh its drawbacks, as the health and prosperity of many people in the industrial world make clear. Quite apart from its benefits in a Darwinian sense, the modern world created by human effort offers freedoms and pleasures unknown in traditional societies. Alienating as they may be, cities are also exciting and fun. Kinship networks offer psychological support during child rearing, but the obligation to support is reciprocal, and many people prefer their family ties loosely knotted. Delayed reproduction may have medical risks, but careers can bring rewards that breast-feeding cannot.

What is more, it may be possible to relieve some of the problems of the novel contemporary environment without returning to the Stone Age, by mimicking some of its key features. Cumulative trauma disorders such as carpal tunnel syndrome are currently treated with drugs and surgery. But they also improve when the sufferer's job is redesigned to allow a greater range of motion—making it perhaps more like the ancestral activities of root grubbing and spear throwing. The risk of breast cancer may one day be reduced by hormone treatments that mimic the cancer-reducing effects of the traditional reproductive pattern, without its career-reducing effects as well.

Alienation is a more subtle problem, calling for a more imaginative solution. The novelist Kurt Vonnegut offered one in *Slapstick, or Lonesome No More!* The second part of the title is the campaign slogan of Wilbur Daffodil-11 Swain, the last president of the U.S. His sole issue is the loneliness of his compatriots, and his solution is to engage the computers of the federal government in recreating kinship networks like the ones of prehistory.

In Vonnegut's fantasy everyone gets a new middle name, corresponding to something in nature - Chipmunk, Hollyhock, Raspberry, Uranium - and a number. By name and number everyone is instantly linked to 10,000 brothers and sisters and 190,000 cousins, all obligated to help out fellow clan members. That's a lot of kinfolk, but individually the obligations are mild. And, as Swain explains, "We need all the help we can get in a country as big and clumsy as ours."

People may never shed the need for kinship networks, but perhaps some day in the distant future adaptations to the modern environment will begin to appear. As sperm banks account for more and more babies, for instance, men may eventually evolve a propensity to find test tubes downright arousing. By the same token, it is not inconceivable that the division of labor could lead to the development or the atrophy of certain physical characteristics in human beings. But, surely, it will be a long time before laboratory supply catalogs are sold at convenience stores and armadillos stop littering the Texas highways.

9

WHAT ARE FRIENDS FOR?[1]

Barbara Smuts

Barbara Smuts challenges the long-held idea that before the development of sexual division of labor, human males and females had little to do with each other except for sex. Her studies of baboons reveal new ideas about the origin of "friendship" between males and females and shows how essential non-sexually motivated friendships are to the well-being of female and infant baboons. She found that in some cases female baboons and their infants' actual survival depends on which males they selected as friends and how long friendships lasted.

Virgil, a burly adult male olive baboon, closely followed Zizi, a middle-aged female easily distinguished by her grizzled coat and square muzzle. On her rump Zizi sported a bright pink swelling, indicating that she was sexually receptive and probably fertile. Virgil's extreme attentiveness to Zizi suggested to me—and all rival males in the troop—that he was her current and exclusive mate.

Zizi, however, apparently had something else in mind. She broke away from Virgil, moved rapidly through the troop, and presented her alluring sexual swelling to one male after another. Before Virgil caught up with her, she had managed to announce her receptive condition to several of his rivals. When Virgil tried to grab her, Zizi screamed and dashed into the bushes with Virgil in hot pursuit. I heard sounds of chasing and fighting coming from the thicket. Moments later Zizi emerged from the bushes with an older male named Cyclops. They remained together for several days, copulating often. In Cyclops' presence, Zizi no longer approached or even glanced at other males.

Primatologists describe Zizi and other olive baboons (*Papio cynocephalus anubis*) as promiscuous, meaning that both males and females usually mate with several members of the opposite sex within a short period of time. Promiscuous mating behavior characterizes many of the larger, more familiar primates, including chimpanzees, rhesus macaques, and gray langurs, as well as olive, yellow, and chacma baboons, the three subspecies of savanna baboon. In colloquial usage, promiscuity often connotes wanton and random sex, and several early studies of primates supported this stereotype. However, after years of laboriously recording thousands of copulations under natural conditions, the Peeping Toms of primate fieldwork have shown that, even in promiscuous species, sexual pairings are far from random.

Some adult males, for example, typically copulate much more often than others. Primatologists have explained these differences in terms of competition: the most dominant males monopolize females and prevent lower-ranking rivals from mating. But exceptions are frequent. Among baboons, the exceptions often involve scruffy, older males who mate in full view of younger, more dominant rivals.

A clue to the reason for these puzzling exceptions emerged when primatologists began to question an implicit assumption of the dominance hypothesis that females were merely passive objects of male competition. But what if females were active arbiters in this system? If females preferred some males over others and were able to express these preferences, then models of mating activity based on male dominance alone would be far too simple.

Once researchers recognized the possibility of female choice, evidence for it turned up in species after species. The story of Zizi, Virgil, and Cyclops is one of hundreds of examples of female primates rejecting the sexual advances of particular males and enthusiastically cooperating with others. But what is the basis for female choice? Why might they prefer some males over others?

This question guided my research on the Eburru Cliffs troop of olive baboons, named after one of their favorite sleeping sites, a sheer rocky outcrop rising several hundred feet above the floor of the Great Rift Valley, about 100 miles northwest of Nairobi, Kenya. The 120 members of Eburru Cliffs spent their days wandering through open grassland studded with occasional acacia thorn trees. Each night they retired to one of a dozen sets of cliffs that provided protection from nocturnal predators such as leopards.

Most previous studies of baboon sexuality had focused on females who, like Zizi, were at the peak of sexual receptivity. A female baboon does not mate when she is pregnant or lactating, a period of abstinence lasting about eighteen months. The female then goes into estrus, and for about two weeks out of every thirty-five-day cycle, she mates. Toward the end of this two-week period she may ovulate, but usually the female undergoes four or five estrous cycles before she conceives. During pregnancy, she once again resumes a chaste existence. As a result, the typical female baboon is sexually active for less than 10 percent of her adult life. I thought that by focusing on the other 90 percent, I might learn something new. In particular, I suspected that routine, day-to-day relationships between males and pregnant or lactating (non-estrous) females might provide clues to female mating preferences.

Nearly every day for sixteen months, I joined the Eburru Cliffs baboons at their sleeping cliffs at dawn and traveled several miles with them while they foraged for roots, seeds, grass, and occasionally, small prey items, such as baby gazelles or hares (see "Predatory Baboons of Kekopey," *Natural History,* March 1976). Like all savanna baboon troops, Eburru Cliffs functioned as a cohesive unit organized around a core of related females, all of whom were born in the troop. Unlike the females, male savanna baboons leave their natal troop to join another where they may remain for many years, so most of the Eburru Cliffs adult males were immigrants. Since membership in the troop remained relatively constant during the period of my study, I learned to identify each individual. I relied on differences in size, posture, gait, and especially facial features. To the practiced observer, baboons look as different from one another as human beings do.

As soon as I could recognize individuals, I noticed that particular females tended to turn up near particular males again and again. I came to think of these pairs as friends. Friendship among animals is not a well documented phenomenon, so to convince skeptical colleagues that baboon friendship was real, I needed to develop objective criteria for distinguishing friendly pairs.

I began by investigating grooming, the amiable simian habit of picking through a companion's fur to remove dead skin and ectoparasites (see "Little Things That Tick Off Baboons,"

Natural History, February 1984). Baboons spend much more time grooming than is necessary for hygiene, and previous research had indicated that it is a good measure of social bonds. Although eighteen adult males lived in the troop, each non-estrous female performed most of her grooming with just one, two, or occasionally three males. For example, of Zizi's twenty-four grooming bouts with males, Cyclops accounted for thirteen, and a second male, Sherlock, accounted for all the rest. Different females tended to favor different males as grooming partners.

Another measure of social bonds was simply who was observed near whom. When foraging, traveling, or resting, each pregnant or lactating female spent a lot of time near a few males and associated with the others no more often than expected by chance. When I compared the identities of favorite grooming partners and frequent companions, they overlapped almost completely. This enabled me to develop a formal definition of friendship: any male that scored high on both grooming and proximity measures was considered a friend.

Virtually all baboons made friends; only one female and the three males who had most recently joined the troop lacked such companions. Out of more than 600 possible adult female-adult male pairs in the troop, however, only about one in ten qualified as friends; these really were special relationships.

Several factors seemed to influence which baboons paired up. In most cases, friends were unrelated to each other, since the male had immigrated from another troop. (Four friendships, however, involved a female and an adolescent son who had not yet emigrated. Unlike other friends, these related pairs never mated.) Older females tended to be friends with older males; younger females with younger males. I witnessed occasional May–December romances, usually involving older females and young adult males. Adolescent males and females were strongly rule-bound, and with the exception of mother-son pairs, they formed friendships only with one another.

Regardless of age or dominance rank, most females had just one or two male friends. But among males, the number of female friends varied greatly from none to eight. Although high-ranking males enjoyed priority of access to food and sometimes mates, dominant males did not have more female friends than low-ranking males. Instead it was the older males who had lived in the troop for many years who had the most friends. When a male had several female friends, the females were often closely related to one another. Since female baboons spend a lot of time near their kin, it is probably easier for a male to maintain bonds with several related females at once.

When collecting data, I focused on one non-estrous female at a time and kept track of her every movement toward or away from any male; similarly, I noted every male who moved toward or away from her. Whenever the female and a male moved close enough to exchange intimacies, I wrote down exactly what happened. When foraging together, friends tended to remain a few yards apart. Males more often wandered away from females than the reverse, and females, more often than males, closed the gap. The female behaved as if she wanted to keep the male within calling distance, in case she needed his protection. The male, however, was more likely to make approaches that brought them within actual touching distance. Often, he would plunk himself down right next to his friend and ask her to groom him by holding a pose with exaggerated stillness. The female sometimes responded by grooming, but more often, she exhibited the most reliable sign of true intimacy: she ignored her friend and simply continued whatever she was doing.

In sharp contrast, when a male who was not a friend moved close to a female, she dared not ignore him. She stopped whatever she was doing and held still, often glancing surreptitiously at the intruder. If he did not move away, she sometimes lifted her tail and presented her rump. When a female is not in estrus, this is a gesture of appeasement, not sexual enticement. Immediately after this respectful acknowledgement of his presence, the female would slip away. But such tense interactions with nonfriend males were rare, because females usually moved away before the males came too close.

These observations suggest that females were afraid of most of the males in their troop, which is not surprising: male baboons are twice the size of females, and their canines are longer and sharper than those of a lion. All Eburru Cliffs males directed both mild and severe aggression toward females. Mild aggression, which usually involved threats and chases but no body contact, occurred most often during feeding competition or when the male redirected aggression toward a female after losing a fight with another male. Females and juveniles showed aggression toward other females and juveniles in similar circumstances and occasionally inflicted superficial wounds. Severe aggression by males, which involved body contact and sometimes biting, was less common and also more puzzling, since there was no apparent cause.

An explanation for at least some of these attacks emerged one day when I was watching Pegasus, a young adult male, and his friend Cicily, sitting together in the middle of a small clearing. Cicily moved to the edge of the clearing to feed, and a higher-ranking female, Zora, suddenly attacked her. Pegasus stood up and looked as if he were about to intervene when both females disappeared into the bushes. He sat back down, and I remained with him. A full ten minutes later, Zora appeared at the edge of the clearing; this was the first time she had come into view since her attack on Cicily. Pegasus instantly pounced on Zora, repeatedly grabbed her neck in his mouth and lifted her off

the ground, shook her whole body, and then dropped her. Zora screamed continuously and tried to escape. Each time, Pegasus caught her and continued his brutal attack. When he finally released her five minutes later she had a deep canine gash on the palm of her hand that made her limp for several days.

This attack was similar in form and intensity to those I had seen before and labeled "unprovoked." Certainly, had I come upon the scene after Zora's aggression toward Cicily, I would not have understood why Pegasus attacked Zora. This suggested that some, perhaps many, severe attacks by males actually represented punishment for actions that had occurred some time before.

Whatever the reasons for male attacks on females, they represent a serious threat. Records of fresh injuries indicated that Eburru Cliffs adult females received canine slash wounds from males at the rate of one for every female each year, and during my study, one female died of her injuries. Males probably pose an even greater threat to infants. Although only one infant was killed during my study, observers in Botswana and Tanzania have seen recent male immigrants kill several young infants.

Protection from male aggression, and from the less injurious but more frequent aggression of other females and juveniles, seems to be one of the main advantages of friendship for a female baboon. Seventy times I observed an adult male defend a female or her offspring against aggression by another troop member, not infrequently a high-ranking male. In all but six of these cases, the defender was a friend. Very few of these confrontations involved actual fighting; no male baboon, subordinate or dominant, is anxious to risk injury by the sharp canines of another.

Males are particularly solicitous guardians of their friends' youngest infants. If another male gets too close to an infant or if a juvenile female plays with it too roughly, the friend may intervene. Other troop members soon learn to be cautious when the mother's friend is nearby, and his presence provides the mother with a welcome respite from the annoying pokes and prods of curious females and juveniles obsessed with the new baby. Male baboons at Gombe Park in Tanzania and Amboseli Park in Kenya have also been seen rescuing infants from chimpanzees and lions. These several forms of male protection help to explain why females in Eburru Cliffs stuck closer to their friends in the first few months after giving birth than at any other time.

The male-infant relationship develops out of the male's friendship with the mother, but as the infant matures, this new bond takes on a life of its own. My co-worker Nancy Nicolson found that by about nine months of age, infants actively sought out their male friends when the mother was a few yards away, suggesting that the male may function as an alternative caregiver. This seemed to be especially true for infants undergoing unusually early or severe weaning. (Weaning is generally a gradual, prolonged process, but there is tremendous variation among mothers in the timing and intensity of weaning. See "Mother Baboons," *Natural History,* September 1980.) After being rejected by the mother, the crying infant often approached the male friend and sat huddled against him until its whimpers subsided. Two of the infants in Eburru Cliffs lost their mothers when they were still quite young. In each case, their bond with the mother's friend subsequently intensified, and—perhaps as a result—both infants survived.

A close bond with a male may also improve the infant's nutrition. Larger than all other troop members, adult males monopolize the best feeding sites. In general, the personal space surrounding a feeding male is inviolate, but he usually tolerates intrusions by the infants of his female friends, giving them access to choice feeding spots.

Although infants follow their male friends around rather than the reverse, the males seem genuinely attached to their tiny companions. During feeding, the male and infant express their pleasure in each other's company by sharing spirited, antiphonal grunting duets. If the infant whimpers in distress, the male friend is likely to cease feeding, look at the infant, and grunt softly, as if in sympathy, until the whimpers cease. When the male rests, the infants of his female friends may huddle behind him, one after the other, forming a "train," or, if feeling energetic, they may use his body as a trampoline.

When I returned to Eburru Cliffs four years after my initial study ended, several of the bonds formed between males and the infants of their female friends were still intact (in other cases, either the male or the infant or both had disappeared). When these bonds involved recently matured females, their long-time male associates showed no sexual interest in them, even though the females mated with other adult males. Mothers and sons, and usually maternal siblings, show similar sexual inhibitions in baboons and many other primate species.

The development of an intimate relationship between a male and the infant of his female friend raises an obvious question: Is the male the infant's father? To answer this question definitely we would need to conduct genetic analysis, which was not possible for these baboons. Instead, I estimated paternity probabilities from observations of the temporary (a few hours or days) exclusive mating relationships, or consortships, that estrous females form with a series of different males. These estimates were apt to be fairly accurate, since changes in the female's sexual swelling allow one to pinpoint the timing of conception to within a few days. Most females consorted with only two or three males during this period, and these males were termed likely fathers.

In about half the friendships, the male was indeed likely to be the father of his friend's most recent infant, but in the other half he was not—in fact, he had never been seen mating with the female. Interestingly, males who were friends with the mother but not likely fathers nearly always developed a rela-

tionship with her infant, while males who had mated with the female but were not her friend usually did not. Thus friendship with the mother, rather than paternity, seems to mediate the development of male-infant bonds. Recently, a similar pattern was documented for South American capuchin monkeys in a laboratory study in which paternity was determined genetically.

These results fly in the face of a prominent theory that claims males will invest in infants only when they are closely related. If males are not fostering the survival of their own genes by caring for the infant, then why do they do so? I suspected that the key was female choice. If females preferred to mate with males who had already demonstrated friendly behavior, then friendships with mothers and their infants might pay off in the future when the mothers were ready to mate again.

To find out if this was the case, I examined each male's sexual behavior with females he had befriended before they resumed estrus. In most cases, males consorted considerably more often with their friends than with other females. Baboon females typically mate with several different males, including both friends and nonfriends, but prior friendship increased a male's probability of mating with a female above what it would have been otherwise.

This increased probability seemed to reflect female preferences. Females occasionally overtly advertised their disdain for certain males and their desire for others. Zizi's behavior, described above, is a good example. Virgil was not one of her friends, but Cyclops was. Usually, however, females expressed preferences and aversions more subtly. For example, Delphi, a petite adolescent female, found herself pursued by Hector, a middle-aged adult male. She did not run away or refuse to mate with him, but whenever he wasn't watching, she looked around for her friend Homer, an adolescent male. When she succeeded in catching Homer's eye, she narrowed her eyes and flattened her ears against her skull, the friendliest face one baboon can send another. This told Homer she would rather be with him. Females expressed satisfaction with a current consort partner by staying close to him, initiating copulations, and not making advances toward other males. Baboons are very sensitive to such cues, as indicated by an experimental study in which rival hamadryas baboons rarely challenged a male-female pair if the female strongly preferred her current partner. Similarly, in Eburru Cliffs, males were less apt to challenge consorts involving a pair that shared a long-term friendship.

Even though females usually consorted with their friends, they also mated with other males, so it is not surprising that friendships were most vulnerable during periods of sexual activity. In a few cases, the female consorted with another male more often than with her friend, but the friendship survived nevertheless. One female, however, formed a strong sexual bond with a new male. This bond persisted after conception, replacing her previous friendship.

My observations suggest that adolescent and young adult females tend to have shorter, less stable friendships than do older females. Some friendships, however, last a very long time. When I returned to Eburru Cliffs six years after my study began, five couples were still together. It is possible that friendships occasionally last for life (baboons probably live twenty to thirty years in the wild), but it will require longer studies, and some very patient scientists, to find out.

By increasing both the male's chances of mating in the future and the likelihood that a female's infant will survive, friendship contributes to the reproductive success of both partners. This clarifies the evolutionary basis of friendship-forming tendencies in baboons, but what does friendship mean to a baboon? To answer this question we need to view baboons as sentient beings with feelings and goals not unlike our own in similar circumstances. Consider, for example, the friendship between Thalia and Alexander.

The affair began one evening as Alex and Thalia sat about fifteen feet apart on the sleeping cliffs. It was like watching two novices in a singles bar. Alex stared at Thalia until she turned and almost caught him looking at her. He glanced away immediately, and then she stared at him until his head began to turn toward her. She suddenly became engrossed in grooming her toes. But as soon as Alex looked away, her gaze returned to him. They went on like this for more than fifteen minutes, always with split-second timing. Finally, Alex managed to catch Thalia looking at him. He made the friendly eyes-narrowed, ears-back face and smacked his lips together rhythmically. Thalia froze, and for a second she looked into his eyes. Alex approached, and Thalia, still nervous, groomed him. Soon she calmed down, and I found them still together on the cliffs the next morning. Looking back on this event months later, I realized that it marked the beginning of their friendship. Six years later, when I returned to Eburru Cliffs, they were still friends.

If flirtation forms an integral part of baboon friendship, so does jealousy. Overt displays of jealousy, such as chasing a friend away from a potential rival, occur occasionally, but like humans, baboons often express their emotions in more subtle ways. One evening a colleague and I climbed the cliffs and settled down near Sherlock, who was friends with Cybelle, a middle-aged female still foraging on the ground below the cliffs. I observed Cybelle while my colleague watched Sherlock, and we kept up a running commentary. As long as Cybelle was feeding or interacting with females, Sherlock was relaxed, but each time she approached another male, his body would stiffen, and he would stare intently at the scene below. When Cybelle presented politely to a male who had recently tried to befriend her, Sherlock even made threatening sounds under his breath. Cybelle was not in estrus at the time, indicating that male baboon jealousy extends beyond the sexual arena to include affiliative interactions

between a female friend and other males.

Because baboon friendships are embedded in a network of friendly and antagonistic relationships, they inevitably lead to repercussions extending beyond the pair. For example, Virgil once provoked his weaker rival Cyclops into a fight by first attacking Cyclops' friend Phoebe. On another occasion, Sherlock chased Circe, Hector's best friend, just after Hector had chased Antigone, Sherlock's friend.

In another incident, the prime adult male Triton challenged Cyclops' possession of meat. Cyclops grew increasingly tense and seemed about to abandon the prey to the younger male. Then Cyclops' friend Phoebe appeared with her infant Phyllis. Phyllis wandered over to Cyclops. He immediately grabbed her, held her close, and threatened Triton away from the prey. Because any challenge to Cyclops now involved a threat to Phyllis as well, Triton risked being mobbed by Phoebe and her relatives and friends. For this reason, he backed down. Males frequently use the infants of their female friends as buffers in this way. Thus, friendship involves costs as well as benefits because it makes the participants vulnerable to social manipulation or redirected aggression by others.

Finally, as with humans, friendship seems to mean something different to each baboon. Several females in Eburru Cliffs had only one friend. They were devoted companions. Louise and Pandora, for example, groomed their friend Virgil and no other male. Then there was Leda, who, with five friends, spread herself more thinly than any other female. These contrasting patterns of friendship were associated with striking personality differences. Louise and Pandora were unobtrusive females who hung around quietly with Virgil and their close relatives. Leda seemed to be everywhere at once, playing with infants, fighting with juveniles, and making friends with males. Similar differences were apparent among the males. Some devoted a great deal of time and energy to cultivating friendships with females, while others focused more on challenging other males. Although we probably will never fully understand the basis of these individual differences, they contribute immeasurably to the richness and complexity of baboon society.

Male-female friendships may be widespread among primates. They have been reported for many other groups of savanna baboons, and they also occur in rhesus and Japanese macaques, capuchin monkeys, and perhaps in bonobos (pygmy chimpanzees). These relationships should give us pause when considering popular scenarios for the evolution of male-female relationships in humans. Most of these scenarios assume that, except for mating, males and females had little to do with one another until the development of a sexual division of labor, when, the story goes, females began to rely on males to provide meat in exchange for gathered food. This, it has been argued, set up new selection pressures favoring the development of long-term bonds between individual males and females, female sexual fidelity, and as paternity certainty increased, greater male investment in the offspring of these unions. In other words, once women began to gather and men to hunt, presto—we had the nuclear family.

This scenario may have more to do with cultural biases about women's economic dependence on men and idealized views of the nuclear family than with the actual behavior of our hominid ancestors. The nonhuman primate evidence challenges this story in at least three ways.

First, long-term bonds between the sexes can evolve in the absence of a sexual division of labor or food sharing. In our primate relatives, such relationships rest on exchanges of social, not economic, benefits.

Second, primate research shows that highly differentiated, emotionally intense male-female relationships can occur without sexual exclusivity. Ancestral men and women may have experienced intimate friendships long before they invented marriage and norms of sexual fidelity.

Third, among our closest primate relatives, males clearly provide mothers and infants with social benefits even when they are unlikely to be the fathers of those infants. In return, females provide a variety of benefits to the friendly males, including acceptance into the group and, at least in baboons, increased mating opportunities in the future. This suggests that efforts to reconstruct the evolution of hominid societies may have overemphasized what the female must supposedly do (restrict her mating to just one male) in order to obtain male parental investment.

Maybe it is time to pay more attention to what the male must do (provide benefits to females and young) in order to obtain female cooperation. Perhaps among our ancestors, as in baboons today, sex and friendship went hand in hand. As for marriage—well, that's another story.

10

POLITICAL ANIMAL[1]

Meredith F. Small

For a long time, the study of the evolution of human intelligence focused on tool use. As Meredith Small reports, this is beginning to be rethought. A new theory is that humans and other primates have large brains and high intelligence not so much to manipulate tools, but rather to enable them to deal with complex social situations.

Almost four million years ago hairy creatures with long arms, low brows and jutting faces stood up on two legs and began to stroll across the African savanna. Less than four feet tall at their full bipedal height, these hominids, now called australopithecines (meaning southern apes), actually were more human than ape, but they shared an important feature with their simian ancestors: they had a small brain, measuring scarcely 450 cubic centimeters, a bit smaller than a softball and not quite a third the volume of the modern human brain. Although next to nothing is known of their daily life and social behavior, it is reasonably certain that the australopithecines underwent an adaptive radiation about three million years ago and that eventually several species coexisted.

It was from one of these small-brained groups that our own genus, *Homo,* evolved some two million years ago. The first human species, known as *Homo habilis* (handy man)—a sobriquet conferred in the early 1960s by the English paleontologist Louis S. B. Leakey for the animal's knack of fashioning stone tools—flourished in eastern and southern Africa. Above all else the trait that distinguished the new humans from their forebears was a substantially larger brain.

H. habilis's evolutionary successor was *Homo erectus* (upright man), who made his appearance in the Pleistocene, about 1.5 million years ago. It was *H. erectus,* the fossil record suggests, that radiated north from Africa and made the first forays into Europe and Asia. Though he retained many simian features, he had a much more developed brain than any of his antecedents—perhaps as large as 750 cubic centimeters. This encephalization con-

[1]This article is reprinted by permission of *The Sciences* and is from the March/April 1990 issue. Individual subscriptions are $28 per year. Write to: *The Sciences*, 2 East 63rd Street, New York, NY 10021.

tinued steadily in the next several hundred millennia, until, about 100,000 years ago, *H. erectus* gave way to *Homo sapiens* sapien— modern man—who had all but shed his apelike appearance and whose brain had burgeoned to its present volume of 1,400 cubic centimeters.

The enormous increase in the growth and sophistication of the hominid brain over a relatively short period in evolution (it doubled in size in roughly a million years) has long intrigued investigators. Human beings have the largest brains, relative to body size. In absolute size the brains of whales, dolphins and elephants are larger than the human brain, but they are far less complex. Clearly the large human brain and the power of reason it confers have been crucial to our survival and success. But why did natural selection favor humans with such a unique mental development?

Until recently the most commonly held view among anthropologists was that the rapid growth of the human brain was a result of some combination of the beginning of tool use, the rise of group hunting and the development of language. And to be sure, it must be more than coincidence that the most dramatic growth of hominid brain tissue took place in the million years or so of evolution from *H. habilis* through *H. erectus.* For it was in that period that tools, a carnivorous diet (instead of a herbivorous one), the consequent need for cooperative tracking of game, and, it

is thought, a spoken language became essential features of hominid life.

Nevertheless, there is a competing body of research, initiated in the 1960s and greatly intensified in the past several years, suggesting that although the tool-hunting language connection may have accelerated human brain development, it was not the only driving force. Indeed, the fossil record indicates that in the matter of brain growth we humans are not unique. Rather we represent the extreme end of a sixty-million-year primate continuum, throughout which our biological order has consistently outstripped our mammalian competitors in intelligence. What is it then about being a primate that has fostered superior mental evolution? Field and laboratory studies conducted on apes, monkeys and lemurs have demonstrated that those animals live remarkably complex social lives: they recognize kinship, form long-term friendships and make strategic social decisions. A growing number of investigators believe that this social acumen—which, after all, provided the foundation for such late hominid refinements as cooperative hunting and language—may be the fundamental selective force behind the evolution of primate intelligence.

In the early 1960s, when Louis and Mary Leakey unearthed stone tools —essentially sharpened flakes of stone— alongside bones of *H. habilis* in Tanzania's (then Tanganyika) Olduvai Gorge, the find provoked enormous scholarly interest in the significance of toolmaking to human evolution. Subsequent discoveries in Africa by the Leakeys and others gave rise to a school of thought according to which the design, manufacture and use of utensils were considered the first milestones in the emergence of mankind. Certainly the capacity to envision a three-dimensional object, to foresee its potential applications, and then to set about creating the tool and putting it to work were far beyond the intellectual endowments of the ape. It thus seemed logical that handy man's time on earth coincided with such a sharp increase in hominid brain development. In particular, scholars noted, one of the regions of the human brain that underwent the greatest growth and sophistication in that period was the sensory-motor cortex, the area charged with controlling our hands.

Although the tool-use theory of human brain development still appears in some textbooks on evolution, it no longer holds sway among most scholars. Crucial in debunking the theory were long-term studies of African chimpanzees conducted by the English primatologist Jane Goodall, among other investigators. In her 1986 book, *The Chimpanzees of Gombe,* Goodall notes two extracts from a diary she had compiled a quarter-century before. In the entry for November 4, 1960, she describes watching a chimpanzee (which she had named David Greybeard) hovering around a termite mound. After a few moments, the animal "very deliberately, pulled a thick grass stalk toward

him and broke off a piece about 45 centimeters long." Then Greybeard loped out of view. Two days later Goodall encountered two other male chimpanzees at the termite mound, each with his own length of grass—which she refers to as "straw." This time she saw something more:

> It [the straw] was held in the left hand, poked into the mound, and then removed coated with termites. The straw was raised to the mouth and the insects [were] picked off with the lips along the length of the straw, starting in the middle.

More than a decade passed before the idea gained acceptance, but Goodall's observation revealed for the first time that toolmaking and tool use are not uniquely human activities. Admittedly grass dipsticks are crude tools compared with hand axes; nevertheless it is now clear that chimpanzees too have the foresight to craft implements for improving their lives. Although Goodall acknowledged that the invention of progressively intricate and specialized tools marked "a crucial step in our evolution," she maintained that it is not what separates man from the apes.

Other adaptive skills might also account for the human encephalization. Perhaps *H. habilis's* shift from a preference for vegetable matter to a reliance on meat led to an increase in intellect in that stage of our past. Tracking large, often dangerous herds of game, for example, and cooperating in organized group hunts require sophisticated thought processes. Even more plausible is the possibility that the early hominids were scavengers who had to use their wits to compete with scavenging wolves, hyenas, lions and other social carnivores, or even with the primary predator, for rights to a carcass. But a tie between selection for large brain size and meat eating is equivocal. The complexities of group hunting or scavenging doubtless sped our journey toward reason, but as with tool use these activities are not peculiar to the genus *Homo* or even to the primate order at large. Many other social carnivores both track transient food resources and actively cooperate to fell prey. More likely, many investigators began to believe, the rapid neural expansion in the hominid lineage was prompted by a feedback loop involving toolmaking, hunting and the development of speech.

The increasing complexity of their lives also made it highly advantageous for hominids to develop an effective system of communications means of conveying information about how to make tools and weapons, where to find food, how to coordinate hunting expeditions, and other aspects of day-to-day existence. Our ancestors' morphological response to this challenge culminated in a spoken language. Exactly when this transpired is a mysterious and widely debated issue. Concrete proof of any hypothesis seems impossible, since most of the anatomical accessories for human speech, made of muscle and cartilage,

have disappeared from the fossil record. Nevertheless, it seems likely that speech evolved relatively late in the evolution of *Homo*.

Although the human ability to articulate abstract ideas with vocal symbols is unique among living things, humans are not the only creatures with a signaling system. A host of other highly social animals—including insects—communicate through noises, body language or chemical secretions. They also have an uncanny ability to keep track of their food resources. A spoken language, to be sure, enhanced the quality of hominid life and may have been an invaluable ally in the harsh natural world. But it was not necessary for survival.

Indisputably then, toolmaking, hunting and speech combined in some way to develop the evolving hominid brain. Manual dexterity, tactical planning, language, learning and memory all point to an increase in cerebral capacity and complexity—and so to enhanced adaptiveness in the hominid environment. This increasing cultural sophistication no doubt helped foster the neural explosion that took place between the time of *H. habilis* and that of *H. sapiens*. But to assume that this lateblooming surge of brain tissue represents the whole of the evolution of human intellect is to take a narrow view. Such a hypothesis ignores the reality that consistent brain growth was nothing new for primates; rather it was a characteristic trait of the primate order tens of millions of years before the hominids' debut on the evolutionary stage.

As far back as the Eocene, sixty million years ago, the brains of the ancestral prosimians were expanding—in relative as well as absolute size—both in the temporal lobe and in the cerebellum. The primate brain became broader and more spherical. The ancestral prosimians were primarily arboreal creatures, and much of the increase in brain size reflects advances in visual acuity that were important for flying through space. Fossil remains indicate that a tarsier-like prosimian—assumed to be the transitional primate between the prosimians and the anthropoids (monkeys and apes)—underwent substantial brain expansion: during the Eocene alone, a span of twenty million years, this ancestral tarsier's brain increased in size by sixty-five percent. The upward trend in brain size and, presumably, intelligence continued throughout the Oligocene (the age of monkeys, which began forty million years ago) and the Miocene (which began twenty-five million years ago, and during which apes were the dominant primates). The monkeys and the apes of the Oligocene and the Miocene probably had color vision, manual dexterity and excellent motor control in order to conduct their arboreal lives.

Taken as a whole, the primate fossil record suggests that the spurt of hominid brain growth is only the steep rise of an already positive slope. The consistent and precipitous increase in brain size among fossil primates represents anatomical and intellectual specialization of the entire order—not

merely of its human membership. But what does it mean to have a larger brain? Is there necessarily a direct relation between quantity and quality of brain tissue?

The connection between brain size and intelligence and, indeed, the very definition of intelligence have been points of considerable controversy. To a large extent, modern notions about the parallel growth of the brain and the primate mind are traceable to broad assumptions put forth by Othniel Charles Marsh, a nineteenth-century paleontologist from Yale University who once combed the American West for fossils under the guidance of William F. ("Buffalo Bill") Cody. In 1886 Marsh proposed that brain size increased gradually in relation to body size through geologic time and that the growth was accompanied by an increase in the complexity of cerebral convolutions and connections.

In recent years the influential neuroanatomist Harry Jerison of the University of California at Los Angeles has argued that "gross brain size" is a "natural biological statistic" for estimating the number of neurons and glial cells in the brain. More precisely, Jerison suggests, the mass of a particular area of the brain is a measure of the extent to which an individual can perform the tasks that the region controls. But, as other workers have cautioned, a complete understanding of the brain and intelligence will be possible only when neuroanatomists have detailed the brain's microorganization and local circuitry, features that—contrary to

Marsh's durable, century-old theory—may prove to have little or nothing to do with overall brain size. Furthermore, the correlation between brain and intellect awaits a satisfying, quantitative definition of animal intelligence, which has generally been sidestepped by comparative psychologists and animal behaviorists. Does intelligence stop at information processing (attention, learning, memory, concept formation)? Or should the definition also embrace emotion, aggression, motivation and biological rhythms? These are open questions, though most experts would agree that whatever else constitutes intelligence, the brighter creatures among us can reason, remember, strategize and alter their behavior according to novel situations.

Acknowledging the considerable scholarly murkiness about the connection between brain and mind, one is left with the following: some selective pressure has been driving the persistent growth of the primate brain since Eocene times. Increasingly, workers are tracing this trend to one theme that runs consistently through the primate order, from the relatively small-brained prosimians to human beings. In contrast with the vast mammalian majority, most primates live in some kind of group. In contrast with schools of fishes or herds of ungulates, the primate groups are not mere aggregations but true social organizations, involving complicated interactions between members and usually maintaining long-term cohesiveness from generation to generation through a dynamic web of interpersonal intrigue.

The sense of community comes at a price, of course: group members force a competition at all levels for food, mates and comfortable places to sleep. Nevertheless, primate social life has endured, and one can only assume that the benefits, such as protection from predators, sharing parental tasks, and more efficient foraging, far outweigh the inconveniences. It may well be that social intelligence, the ability to exploit relationships within one's own group—whether among a troop of lemurs on Madagascar, or at a cocktail party in Manhattan —has energized the growth of the primate brain and the expansion of the primate mind.

In 1966 the primatologist Alison Jolly, now at Princeton University, published a paper in the journal *Science,* titled "Lemur social behavior and primate intelligence," which stands as the first study linking sociality to the evolving primate brain. Lemurs, whose brains are smaller than those of most other primates, traditionally fail miserably on standard laboratory tests of animal intelligence. As Jolly pointed out, however, the tests more often than not involve the manipulation of some sort of gadgetry—bells, buttons or the like—for a reward, typically food. She suggested that a more appropriate measure of their mental capacity is their ability to form and sustain intricate social bonds.

Like the monkeys and the apes, which so outclass them on the standard tests, lemurs live in troops made up of a diverse blend of sexes and ages. The troops are organized in female-dominated hierarchies, and they display various cohesive behaviors, including play, mutual grooming, intramural spats and stink fights (during which a male wipes urine on his tail and shakes it at another male), and group response to hostile carnivores, usually expressed by gathering round to mob the predator. This knack for functioning as a social group, day in and day out, is a special kind of intelligence, more subtle than that required to push buttons—a social acumen calling for a good memory, the ability to recognize and categorize others and the capacity to act on that knowledge.

Detailed observations of several primate species in the past two decades have borne out Jolly's contention: primates are indeed socially sophisticated creatures that maintain consistent, tightly reinforced relationships with troopmates. Three of the most thoroughly studied social animals are Old World monkeys—macaques, vervet monkeys and baboons of the savanna. These primates live in female-bonded societies: the males are transients that migrate to other troops on reaching sexual maturity, but the females remain lifelong members of the groups in which they were born.

Serving as the infrastructure of these societies are complex female dominance hierarchies, which tend to be remarkably stable—an entrenched simian caste system perpetuated over the course of generations. From infancy each female learns her place in the scheme by experiencing the interactions between her mother and other females. A baby macaque, for instance, spends its first three months of life riding on its mother's back, where it may find itself swept into the midst of a fight, with a front row seat from which to view the behavior of the combatants and to see how its mother fares in the altercation. My work on Barbary macaques has demonstrated that this period of infant socialization is crucial to development. Barbary infants are passed among group members like squeaky toys; males, females and juveniles try their best to gain access to the pink and black babies. For infants these interactions form the macaque social web: personalities are shaped, relationships are established and long-term bonds begin to form. In other words, the infant gets a vivid seminar in the fabric of monkey life.

The bonds of blood are strong among Old World monkeys. One of the most apparent expressions of this intimacy is physical closeness: relatives typically travel, feed and sleep together. Mutual grooming, another common gesture of familiarity, most often takes place between mothers and offspring but also is engaged in by more distant relations—aunts and nieces, as well as males who have not yet abandoned the group. In hostile encounters, relatives always back up one another. Indeed, in the occasional instances when lower-ranking females mount successful coups against their superiors, they usually do so with the aid of a gang of nearby kin.

Friendships and alliances between monkeys often transcend the bounds of kinship. For example, the primatologist Barbara Smuts of the University of Michigan has shown that among certain baboons, males and females from different lineages carry on chaste friendships—at least in the beginning of a relationship. A female will typically associate with one or two males year round, grooming, feeding and sleeping with them. For most of this time she is either pregnant or lactating and is not sexually receptive. Then, when in estrus, she likely will favor her long-term pals as mates. In general, it is common for Old World monkeys to form alliances with members of other families. This clearly is a case of "you scratch my back, and I'll scratch yours"; alliances are forged and maintained through the principle of reciprocal altruism: a favor, whether it involves grooming in peacetime or defensive assistance in conflict, does not go unreturned.

Whenever friendships, alliances or other such relationships among monkeys were discussed two decades ago, there was the suspicion that the discussant was a wayward primatologist guilty of anthropomorphism, or projecting human social values onto baboons and other simians. These doubts were dispelled, at least in part, by work conducted in Kenya during the late 1970s on the small vervet monkey.

In a series of elegant field experiments Dorothy Cheney and Robert Seyfarth of the University of Pennsylvania asked a basic question: Are monkeys conscious of relationships? Cheney and Seyfarth played audiotape recordings of the screams of an imperiled juvenile vervet through a loudspeaker they had placed in a bush. The young monkey's mother and two female companions were next to the bush, and when the mother heard her offspring's recorded cries, she immediately turned toward the loudspeaker. Her behavior was hardly surprising, since most female mammals respond to the sounds of their offspring in distress. What was intriguing was the reaction of the two companions: on hearing the screams, they turned their heads not toward the loudspeaker but toward the mother. In other words, they could recognize the vocalization of the young vervet, and they could associate that juvenile with its mother.

A similar study by Sarah and Harold Gouzoules of Rockefeller University in New York focused on the rhesus macaques of Cayo Santiago, an island near Puerto Rico. The Gouzouleses discovered that mothers' responses varied with nuances in juveniles' screams. When their offspring were menaced by relatives, mothers responded with little more than indifference. Only when the young were threatened by nonkin macaques were their mothers roused to intervention. The investigators concluded that screams carry specific information about social relationships that macaques process when deciding on a course of action.

Working again with vervets, Cheney and Seyfarth probed further the subtleties of primate social awareness, this time paying attention to patterns of aggression. They noted that if monkey A threatened monkey B, it was likely that A would also threaten a relative of B later in the day. Even more intriguing was that a relative of A would also typically seek out and menace an unsuspecting member of B's troop, hinting that the original skirmish might escalate into a feud reminiscent of the battles between the Hatfields and the McCoys in the Appalachian hills. These observations support the idea that vervets have a concept of affiliation between individuals in their groups. In short, they know one another.

Another study, published in 1988 by Verena Dasser of the University of Zurich, proved that Javanese lion-tailed macaques also recognize relationships between troopmates. Dasser spent one year training her two female subjects to respond to slides depicting the mothers and juveniles in their group. The macaques were then tested on their ability to match slides of each mother with those of their offspring. Dasser's monkeys passed with flying colors: one answered correctly fourteen times in fourteen tries, and the other successfully linked mother and offspring twenty times out of twenty-two.

Discerning these complex social relationships, including kin associations, nonkin alliances, long-term friendships and interfamily grudges, requires intelligence of a reasonably high order. To be sure, just to keep track of it all requires a voluminous memory. These monkeys not only must remember who's who in the group but also must keep daily mental scorecards of their troopmates' actions. A bitter foe one day may be an ally the next, and vice versa. This knack for recognizing and cataloguing relationships, which primatologists call social cognition, seems impressive enough. But what a growing number of investigators believe is that the true distinction of primates is their dark side: an ability to manipulate others for personal gain.

As early as 1967 the Swiss ethologist Hans Kummer outlined what he called tripartite relations in the Hamadryas baboon of Ethiopia. Kummer observed that one Hamadryas, when embroiled in a conflict with another, is apt to use a third baboon—previously uninvolved in the fracas—to deceive the enemy. In other words, one baboon is able to use another for its own benefit.

Recently two psychologists, Andrew Whiten and Richard W. Byrne of the University of Saint Andrews in Fife, Scotland, suggested that social manipulation could be a prominent force in the evolution of primate intelligence. During fieldwork in South Africa Whiten and Byrne noted several expressions of what they describe as Machiavellian deception among baboons. In one instance a juvenile spied an adult female digging for corms, a kind of grass bulb or tuber—and a valued food resource that juveniles normally find hard to get. Although the young baboon was entirely unprovoked, it shrieked as if it were being attacked, prompting its mother to rush to the rescue and chase the feeding adult down the hill. Having duped both its mother and the unwitting feeder, the devious juvenile moved in to feast on the remaining corms.

Other investigators have cited cases of similar primate behavior that, if not quite worthy of the Borgia popes, nonetheless smacks of double-dealing. In a 1985 article Shirley C. Strum of the University of California at San Diego tells a steamy vignette about olive baboons, the plot of which—including the crucial ingredients sex, thievery and a corpse—might have been lifted from a grade-B movie:

> One of the female baboons. . . grew particularly fond of meat, although the males do most of the hunting. A male, one who does not willingly share, caught an antelope. The female edged up to him and groomed him until he lolled back under her attentions. She then snatched the antelope carcass and ran.

Taken together, these and other pieces of experimental and anecdotal evidence support the notion that primates are socially intelligent animals. Macaques, vervet monkeys and baboons recognize and differentiate between troopmates; they adhere to sophisticated hierarchies; they form and maintain relationships that benefit them in daily activities; and on occasion they manipulate others to serve their own desires. Members of the primate order have especially long periods of infant dependency compared with other mammals, because, it is believed, juveniles need the time to learn the ropes of their uniquely intricate social world.

What remains to be seen is whether this knowledge serves them well in the evolutionary sense. Any proposal that the need for these social machinations must have favored large and complex primate brains is equivocal, because no one has yet demonstrated a direct relation between social acumen and individual reproductive success. Until this critical information is in our grasp we must tread lightly when suggesting that social intelligence is the sole—or even the major—driving force behind the evolution of the primate brain. Still, it is incontestable that we are social animals and that knowing who we are, where we stand and how to get what we want - even at the expense of others - is key to survival for all primates, monkeys and humans alike.

11

NEW WOMEN OF THE ICE AGE[1]

Heather Pringle

For a long time, the study of human origins focused primarily on males and their typical activities, such as big-game hunting and stone tool manufacture. Recently, however, a new generation of archaeologists has been looking more at female hominids. As Heather Pringle reports, such research is raising questions about such issues as religion and the sexual division of labor during the Paleolithic.

The Black Venus of Dolni Vestonice, a small, splintered figurine sensuously fashioned from clay, is an envoy from a forgotten world. It is all soft curves, with breasts like giant pillows beneath a masked face. At nearly 26,000 years old, it ranks among the oldest known portrayals of women, and to generations of researchers, it has served as a powerful—if enigmatic—clue to the sexual politics of the Ice Age.

Excavators unearthed the Black Venus near the Czech village of Dolni Vestonice in 1924, on a hillside among charred, fractured mammoth bones and stone tools. (Despite its nickname, the Black Venus is actually reddish—it owes its name to the ash that covered it when it was found.) Since the mid-nineteenth century, researchers had discovered more than a dozen similar statuettes in caves and open-air sites from France to Russia. All were cradled in layers of earth littered with stone and bone weaponry, ivory jewelry, and the remains of extinct Ice Age animals. All were depicted naked or nearly so. Collectively, they came to be known as Venus figurines, after another ancient bare-breasted statue, the Venus de Milo. Guided at least in part by prevailing sexual stereotypes, experts interpreted the meaning of the figurines freely. The Ice Age camps that spawned this art, they concluded, were once the domain of hardworking male hunters and secluded, pampered women who spent their days in idleness like the harem slaves so popular in nineteenth-century art.

Over the next six decades, Czech archeologists expanded the excavations at Dolni Vestonice, painstakingly combing the site square meter by square meter. By the 1990s they had unearthed thousands of bone, stone, and

---

[1]Originally published in *Discover* (April 1998). Reprinted with permission from the publisher.

clay artifacts and had wrested 19 radio-carbon dates from wood charcoal that sprinkled camp floors. And they had shaded and refined their portrait of Ice Age life. Between 29,000 and 25,000 years ago, they concluded, wandering bands had passed the cold months of the year repeatedly at Dolni Vestonice. Armed with short-range spears, the men appeared to have been specialists in hunting tusk-wielding mammoths and other big game, hauling home great mountains of meat to feed their dependent mates and children. At night men feasted on mammoth steaks, fed their fires with mammoth bone, and fueled their sexual fantasies with tiny figurines of women carved from mammoth ivory and fired from clay. It was the ultimate man's world.

Or was it? Over the past few months, a small team of American archeologists has raised some serious doubts. Amassing critical and previously overlooked evidence from Dolni Vestonice and the neighboring site of Pavlov, Olga Soffer, James Adovasio, and David Hyland now propose that human survival there had little to do with manly men hurling spears at big-game animals. Instead, observes Soffer, one of the world's leading authorities on Ice Age hunters and gatherers and an archeologist at the University of Illinois in Champaign–Urbana, it depended largely on women, plants, and a technique of hunting previously invisible in the archeological evidence—net hunting. "This is not the image we've always had of Upper Paleolithic macho guys out killing animals up close and personal," Soffer explains. "Net hunting

is communal, and it involves the labor of children and women. And this has lots of implications."

Many of these implications make her conservative colleagues cringe because they raise serious questions about the focus of previous studies. European archeologists have long concentrated on analyzing broken stone tools and butchered big-game bones, the most plentiful and best preserved relics of the Upper Paleolithic era (which stretched from 40,000 to 12,000 years ago). From these analyses, researchers have developed theories about how these societies once hunted and gathered food. Most researchers ruled out the possibility of women hunters for biological reasons. Adult females, they reasoned, had to devote themselves to breast-feeding and tending infants. "Human babies have always been immature and dependent," says Soffer. "If women are the people who are always involved with biological reproduction and the rearing of the young, then that is going to constrain their behavior. They have to provision that child. For fathers, provisioning is optional."

To test theories about Upper Paleolithic life, researchers looked to ethnography, the scientific description of modern and historical cultural groups. While the lives of modern hunters do not exactly duplicate those of ancient hunters, they supply valuable clues to universal human behavior. "Modern ethnography cannot be used to clone the past," says Soffer. "But people have always had to solve problems. Nature and social relationships present problems to people. We use ethnography to look for theoretical insights into human behavior, test them with ethnography, and if they work, assume that they represent a universal feature of human behavior."

But when researchers began turning to ethnographic descriptions of hunting societies, they unknowingly relied on a very incomplete literature. Assuming that women in surviving hunting societies were homebodies who simply tended hearths and suckled children, most early male anthropologists spent their time with male informants. Their published ethnographies brim with descriptions of males making spears and harpoons and heaving these weapons at reindeer, walruses, and whales. Seldom do they mention the activities of women. Ethnography, it seemed, supported theories of ancient male big-game hunters. "When they talked about primitive man, it was always 'he,'" says Soffer. "The 'she' was missing."

Recent anthropological research has revealed just how much Soffer's colleagues overlooked. By observing women in the few remaining hunter-gatherer societies and by combing historical accounts of tribal groups more thoroughly, anthropologists have come to realize how critical the female half of the population has always been to survival. Women and children have set snares, laid spring traps, sighted game and participated in animal drives and surrounds—forms of hunting that endangered neither young mothers nor their offspring. They dug starchy roots and collected other plant carbohydrates essential to survival. They even hunted, on occasion, with the projectile points

traditionally deemed men's weapons. "I found references to Inuit women carrying bows and arrows, especially the blunt arrows that were used for hunting birds," says Linda Owen, an archeologist at the University of Tubingen in Germany.

The revelations triggered a volley of new research. In North America, Soffer and her team have found tantalizing evidence of the hunting gear often favored by women in historical societies. In Europe, archeobotanists are analyzing Upper Paleolithic hearths for evidence of plant remains probably gathered by women and children, while lithics specialists are poring over stone tools to detect new clues to their uses. And the results are gradually reshaping our understanding of Ice Age society. The famous Venus figurines, say archeologists of the new school, were never intended as male pornography: instead they may have played a key part in Upper Paleolithic rituals that centered on women. And such findings, pointing toward a more important role for Paleolithic women than had previously been assumed, are giving many researchers pause.

Like many of her colleagues, Soffer clearly relishes the emerging picture of Upper Paleolithic life. "I think life back then was a hell of a lot more egalitarian than it was with your later peasant societies," she says. "Of course the Paleolithic women were pulling their own weight." After sifting through Ice Age research for nearly two decades, Soffer brings a new critical approach to the notion—flattering to so many of her male colleagues—of mighty male mammoth hunters. "Very few archeologists are hunters," she notes, so it never occurred to most of them to look into the mechanics of hunting dangerous tusked animals. They just accepted the ideas they'd inherited from past work.

But the details of hunting bothered Soffer. Before the fifth century B.C., no tribal hunters in Asia or Africa had ever dared make their living from slaying elephants; the great beasts were simply too menacing. With the advent of the Iron Age in Africa, the situation changed. New weapons allowed Africans to hunt elephants and trade their ivory with Greeks and Romans. A decade ago, keen to understand how prehistoric bands had slaughtered similar mammoths, Soffer began studying Upper Paleolithic sites on the Russian and Eastern European plains. To her surprise, the famous mammoth bone beds were strewn with cumbersome body parts, such as 220-pound skulls, that sensible hunters would generally abandon. Moreover, the bones exhibited widely differing degrees of weathering, as if they had sat on the ground for varying lengths of time. To Soffer, it looked suspiciously as if Upper Paleolithic hunters had simply camped next to places where the pachyderms had perished naturally--such as water holes or salt licks–and mined the bones for raw materials.

Soffer began analyzing data researchers had gathered describing the sex and age ratios of mammoths excavated from four Upper Paleolithic sites. She found many juveniles, a smaller number of adult females, and hardly any males. The distribution mirrored the death pattern other researchers had observed at African water holes, where the weakest animals perished closest to the water and the strongest farther off. "Imagine the worst time of year in Africa, which is the drought season," explains Soffer. "There is no water, and elephants need an enormous amount. The ones in the worst shape—your weakest, your infirm, your young—are going to be tethered to that water before they die. They are in such horrendous shape, they don't have any extra energy to go anywhere. The ones in better shape would wander off slight distances and then keel over farther away. You've got basket cases and you've got ones that can walk 20 feet."

To Soffer, the implications of this study were clear. Upper Paleolithic bands had pitched their camps next to critical resources such as ancient salt licks or water holes. There the men spent more time scavenging bones and ivory from mammoth carcasses than they did risking life and limb by attacking 6,600-pound pachyderms with short-range spears. "If one of these Upper Paleolithic guys killed a mammoth, and occasionally they did," concedes Soffer dryly, "they probably didn't stop talking about it for ten years."

But if Upper Paleolithic families weren't often tucking into mammoth steaks, what were they hunting and how? Soffer found the first unlikely clue in 1991, while sifting through hundreds of tiny clay fragments recovered from the Upper Paleolithic site of Pavlov, which lies just a short walk from Dolni Vestonice. Under a magnifying lens, Soffer noticed something strange on a few of the fragments: a series of parallel lines impressed on their surfaces. What could have left such a regular pattern? Puzzled, Soffer photographed the pieces, all of which had been unearthed from a zone sprinkled with wood charcoal that was radiocarbon-dated at between 27,000 and 25,000 years ago.

When she returned home, Soffer had the film developed. And one night on an impulse, she put on a slide show for a visiting colleague, Jim Adovasio. "We'd run out of cable films," she jokes. Staring at the images projected on Soffer's refrigerator, Adovasio, an archeologist at Mercyhurst College in Pennsylvania and an expert on ancient fiber technology, immediately recognized the impressions of plant fibers. On a few, he could actually discern a pattern of interlacing fibers—weaving.

Without a doubt, he said, he and Soffer were gazing at textiles or basketry. They were the oldest—by nearly 7,000 years—ever found. Just how these pieces of weaving got impressed in clay, he couldn't say. "It may be that a lot of these [materials] were lying around on clay floors," he notes. "When the houses burned, the walked-in images were subsequently left in the clay floors."

Soffer and Adovasio quickly made arrangements to fly back to the Czech Republic. At the Dolni Vestonice branch of the Institute of Archeology, Soffer sorted through nearly 8,400 fired clay pieces, weeding out the rejects. Adovasio made positive clay casts of 90. Back in Pennsylvania, he and his Mer-

cyhurst colleague David Hyland peered at the casts under a zoom stereomicroscope, measuring warps and wefts. Forty-three revealed impressions of basketry and textiles. Some of the latter were as finely woven as a modern linen tablecloth. But as Hyland stared at four of the samples, he noted something potentially more fascinating: impressions of cordage bearing weaver's knots, a technique that joins two lengths of cord and that is commonly used for making nets of secure mesh. It looked like a tiny shred of a net bag, or perhaps a hunting net. Fascinated, Soffer expanded the study. She spent six weeks at the Moravian Museum in Brno, sifting through the remainder of the collections from Dolni Vestonice. Last fall, Adovasio spied the telltale impressions of Ice Age mesh on one of the new casts.

The mesh, measuring two inches across, is far too delicate for hunting deer or other large prey. But hunters at Dolni Vestonice could have set nets of this size to capture hefty Ice Age hares, each carrying some six pounds of meat, and other furbearers such as arctic fox and red fox. As it turns out, the bones of hares and foxes litter camp floors at Dolni Vestonice and Pavlov. Indeed, this small game accounts for 46 percent of the individual animals recovered at Pavlov. Soffer, moreover, doesn't rule out the possibility of turning up bits of even larger nets. Accomplished weavers in North America once knotted mesh with which they captured 1,000-pound elk and 300-pound bighorn sheep. "In fact, when game officials have to move sheep out west, it's by nets," she adds. "You throw nets on them and they just lie down. It's a very safe way of hunting."

In many historical societies, she observes, women played a key part in net hunting since the technique did not call for brute strength nor did it place young mothers in physical peril. Among Australian aborigines, for example, women as well as men knotted the mesh, laboring for as much as two or three years on a fine net. Among native North American groups, they helped lay out their handiwork on poles across a valley floor. Then the entire camp joined forces as beaters. Fanning out across the valley, men, women, and children alike shouted and screamed, flushing out game an driving it in the direction of the net. "Everybody and their mother could participate," says Soffer. "Some people were beating, others were screaming or holding the net. And once you got the net on these animals, they were immobilized. You didn't need brute force. You could club them, hit them any old way."

People seldom returned home empty-handed. Researchers living among the net-hunting Mbuti in the forests of Congo report that they capture game every time they lay out their woven traps, scooping up 50 percent of the animals encountered. "Nets are a far more valued item in their panoply of food-producing things than bows and arrows are," says Adovasio. So lethal are these traps that the Mbuti generally rack up more meat than they can consume, trading the surplus with neighbors. Other net hunters traditionally smoked or dried their catch and stored it

for leaner times. Or they polished it off immediately in large ceremonial feasts. The hunters of Dolni Vestonice and Pavlov, says Soffer, probably feasted during ancient rituals. Archeologists unearthed no evidence of food storage pits at either site. But there is much evidence of ceremony. At Dolni Vestonice, for example, many clay figurines appear to have been ritually destroyed in secluded parts of the site.

Soffer doubts that the inhabitants of Dolni Vestonice and Pavlov were the only net makers in Ice Age Europe. Camps stretching from Germany to Russia are littered with a notable abundance of small-game bones, from hares to birds like ptarmigan. And at least some of their inhabitants whittled bone tools that look much like the awls and net spacers favored by historical net makers. Such findings, agree Soffer and Adovasio, reveal just how shaky the most widely accepted reconstructions of Upper Paleolithic life are. "These terribly stilted interpretations," says Adovasio, "with men hunting big animals all the time and the poor females waiting at home for these guys to bring home the bacon—what crap."

In her home outside Munich, Linda Owen finds other faults with this traditional image. Owen, an American born and raised, specializes in the microscopic analysis of stone tools. In her years of work, she often noticed that many of the tools made by hunters who roamed Europe near the end of the Upper Paleolithic era, some 18,000 to 12,000 years ago, resembled pounding stones and other gear for harvesting and processing plants. Were women and children gathering and storing wild plant foods?

Most of her colleagues saw little value in pursuing the question. Indeed, some German archeologists contended that 90 percent of the human diet during the Upper Paleolithic era came from meat. But as Owen began reading nutritional studies, she saw that heavy meat consumption would spell death. To stoke the body's cellular engines, human beings require energy from protein, fat, or carbohydrates. Of these, protein is the least efficient. To burn it, the body must boost its metabolic rate by 10 percent, straining the liver's ability to absorb oxygen. Unlike carnivorous animals, whose digestive and metabolic systems are well adapted to a meat-only diet, humans who consume more than half their calories as lean meat will die from protein poisoning. In Upper Paleolithic times, hunters undoubtedly tried to round out their diets with fat from wild game. But in winter, spring, and early summer, the meat would have been very lean. So how did humans survive?

Owen began sifting for clues through anthropological and historical accounts from subarctic and arctic North America. These environments, she reasoned, are similar to that of Ice Age Europe and pose similar challenges to their inhabitants. Even in the far north, Inuit societies harvested berries for winter storage and gathered other plants for medicines and for fibers. To see if any of the flora that thrived in Upper Paleolithic Europe could be put to similar uses, Owen drew up a list of plants economically important to people living in cold-climate regions of North America and Europe and compared it with a list of species that botanists had identified from pollen trapped in Ice Age sediment cores from southern Germany. Nearly 70 plants were found on both lists. "I came up with just a fantastic list of plants that were available at that time. Among others, there were a number of reeds that are used by the Eskimo and subarctic people in North America for making baskets. There are a lot of plants with edible leaves and stems, and things that were used as drugs and dyes. So the plants were there."

The chief plant collectors in historical societies were undoubtedly women. "It was typically women's work," says Owen. "I did find several continents that the men on hunting expeditions would gather berries or plants for their own meals, but they did not participate in the plant-gathering expeditions. They might go along, but they would be hunting or fishing."

Were Upper Paleolithic women gathering plants? The archeological literature was mostly silent on the subject. Few archeobotanists, Owen found, had ever looked for plant seeds and shreds in Upper Paleolithic camps. Most were convinced such efforts would be futile in sites so ancient. At University College London, however, Owen reached a determined young archeobotanist, Sarah Mason, who had analyzed a small sample of charcoal-like remains from a 26,390-year-old hearth at Dolni Vestonice.

The sample held more than charcoal. Examining it with a scanning electron microscope, Mason and her colleagues found fragments of fleshy plant taproots with distinctive secretory cavities—trademarks of the daisy and aster family, which boasts several species with edible roots. In all likelihood, women at Dolni Vestonice had dug the roots and cooked them into starchy meals. And they had very likely simmered other plant foods too. Mason and her colleagues detected a strange pulverized substance in the charred sample. It looked as if the women had either ground plants into flour and then boiled the results to make gruel or pounded vegetable material into a mush for their babies. Either way, says Soffer, the results are telling. "They're stuffing carbohydrates."

Owen is pursuing the research further. "If you do look," she says, "you can find things." At her urging, colleagues at the University of Tubingen are now analyzing Paleolithic hearths for botanical remains as they unearth them. Already they have turned up more plants, including berries, all clearly preserved after thousands of years. In light of these findings, Owen suggests that it was women, not men, who brought home most of the calories to Upper Paleolithic families. Indeed, she estimates that if Ice Age females collected plants, bird eggs, shellfish, and edible insects, and if they hunted or trapped small game and participated in the hunting of large game—as northern women did in historical times—they most likely contributed 70 percent of the consumed calories.

Moreover, some women may have enjoyed even greater power, judging from the most contentious relics of Ice Age life: the famous Venus figurines. Excavators have recovered more than 100 of the small statuettes, which were crafted between 29,000 and 23,000 years ago from such enduring materials as bone, stone, antler, ivory, and fired clay. The figurines share a strange blend of abstraction and realism. They bare prominent breasts, for example, but lack nipples. Their bodies are often minutely detailed down to the swaying lines of their backbones and the tiny rolls of flesh—fat folds—beneath their shoulder blades, but they often lack eyes, mouths, and any facial expression. For years researchers viewed them as a male art form. Early anthropologists, after all, had observed only male hunters carving stone, ivory, and other hard materials. Females were thought to lack the necessary strength. Moreover, reasoned experts, only men would take such loving interest in a woman's body. Struck by the voluptuousness of the small stone, ivory, and clay bodies, some researchers suggested they were Ice Age erotica, intended to be touched and fondled by their male makers. The idea still lingers. In the 1980s, for example, the well-known American paleontologist Dale Guthrie wrote a scholarly article comparing the postures of the figurines with the provocative poses of *Playboy* centerfolds.

But most experts now dismiss such contentions. Owen's careful scouring of ethnographic sources, for example, revealed that women in arctic and subarctic societies did indeed work stone and ivory on occasion. And there is little reason to suggest the figurines figured as male erotica. The Black Venus, for example, seems to have belonged to a secret world of ceremony and ritual far removed from everyday sexual life.

The evidence, says Soffer, lies in the raw material from which the Black Venus is made. Clay objects sometimes break or explode when fired, a process called thermal-shock fracturing. Studies conducted by Pamela Vandiver of the Smithsonian Institution have demonstrated that the Black Venus and other human and animal figurines recovered from Dolni Vestonice—as well as nearly 2,000 fired ceramic pellets that litter the site—were made from a local clay that is resistant to thermal-shock fracturing. But many of the figurines, including the celebrated Black Venus, bear the distinctive jagged branching splinters created by thermal shock. Intriguingly, the fired clay pellets do not.

Curious, Vandiver decided to replicate the ancient firing process. Her analysis of the small Dolni Vestonice kilns revealed that they had been fired to temperatures around 1450 degrees Fahrenheit—similar to those of an ordinary hearth. So Vandiver set about making figurines of local soil and firing them in a similar earthen kiln, which a local archeological crew had built nearby. To produce thermal shock, she had to place objects larger than half an inch on the hottest part of the fire; moreover, the pieces had to be so wet they barely held their shape.

To Vandiver and Soffer, the experiment—which was repeated several times back at the Smithsonian Institution —suggests that thermal shock was no accident. "Stuff can explode naturally in the kiln," says Soffer, "or you can make it explode. Which was going on at Dolni Vestonice? We toyed with both ideas. Either we're dealing with the most inept potters, people with two left hands, or they are doing it on purpose. And we reject the idea that they were totally inept, because other materials didn't explode. So what are the odds that this would happen only with a very particular category of objects?"

These exploding figurines could well have played a role in rituals, an idea supported by the location of the kilns. They are situated far away from the dwellings, as ritual buildings often are. Although the nature of the ceremonies is not clear, Soffer speculates that they might have served as divination rites for discerning what the future held. "Some stuff is going to explode. Some stuff is not going to explode. It's evocative, like picking petals off a daisy. She loves me, she loves me not."

Moreover, ritualists at Dolni Vestonice could have read significance into the fracturing patterns of the figurines. Many historical cultures, for example, attempted to read the future by a related method called scapulimancy. In North America, Cree ceremonialists often placed the shoulder blade, or scapula, of a desired animal in the center of a lodge. During the ceremonies, cracks began splintering the bone: a few of these fractures leaked droplets of fat. To Cree hunters, this was a sign that they would find game if they journeyed in the directions indicated by the cracks.

Venus figurines from other sites also seem to have been cloaked in ceremony. "They were not just something made to look pretty," says Margherita Mussi, an archeologist at the University of Rome–La Sapienza who studies Upper Paleolithic figurines. Mussi notes that several small statuettes from the Grimaldi Cave carvings of southern Italy, one of the largest troves of Ice Age figurines ever found in Western Europe, were carved from rare materials, which the artists obtained with great difficulty, sometimes through trade or distant travel. The statuettes were laboriously whittled and polished, then rubbed with ocher, a pigment that appears to have had ceremonial significance, suggesting that they could have been reserved for special events like rituals.

The nature of these rites is still unclear. But Mussi is convinced that women took part, and some archeologists believe they stood at the center. One of the clearest clues, says Mussi, lies in a recently rediscovered Grimaldi figurine known as Beauty and the Beast. This greenish yellow serpentine sculpture portrays two arched bodies facing away from each other and joined at the head, shoulders, and lower extremities. One body is that of a Venus figurine. The other is a strange creature that combines the triangular head of a reptile, the pinched waist of a wasp, tiny arms, and horns. "It is clearly not a creature of this world," says Mussi.

The pairing of woman and supernatural beast, adds Mussi, is highly significant. "I believe that these women were related to the capacity of communicating with a different world," she says. "I think they were believed to be the gateway to a different dimension." Possessing powers that far surpassed others in their communities, such women may have formed part of a spiritual elite, rather like the shamans of ancient Siberia. As intermediaries between the real and spirit worlds, Siberian shamans were said to be able to cure illnesses and intercede on behalf of others for hunting success. It is possible that Upper Paleolithic women performed similar services for their followers.

Although the full range of their activities is unlikely ever to be known for certain, there is good reason to believe that Ice Age women played a host of powerful roles—from plant collectors and weavers to hunters and spiritual leaders. And the research that suggests those roles is rapidly changing our mental images of the past. For Soffer and others, these are exciting times. "The data do speak for themselves," she says finally. "They answer the questions we have. But if we don't envision the questions, we're not going to see the data."

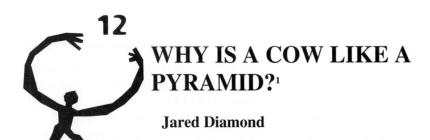

12

WHY IS A COW LIKE A PYRAMID?[1]

Jared Diamond

Some things, like pyramids, were probably invented independently many times and in many places around the world. Other things, perhaps including the wheel, appear to have been invented just once and then diffused around the world. As Jared Diamond reports, recent studies of bovine genetics suggest that the history of cattle may include a little of both processes: They appear to have been domesticated at least twice in Eurasia and then diffused and interbred in such places as Africa and, much more recently, the Americas.

How many times in history did people "invent" pyramids? Think of Mexico's Pyramids of the Sun and the Moon at Teotihuacan or of other pyramids built by American Indians centuries before Columbus's arrival. The resemblance of the American structures to the earlier pyramids of Egypt is so obvious that we call them by the same name. Does this suggest that Egyptians reached the New World in ancient times and taught Mexicans the art of pyramid construction?

Many similar parallels exist between ancient Old World and New World civilizations. Do they also imply diffusion of inventions between the hemispheres? Author Thor Heyerdahl (and many others) have attributed such parallels to transatlantic contacts between American Indians and such seafaring Old World peoples as Egyptians and Phoenicians.

But there are doubters who reason as follows: Suppose you were an ancient emperor who wished to build the largest and highest structure ever seen in order to advertise your power, mobilize your work force, or unify your empire. In ancient times, the tallest building that you could have built would have been a pyramid. American Indians were as capable of figuring that out as were Egyptians. Indeed, most scholars now think that Egyptian and Mexican pyramids were "invented" independently, mainly because the structures had differing functions (tombs in Egypt, temple

[1]Reprinted with permission from *Natural History* (July, 1995). Copyright © the American Museum of Natural History (1995).

bases in Mexico) and were built of different materials.

Such debates about the relative roles of independent invention and diffusion pop up again and again among historians, archeologists, and anthropologists. Both capabilities are facts of human nature. On the one hand, humans are inventive. If person A thinks of a new idea or invention in Boston on Wednesday, then person B could think of it in Dar es Salaam on Thursday. Independent brainstorms happen all the time. But humans also spread and receive ideas. Whenever people travel or emigrate, they bring things and ideas with them, and other people are always on the lookout for new things and ideas.

At scholarly meetings, the arguments rage ad nauseam. Some scholars like inventionist interpretations; others prefer diffusionist ones. The debate quickly becomes polarized because one's answer to it reflects one's whole Weltanschauung and one's view about the role of rare geniuses.

Some recent discoveries, however, may actually have succeeded in resolving one such historical debate: the origins of domestic cattle. The domestication of cattle was one of the most important events in human history, far more important than the construction of the first pyramid. As sources of meat, milk, and milk products, cattle have been the most valuable domestic animal species in much of the Old World for much of history and remain so on all continents today. And by drawing plows and providing manure, cattle made agriculture possible on land that farmers had previously been unable to till. Cattle also revolutionized land transport by providing a way to move goods in bulk.

Today, domestic cattle are very diverse, with about 800 recognized breeds. All derive from a now-extinct wild species called aurochs. Formerly widespread over Eurasia and North Africa, and similar to cattle except for its larger size, the last surviving aurochs is thought to have been killed in Poland in 1627. Was the domestication of this prize beast achieved by some genius herders just once in human history? If so, who were they, and when and where did they live? Did that one ancestral domesticated breed then spread over the Old World in ancient times, and are all modern cattle breeds descended from it? Or if one tribe of geniuses was able to domesticate the aurochs in Turkey, did some other tribe of geniuses do it in India at another time? The debate about domestic cattle origins is thus a model for similar debates about the origins of pyramids, wheels, and writing.

Even those of us who have never been to India know from pictures that Indian cattle look different from the European (actually western Eurasian) varieties now widespread in the Americas. Indian cattle, or zebu, have humps; many, but not all, traditional African breeds are also humped but European cattle aren't. Did ancient herders of the western and eastern subspecies of wild aurochs independently domesticate the ancestors of different modern breeds? And if so, can we believe the evidence of our eyes and conclude that humped

African cattle are most closely related to humped Indian breeds? Or was there instead a single domestication of aurochs, with humped and humpless breeds developing afterward?

Anatomists, physiologists, archeologists, cytogeneticists, and biochemists have been debating this question for decades. Anatomists note that Indian, African, and European cattle differ from one another in more than their humps. Further complicating the issue is the consideration that the anatomy of their humps differs between African and Indian breeds. Could both have acquired the feature independently through convergent evolution, just as birds and bats independently evolved wings? Physiologists note that Indian cattle and many African breeds have similar physiological adaptations to a hot, dry climate, and that these aren't found in European cattle. Cytogeneticists and biochemists note differences in the chromosomes and proteins of European and Indian cattle. The question is, did all those intercontinental differences arise in the 8,000 years since cattle were domesticated? Or do the differences instead stem from independent domestications of already differing wild aurochs populations?

The earliest, widely accepted archeological evidence for domesticated cattle places them in Anatolia (modern Turkey) by approximately 5800 B.C. By 2500 B.C., both humped and humpless cattle inhabited the Indus Valley, as evidenced by finds from archeological sites. Even before that, humped cattle were depicted in Mesopotamian art,

raising the possibility that they reached India from the west (rather than vice versa). A further complication is that some archeologists believe they have found bones of domesticated cattle in ancient North African sites that are possibly older than the oldest Eurasian sites providing similar evidence. This suggests independent domestication of cattle by Africans. Other archeologists, perhaps the majority, consider those bones to be those of wild aurochs.

Recent discoveries that help resolve these questions come from the field of molecular genetics. Recall that our genetic material consists of long molecular strands termed DNA, made up of small units known as nucleotide base pairs. Most DNA of higher animals is confined to cell nuclei, but some occurs in intracellular particles called mitochondria. Mitochondrial DNA evolves more rapidly and varies much more between individuals, populations, and species than does nuclear DNA. As a result, mitochondrial DNA is more useful for tracing relationships of closely related populations, since nuclear DNA may exhibit too little variation to analyze profitably. That's why the controversial "mitochondrial Eve hypothesis" of recent human origins was based on studies of human mitochondrial DNA.

To exploit DNA's potential value for tracing relationships, scientists determine the sequence of nucleotide base pairs in corresponding DNA chains of individuals drawn from different populations or species. This permits them to put a number on the genetic difference between the populations. If researchers see one cow with a hump and another without one, that observation still leaves them wondering whether the cows differ in 0.1 percent, 1 percent, or 10 percent of their genes. But DNA analyses permit such statements as: "Cow *A* and cow *B* differ in 35 out of 900 base pairs analyzed." Extending the analyses to more cows, we can deduce relationships. If cow *C* differs in 38 base pairs from cow *B* but in only 2 base pairs from cow *A*, we conclude that cows *A* and *C* are much more closely related to each other than either is to cow *B*. In addition, anatomical features such as humps may be influenced by diet and environment, but DNA base pair sequences are not. Finally, superficially similar anatomical structures may arise repeatedly and independently through convergent evolution (as did the wings of birds and bats), but two unrelated species are extremely unlikely to evolve identical sequences of 898 DNA base pairs independently of each other.

Those are the principles behind a study of cattle relationships carried out by Ronan Loftus and four colleagues at Trinity College, Dublin. Of the 800 breeds of cattle, the Dublin team selected thirteen in order to sample the spectrum of modern breeds. Six were humpless European breeds, including such familiar ones as Hereford, Jersey, and Friesian. Three were humped zebu breeds from India. The other four were from Africa: two humped breeds from East Africa and one humped and one humpless breed from West Africa. For two individuals of each of the thirteen breeds, the Dubliners determined the base pair sequence of the most variable (and hence the most informative) part of mitochondrial DNA, its so-called D loop. For five more individuals of each breed they sequenced the most variable part of the D loop itself. They also compared D loop DNA in about ten other individuals per breed by a quick-and-dirty method called RFLP (restriction fragment length polymorphism). Finally, they studied bison, a wild, hoofed mammal species related to cattle but in anyone's view less closely related to any cattle breed than either European, Indian, or African cattle are related to one another.

The Dubliners' results were striking. First, they found that, *within* each continent, *all* the studied breeds were very closely related to one another. Within the African, European, and Indian groups, cattle breeds differed, on the average, in only 0.4 percent of their analyzed base pairs. That is scarcely greater than the average difference among individuals of the same breed. But that result isn't so surprising. Everyone agrees that European domesticated breeds were derived from a common ancestor within the last 8,000 years, and have therefore had, at most, only that modest length of time to diverge from one another; and that Indian cattle breeds have similarly had only that time to diverge from one another.

The differences among breeds within a continent were slight, but the gap between Indian and European cattle proved to be enormous. Five percent of the analyzed base pairs differed, fully 12 times the intracontinental difference. What can that 5 percent figure tell us about how long the continental breeds have been separated?

Fortunately, we have a guidepost. The fossil record indicates that the ancestors of cattle and of bison diverged about one million years ago, and possibly earlier. Yet the DNA difference between bison and any cattle breed is only about 6.7 percent, little more than the 5 percent difference between European and Indian breeds. Assuming a constant rate of DNA change, European and Indian cattle must have diverged from each other only slightly less than a million years ago.

Since cattle domestication began much more recently than that, those big differences separating Indian from European cattle must have arisen mainly before domestication rather than after it. That is, Indian and European cattle must have been independently domesticated from geographically separate populations (different subspecies) of wild aurochs, which had already had hundreds of thousands of years to diverge. One aurochs population must have been domesticated somewhere in the eastern part of Eurasia, possibly between eastern Iran and India, and another somewhere in the western part of Eurasia, very likely between Anatolia and Mesopotamia. Most of the differences that can be measured today between Indian and European cattle breeds must already have distinguished the ancestral western and eastern species of aurochs. It was not the case, therefore, that European domestic cattle were derived from In-

dian domestic cattle (or vice versa); the differences between them are much too great to have arisen since a single domestication in the last 8,000 years.

Thus, Ronan Loftus and his Trinity College colleagues seem to have resolved—at least, to my satisfaction—the debate over the respective origins of European and Indian domestic cattle. Those scholars who believed in independent origins were right; those who believed in common origins were wrong. But the Dublin team's findings about the origins of African cattle are likely to come as a surprise to both schools of thought.

First, the sole humpless breed of cattle they studied, the West African N'Dama, proved to be no more different from the three humped breeds of African cattle studied than the three humped breeds were from one another. In both cases, the differences make up a mere 0.4 percent of the base pairs sequenced. Second and even more surprising, all four African breeds, including the three that are humped, are much closer to the humpless European breeds than to the humped Indian breeds. The former difference is only 0.4 percent; the latter a whopping 5 percent. As far as mitochondrial DNA is concerned, a cow's hump is a red herring. Thus, there is no evidence for independent domestication of cattle in Africa. But the source of African cattle was a surprise.

Nevertheless, we can't just stop here, shrug off humps as a red herring, and go back to work satisfied with our new understanding of cattle origins. A hump is still a hump and has to be explained somehow. We still need to understand why Africa's humpless N'Dama cattle are so similar to African humped cattle. We still need to account for the evidence from physiology, cytogenetics, and proteins that seemed to point to an Indian origin of African humped cattle. And we can't dismiss archeological evidence that Indian cattle actually were introduced into Africa, beginning with the Arab invasions of the seventh century and later. What happened to the genes of those introduced Indian cattle, and how did African cattle acquire their hump?

They may have gotten it from Indian cattle, after all. I haven't yet mentioned a catch in the studies of mitochondrial DNA by Loftus and his colleagues. Mitochondrial DNA is inherited only from the mother, most nuclear DNA is inherited as a copy of both the mother's and the father's DNA, and the so-called Y chromosome of our nuclear DNA is inherited only from the father. If male Indian cattle had been introduced to Africa, one would never have been able to deduce it from studies of mitochondrial DNA. No matter how Indian cattle in ancient times were brought to Africa—whether by land over the Suez isthmus, by water across the Red Sea, or across the Indian Ocean from India—the task couldn't have been easy, and there couldn't have been many Indian cattle introduced. The most efficient way for ancient cattle breeders to bring desirable humped cattle to Africa would have been to transport small numbers of males to inseminate the many humpless females already present.

Thus, African cattle may have had a crossbred origin, resulting from an earlier introduction of European and Near Eastern humpless cattle of both sexes, followed by a later introduction of mostly male Indian humped cattle. If this scenario is correct, then modern African breeds would owe their drought and heat tolerance, and (insofar as they have them) their humps, to their Indian great-great- . . . great-grandfathers. But they would still owe their mitochondrial DNA to their great-great- . . . great-grandmothers.

This tale of crossbred cows has many broad implications. I shall mention only three: for other domestic animals, for human population histories, and for the battleground of diffusionists against inventionists.

First, essentially the same debate that I have described for cattle origins arises for the origins of other domesticated animals and plants. Did American Indians and Eurasians get their dogs by independently domesticating wolves? Domestic dogs are apparently at least as ancient in the Americas as in the Old World, so independent domestication seems possible—unless the first ancestral Indians arriving from Asia across the Bering Strait had brought Eurasian dogs with them. Did the Chinese and Mesopotamians domesticate pigs independently? I wouldn't be surprised if some molecular geneticists are already at work on these questions. If they aren't, they ought to be.

Second, one can think of modern "hybrid" human populations whose paternal and maternal genes may have come from predominantly different geographic sources, just as did those of African cattle. For example, in the early nineteenth century the European settlers of Tasmania nearly exterminated that island's Aboriginal. Apparently, the sole survivors were Tasmanian women enslaved or otherwise acquired by white sealers. Today their descendants, numbering in the thousands, are struggling for their rights and their identity within white-dominated Tasmanian society. If their genes were investigated, would the maternal genes of their mitochondrial DNA prove to be mainly Aboriginal Tasmanian, their Y chromosomes mainly European, and their other nuclear genes a mixture? It seems possible that different populations may also have made different relative contributions to paternal and maternal genes of African Americans.

Finally, what general conclusions can we now draw about the battle between the diffusionists and the inventionists? I say, none, because there *is* no general conclusion. Indian and European cattle were "invented" (read "domesticated") independently. African cattle seem instead to have arrived by diffusion, both from India and from western Eurasia. Pyramids were invented independently in Mexico and in Egypt. So were wheels and writing. But wheels seem to have diffused west and east in the Old World from their site of invention near the Black Sea. So did domesticated barley and horses.

Thus, some cows are like pyramids and other cows are like Old World wheels. Every battle of the diffusionists and the inventionists has a separate victor.

13

IN SEARCH OF THE FIRST AMERICANS[1]

Vaughn M. Bryant, Jr.

While many in the world were celebrating the 500th anniversary of Columbus' voyage and his "discovery" of the New World, smaller groups of archaeologists were busy searching for answers to, "when did the first humans really arrive in the Americas?" Vaughn Bryant examines both "solid" and controversial evidence found at a number of archaeological sites in North and South America and explains what types of proof are essential for confirming "when" and "how" the first humans reached these new lands. The author points out which sites he believes are the most likely candidates for being the "oldest" evidence of human occupation in the Americas.

A few years ago, driving through a fierce snowstorm toward Raton, New Mexico, I saw a small road sign on ... les." Incredi-... right was the ... that made us ... inking about ... ent was first

... the icy side ... e abandoned ... ather-beaten ... rocery store ... mp. Ahead, ... loomed an

old frame building with a battered sign hanging by a single nail: "Museum."

In a large, dimly lit, unheated room I saw pioneer farming days to World War II relics—tools, broken toys, military uniforms, old machine guns, photos, all very dusty. Open on a counter next to an empty pickle jar with a faded sign "Donations" lay a guest register with curling pages, its last entry more than a year old.

Slowly, my eyes adjusted to the dim light. In a far corner I saw the skull of an extinct bison hanging on the wall. And, next to this a small, hand-labeled display under clouded glass with badly

Jane Rodgers
Senior Account Manager

69 Oakdale Boulevard
Pleasant Ridge, MI 48069
Tel 248 548 5421
jane_rodgers@mcgraw-hill.com

faded photos of the 1920s excavation of the nearby site that revolutionized American archaeology.

Shivering in the cold, reading the labels and listening to a distant window shutter banging in the wind, I was overcome by wonder. I was really here! Folsom—called by many the most important archaeological breakthrough in the history of North America. And, perhaps it was.

It was here they found the first indisputable evidence of the first Americans, hunters who roamed the vast grasslands of North America when mammoths, mastodons, and now extinct forms of giant bison were common. But, despite its revelations Folsom begged the question: Were they *really* the first Americans? Searching for the answer has fueled a controversy that continues unabated today.

Folsom and Clovis

By the end of the 1880s many scientists firmly believed in the existence of a North American Paleolithic extending hundreds of thousands of years into the past. American archaeologists explored burial mounds, dug up river gravels, examined caves, sifted soils, and scoured riverbanks for traces of ancient artifacts. Newspapers reported exciting accounts of each new find and claimed each to be the oldest. However, in time, it seemed that each new find was flawed when the evidence was systematically examined by the experts. Each site lacked one or more of the three essential elements needed for in-

disputable proof of authenticity. First, a site had to contain tools, weapons, or other artifacts definitely made by humans, or must contain the remains of human skeletons. Second, the human-made materials had to be buried in a way that clearly showed they came from specific layers of undisturbed sediments. And third, the age of the site had to be determined by accurate dating methods.

Undaunted by failures and false leads, the search for new sites in the Americas went on, even though none yet met the three essential criteria. The battle lines soon became well established. On one side were hundreds of amateur archaeologists and some professionals unwavering in their belief that occupation of the Americas was very early. They continued their claims of early human evidence by protesting that the three required elements for site authenticity were too stringent. "After all," they argued, "the older the evidence, the less likely all three elements will still be preserved."

An exception was John Wesley Powell, director of the Smithsonian Institution's Bureau of Ethnology. In 1887 he appointed geologist William Holmes to prepare a detailed report on each new claim of discovery of ancient peoples in the Americas. Powell wanted to counteract the flood of unsubstantiated press reports of new discoveries allegedly dating back tens of thousands of years.

Requests for news of recent archaeological sites and new evidence brought nearly a thousand responses to the Smithsonian Institution, only to be eliminated one-by-one after careful checking. Then, late in the nineteenth century geologist G. Frederick Wright heated up the controversy by using much of the "undocumented" evidence as the basis for two books about the pre-Ice Age cultures in North America. Well-written and widely read, they helped polarize the general public's view and added new pressures on scientists to accept much of the circumstantial evidence.

After the turn-of-the-century, and certainly by the 1920s, the argument had grown so heated that few professional scholars or students dared risk their reputations by questioning the unproved, yet often accepted, belief among scientists that there just wasn't any supportable evidence of humans in the Americas dating beyond 4,000 years of age. Into the midst of that tension, between 1925 and 1928, came the excavations of the Folsom site. Here, finally, was the big breakthrough; not only was Folsom the first American site to meet the three essential elements, but it had also more than doubled the previously accepted 4,000 year date. Folsom's **indisputable** evidence revealed that early Indians had hunted a species of giant bison that became extinct nearly 10,000 years ago. Not only did the Folsom site contain a wealth of bones and stone artifacts, but in one deposit a human-made stone point was found lodged between the ribs of an extinct bison! Soon, in Colorado, Texas, and New Mexico other sites were found containing fossil bones of more extinct bison, or bones of other extinct animals like the camel, mammoth, and a breed of horses which had all disappeared at the same time as the giant bison. In a growing number of these new sites a clear association between extinct animal bones and human-made stone tools and spear points was apparent. Some tools and points matched Folsom's, but others did not, raising new questions about which was oldest.

It was in the early 1930s when evidence in the Colorado site at Dent was first to confirm a clear relationship between extinct mammoths and early American hunters, now known as *Paleoindians*. At Dent another type of large stone spear point was found, one directly under one mammoth pelvis and another in between the bones of a second mammoth. The position of the second mammoth skeleton was especially important because it was nearly complete and articulated (*i.e.,* the bones were positioned as in life), proving that the deposits had remained undisturbed since the animal's death and that the stone point probably caused death. However, the Dent site's age and its relationship to the Folsom group of Paleoindians wouldn't be determined for another 15 years.

During 1949–1950 excavations of another Paleoindian site near Clovis, New Mexico, a Dent-type stone spear point was found among mammoth bones in deposits directly underneath extinct bison bones containing Folsom spear points. The puzzle was solved. The Dent-type spear points, now called

Clovis points, must be the earliest! This discovery also pushed back the existence of humans in the New World to 11,500 years ago.

For some, the Clovis hunters **were** the first Americans. These scientists believed no further searching for older peoples was necessary. There were no American ancestors of Clovis. Yet for others, Clovis represented one link in the middle of a long chain of early American cultures. These scientists pointed to other sites they said proved the Clovis hunters were not the first. The other important issue raised by Clovis was, "how did the first Americans reach the New World?"

The Journey East

In the six decades since Folsom and Clovis sites were first studied and identified, new scientific techniques and refinement of old ones have clarified many of our ideas about the first Americans—who they were, how they got here, the animals they hunted, and the harsh climate they had to overcome.

Physical anthropologists using genetic and blood-grouping studies have compared living American Indians with populations of eastern Asia. Their evidence is overwhelming in confirming that the first Americans were hunters who first came here from Asia. But did they come by land or by sea? Archaeologists like Knut Fladmark of Simon Fraser University, Vancouver, British Columbia, and Ruth Gruhn of the University of Alberta believe that an early crossing to North America was possible by sea and that the first American could have used a coastal route to reach areas as far south as California, while much of the continent was buried beneath glacial ice. Yet, in spite of their argument, most scientists still believe a land crossing is more likely.

Some geologists, like David Hopkins of the University of Alaska, have spent their careers studying the environmental changes in western Alaska, eastern Siberia, and the area in between. Records of glaciation, rises and falls in ancient sea levels, and surface topography suggest to Hopkins that there were two main periods when the Bering Sea was low enough to expose a wide land mass, now called Beringia, connecting Asia with North America. He notes that Beringia was first exposed between 75,000–45,000 years ago and last exposed between 25,000–14,000 years ago. Until recently, no archaeological sites in eastern Siberia had proved older than 40,000 years of age, leaving only the second of Hopkins' periods for serious consideration. However, recent discoveries in Siberia imply that humans may have lived in areas near Beringia as early as 70,000 years ago.

It is reasonable to ask why people would leave Asia and walk to North America over a land bridge. No one knows, but there appears to have been no special reasons for making the crossing. Perhaps the first crossings were made by small groups of Asian hunters and their families who, not aware that the sometimes 1,000-mile-wide region was even a land bridge, followed seasonal migrations of Arctic animals back and forth in Beringia; eventually some peoples became trapped in Alaska when sea levels rose and the land connection flooded. Paleo-ecologists such as Ohio State University's Paul Colinvaux and University of Vermont's Steven Young have each offered ideas about the Beringia environment which tend to confirm this theory. From buried pollen records used as indicators of plants that once grew in Beringia, Colinvaux concludes the land bridge area was an inhospitable, barren region of sparse tundra offering limited plant resources for grazing animals and humans. His research suggests the Beringian climate was unpredictable and forbidding from the beginning of its last opening around 25,000 years ago until just before rising sea levels finally tempered the environment and supported grasslands and scrub vegetation. Those improved conditions around 14,000 years ago, he believes, attracted herds of animals and hunters into the New World. Young, on the other hand, thinks the fossil pollen records, combined with known modern plant distributions in western Alaska, indicate a 10,000-year period that began nearly 25,000 years ago when Beringia vegetation could have supported a variety of large herd animals and the Asian hunters who followed them.

What foods these first Asian travelers ate on their way to the Americas are one of many intriguing questions. Some scholars, such as Dale Guthrie of the University of Alaska, be-lieve the first Americans were hunters who preyed mainly on mastodons, mammoths, giant bison, and similar large herd mammals. Others believe these first people ate a variety of plant foods and relied on small rabbit- and deer-sized animals that they could catch or trap fairly easily. They add that killing a large game animal may have been a rare occasion for these early Americans. Whichever view is correct, knowing the right food preferences would help scientists visualize a clearer picture of the culture and lifestyles of these earlier hunters.

Determining *when* the first people came to the Americas is more difficult than determining *how* they got here. Prior to the development of radiocarbon techniques in the early 1950s, accurate and precise dating of ancient sites was difficult, and often impossible. Even today, some still argue that other dating techniques are reliable such as the degree of surface weathering on stone tools, the depth of sediment accumulation, and changes in the composition of proteins and amino acids still trapped in fossil bones. Of all the dating techniques, however, only dates based on radiocarbon analyses are presently accepted as the best and most conclusive. Even so, radiocarbon dating still has its problems.

Pre-Clovis or Clovis

Volumes of articles and books have been written on the first Americans. Yet, over this issue archaeologists are still split into two groups. The pre-Clovis group suggests an early occupation of the Americas, somewhere between 15,000 and 200,000 years ago. By contrast, the Clovis group claims Clovis-type hunters and their immediate ancestors were first and arrived in the New World no earlier than some 12,000 years ago.

Making the answer so difficult is finding specific evidence that both sides will accept as indisputable records of early Americans. Each group has its distinguished scholars, its own ideas and hypotheses, and a list of sites it feels proves its convictions. Members of the pre-Clovis scholars, including Ruth Gruhn and Alan Bryan of the University of Alberta; George Carter of Texas A&M University; Richard S. MacNeish of the Andover Foundation for Archaeological Research; James Adovasio of Mercyhurst College in Pennsylvania; Richard Morlan of the National Museum of Man in Canada; Jacques Cinq-Mars of the Canadian Museum of Civilization in Quebec; and Tom Dillehay of the University of Kentucky all favor slightly different time periods when, they think, the first pre-Clovis peoples reached the Americas. As a group, however, they all believe the migration across Beringia occurred more than 15,000 years ago and that these hunters and their descendants then moved slowly southward from Alaska into the interior of North America and beyond. In their view, these early Americans took thousands of years to reach areas as distant as the southern tip of South America.

As a group, the pre-Clovis scholars believe that the technological skills of these earliest Americans were not as refined as the later Clovis populations and thus many of the weapons and tools were made of hardened wood, broken bones, antlers, and cracked river cobbles. Finally, these scholars acknowledge, the remains of these pre-Clovis groups are meager, but bone, antler, and wooden tools decay rapidly, so the finding of mere scraps of evidence is thought remarkable considering the age of the sites.

The Clovis-first group is led by members such as C. Vance Haynes and Paul Martin of the University of Arizona; Michael Waters and Thomas Lynch of Texas A&M University; and Larry Agenbroad of North Arizona University. Although each may have a slightly different point of view, the essence of their argument begins 25,000–30,000 years ago in Eastern Europe where hunters learned how to attack and kill large mammoths. They were so successful that soon they concentrated on mammoth hunting. They wandered slowly eastward, following mammoth herds until reaching the tip of eastern Siberia some 15,000–20,000 years ago. In their continued mammoth pursuit, some hunters wandered across Beringia into Alaska just before the land bridge flooded for the last time, some 14,000 years ago.

Then, as the continental glaciers began melting, ice-free corridors opened and provided conduits into the heartland of North America. The Clovis-first group believes that once opened, the mammoth hunters followed their prey southward out of Alaska and along the way developed new types of weapons that are unique to the Americas, like the spear points found at Dent, Colorado, and Clovis, New Mexico. They believe this began about 12,000 years ago and was completed within about 1,000 years. In other words, this means that the new Clovis-type mammoth hunters spread from Alaska through the western part of the continental United States, and on to the southern tip of South America, in record time. Moreover, some, such as Martin and others, believe the skill of the Clovis hunters, combined with their rapid population growth, decimated the mammoth and caused its extinction during this period.

When asked why they don't accept the possibility of much earlier pre-Clovis populations in the New World, the Clovis group says there are no sites with indisputable evidence to support that claim. The Clovis group contends that the evidence associated with the purported pre-Clovis sites is flawed. Either the associations of human artifacts and early dates are inconclusive, or the deposits are mixed and disturbed. In other cases, they claim radiocarbon dates are based on contaminated materials so that the so-called pre-Clovis tools cannot be proved to be the handiwork of humans.

Candidates for Pre-Clovis

Of the numerous pre-Clovis sites and many pieces of evidence discov-

ered during the last 100 years, many have been dismissed by even the ardent pre-Clovis scholars as too problematic or inconclusive. There are, nevertheless, a few key sites that always seem to be mentioned when the issue of the "earliest" Americans is discussed.

Two Arctic sites are often mentioned. The older, a locale in the Yukon's Old Crow Flats, yielded a carved bone tool once believed to show that early ice-age hunters roamed the Yukon-Alaskan borderlands about 27,000 years ago. The age estimate came from a conventional radiocarbon dating of bone material. However, recent retesting of the material by means of accelerator mass spectrometry, a refinement of radiocarbon dating, indicates that what was regarded as the best evidence for pre-Clovis occupation in the Arctic region is actually less than 2,000 years old.

The second Arctic site is the Bluefish Caves located 65 kilometers southwest of Old Crow Flats. There archaeologist Jacquet Cine-Mars found what he believes are ancient bones and stone tools associated with animal bones showing cut marks made by stone knives during butchering. The materials are associated with extinct horse and mammoth bones which yielded radiocarbon dates between 13,000–15,500 years old. Nevertheless, skeptics remain convinced that neither the marks on bones, nor the bone and stone tools date from the pre-Clovis era. Some also suspect that the sediments have been mixed as a result of repeated cycles of freezing and thawing.

Because the continental United States is the most archaeologically investigated region in the New World, it is also the area with the most sites claiming pre-Clovis age. The oldest is the Calico region near Barstow, California. There, in the Mohave Desert, Ruth Simpson of the San Bernardino County Museum and her colleagues found hundreds of flaked stones in deposits ranging in age from 100,000–600,000 years. These finds are hotly debated by skeptics such as Vance Haynes and others who claim all of the flaked stones were chipped by geologic forces, not humans. Nearby in the San Diego region, George Carter spent decades recovering thousands of flaked stones from deposits he believed represented human campsites and fire hearths. Geologically, these deposits range in age from 80,000 to more than 120,000 years. However, like the remains from the Calico region, there is heated debate whether Carter's flaked stones, his ancient campsites, and the burned hearth-like areas are really the products of human activity or natural geologic forces. A third site, the Meadowcroft Rock Shelter in southwestern Pennsylvania, is also under fire from the skeptics who question the validity of its early radiocarbon dates that suggests ancient hunters used the site between 14,000–14,500 years ago. Instead, skeptics argue that the dates and early human remains found there are not associated.

The most recent U.S. pre-Clovis candidate is a site Richard S. MacNeish has been excavating in southeastern New Mexico. His Orogrande Cave contains a long and well-stratified sequence of extinct animal and plant remains extending back nearly 40,000 years. Among the remains are several human palm and hand prints preserved in fire-hardened clay, chipped stones, and a wide variety of broken animal bones. These materials and numerous radiocarbon dates have convinced MacNeish and others of the cave's long record of human occupation spanning more than 30,000 years. Not all who have visited the site are convinced, however; Dena Dincauze of the University of Massachusetts and Vance Haynes, for example, argue that the many stone items are of natural origin because they *do not show the typical* chipping marks expected during human manufacture.

Central America also has several suspected pre-Clovis sites. At the El Bosque site in Nicaragua, Alan Bryan, Ruth Gruhn, and William Irving of the University of Toronto discovered extinct animal bones, chipped stones and large blackened areas with river-pebble concentrations they thought were ancient fire hearths. Radiocarbon dates place the age of the deposits between 18,000–30,000 years, but skeptics argue the dates are based on contaminated materials, the blackened areas were caused by natural brush fires, and the chipped stones are the works of nature, not humans.

Like El Bosque, the Mexican sites of Valsequillo and Tlapacoya contain suspected human-made materials associated with early radiocarbon dates.

At Valsequillo archaeologists Juan Camacho and Cynthia Irwin-Williams excavated a series of sites and in one they found a chipped stone tool in deposits dated 21,000 years ago. At Tlapacoya the bones of extinct animals, suspected fire hearths, and a number of obsidian stone flakes were found in deposits between 21,000–24,000 years old. Many skeptics, however, claim the suspected fire hearths were actually formed by grass fires and that the obsidian flakes are not really related to either the extinct animal bones or the early pre-Clovis dated materials.

In the thin strip of Chile, at the tip of South America, lies the site of Monte Verde. Archaeologist Tom Dillehay has supervised excavations that reveal the remains of a campsite containing wooden, bone, and stone artifacts including the remains of seven mastodons. The first set of radiocarbon dates places the site's age between 12,500-13,000 years. Additional dates from an even lower level suggest an age about 34,000 years old. Although skeptics agree on the high quality of excavation, and on the importance of the site, they raise questions about possible stratigraphic mixing and of the materials selected for radiocarbon dating. Some suspect that the dated samples may have been contaminated. If so, this may explain erroneous dates that seem much too old.

The two other important sites in South America often mentioned in any Clovis vs pre-Clovis discussion is Pikimachay and Pedra Furada. In the early 1970s Richard MacNeish supervised the excavation of the Peruvian rock shelter of Pikimachay. In the bottom deposits he found extinct sloth and horse bones, broken river cobbles, charcoal, and fist-sized pieces of volcanic tufa rocks that he believed had been chipped to form sharp edges. Radiocarbon dates from these bottom levels range from 14,000–20,000 years old, yet Clovis-first scholars remain unconvinced. They question the radiocarbon dates and assert that neither the tufa rocks nor the broken river cobbles are sufficient evidence to validate pre-Clovis human activity.

The final South American location is in northern Brazil, where Niède Guidon of the École des Hautes en Sciences Sociales in Paris excavated the site of Boqueirão da Pedra Furada. In a 70-meter (230-foot)-long rock shelter filled with the oldest known cave art in the Americas, Guidon found hundreds of chipped and broken stones and rock-lined areas that she describes as fire hearths. More than 40 radiocarbon dates now suggest that the deposits range in age from 5,000–33,000 years. Skeptics, most of whom have not yet visited the site, are already claiming that the chipped and broken stones are of natural origin and that the hearths are areas naturally burned during ancient grass fires.

The Fascination of a Mystery

Anthropology teaches us that humans everywhere are curious. Throughout time, peoples have created elaborate ways of explaining mysteries in their lives. Before science, mankind created myths and legends to answer and explain the unexplainable mysteries. Later, people replaced myths and legends with facts. Yet, we're still fascinated by unsolved mysteries. This is why even today some people remain spellbound by the possibility that creatures like the Yeti still roam the Himalayas, or that someday searchers really will find the remains of Noah's Ark. Most scientists tell us neither of these mysteries will ever be solved because both are based on myths, not reality. Yet, the idea that either might somehow be true still catches our curiosity, challenges our mind for answers, and supports the tabloids.

So it is with the quest to find the first Americans. The answer falls somewhere between myth and reality and continues to capture our curiosity and attention. If everyone were suddenly to accept the view that Clovis cultures were the first Americans, then the search would be over. So would be the romantic images conjured up by us when we discuss the possibilities put forth by some in the pre-Clovis group. Did Neanderthals ever live in the Americas? Some in the pre-Clovis group believe they did. What about groups earlier than even the Neanderthals? Maybe, say some of the more liberal of the group. Perhaps the question will never be fully resolved until all scientists are willing to agree on the specific conditions that all early sites must pass. The scientists in the Clovis group have already set forth their rules for sites—a clear association of humans and/or their tools found in undisturbed deposits that can be precisely dated. However, as mentioned earlier, scientists in the pre-Clovis group offer their own reasons why they believe these criteria are unreasonable for the oldest of the early sites.

Some have said, almost jokingly, the issue will never be resolved until we find a site with a human skeleton holding a banner saying, "we are the first Americans!" Realistically, what is needed most is evidence that will satisfy both groups of scientists.

Most of the best evidence has been discovered in the Americas during the last 50 years—and found by accident. Few systematic searches have ever taken place in key areas of the Americas where scientists think the answer to the puzzle might be found. Archaeological searches are expensive and take much time to complete. Finding capable scientists willing to spend the time, and finding the money to conduct the kinds of searches have always been important constraints. Also, some believe the most important areas yet to be searched now lay buried beneath the waters of the American coastal regions.

This point was well-documented during the 1960s when the probable camp site of a group of early Americans was found on the continental shelf off the shores of Chesapeake Bay, at a depth of 43 meters. Exploration of such remote locales, however, must await adequate funding, new excavation techniques, and all the skills underwater archaeologists can focus on a careful exploration of those deposits.

At the start of the 20th century, archaeologists could not imagine the kind of precise information that would soon be applied to the search for the first Americans. Precise dating using radiocarbon techniques, discovering the nature of ancient climates and vegetation through studies of fossil pollen, understanding the role human genetics would play in solving the puzzle, and learning the varieties and habits of long-extinct game animals like mammoths and giant bison were all unknowns less than 100 years ago. Like those scientists of the early 1900s, we cannot foresee the advances that will prove the most important to archaeology. The search for the first people to set foot in the New World may end within our lifetime, or it may not. Until it does conclude, imagination and inquisitiveness will ensure that it remains among science's most alluring mysteries.

14

THE PALEOLITHIC HEALTH CLUB[1]

Vaughn M. Bryant, Jr.

Vaughn Bryant contends that modern humans have lost touch with the essence of the diet and lifestyle that honed the bodies of our prehistoric foraging ancestors. After examining human lifestyles and diets during the developmental stages of humans, the author notes that it is not too late to learn from our ancestors. By making informed choices about our food and exercise habits now, we can enjoy a healthier way of life which should also improve our chances for living a longer and higher-quality life during our later decades.

Paleolithic humans inherited a body that originally evolved for our primate ancestors. Fortunately, several physical traits became advantages. Instead of being physically specialized and restricted to life in only one habitat, our generalized physiology enabled us to adapt to many different environments. It's true that some minor physiological changes have occurred. Some groups living at high altitudes have developed larger lung capacities while others living in hot deserts tend to be tall and thin because it maximizes the body's ability to dissipate heat. Nevertheless, in cold climates we use warm clothes in place of body hair, to travel by sea we use boats in place of gills and flippers, and

to travel overland we use trains, cars, or planes instead of having long legs or wings.

Our hairless bodies and ability to sweat are other advantages. They enable us to work in hot deserts, yet cool ourselves quickly when needed. Our ability to consume and digest both plant and animal food is another advantage, because it enables us to use many different resources and eat almost anything.

The archaeological evidence already tells us quite a bit about our Paleolithic hunting and gathering ancestors. Studies of their skeletons and of the artifacts they left behind tell us important clues about their lifestyles, diets and nutrition. When compared to the skeletons from early farming cultures, the Paleolithic skeletons provide chilling evidence of what has happened to the lives and health of most of the world's post-agricultural and urban peoples.

According to anthropologist George Armelagos of Emory University, high levels of bone porosity in the vault of the skull and around the eye orbits, called *porotic hyperostosis*, are considered good indicators of long-term anemia, commonly attributed to iron deficiency. Although porosity might be caused by other conditions, such as severe hookworm infections, the most frequent link is to long-term reliance on diets that are low in meat and high in carbohydrates, a common occurrence in early farming cultures which relied heavily on diets of cereal grains.

When Dr. Armelagos compared human skeletons from pre-agricultural foraging peoples with those of later farming cultures who lived in the Illinois and Ohio river valleys, the evidence of anemia in the farming group was overwhelming. He found a 400% increase in the occurrence of porotic hyperostosis among skeletons from the farming period, whose reconstructed diets consisted mostly of maize.

Professor Jane Buikstra, of the University of Chicago's anthropology department, notes that humans who experience episodes of severe physical stress often carry a record of those events in the long bones of their arms and legs and in the enamel layers of their teeth. She identifies typical types of stress as periods of prolonged or serious famine, periods of severe infection, or stress caused by malnutrition.

One growth-related stress indicator is known as Harris lines, which can be seen during x-ray or cross-section examinations of human long bones. Although most commonly found in the skeletons of farming cultures, Harris lines occasionally appear in the skeletons of foragers. Many now believe that some types of Harris lines reflect relatively short periods of stress while others indicate prolonged periods of stress.

Dr. Buikstra has noted that studies of North American skeletons from foraging groups and from early farming cultures show noticeable differences. The long bones from the farming groups have thinner cortical thickness, and are shorter, indicating a reduction in body height after the switch to farming. These, she believes, represent the physical effects of chronic malnutrition.

Another reliable indicator of diet and nutritional-related stress is abnormal development in the enamel layer of teeth. One type of tooth abnormality is called *linear enamel hypoplasia* and seems to be caused by severe stress. This condition, which appears as depressed and pitted areas in the enamel layers, is more commonly seen in the teeth of early farming cultures than in those of foragers.

Wilson bands, another type of tooth enamel abnormality, are also linked to stress-induced growth disruptions and are much more prevalent in the skeletons from farming cultures than foraging ones. When the teeth from burials belonging to farming cultures are examined, they show large numbers of enamel abnormalities and large numbers of dental caries. By contrast, rarely is either of these conditions found in the teeth of earlier foraging groups.

Susceptibility to dental caries varies with individuals, but in all cases the potential for infection is greater on diets containing large amounts of refined carbohydrates, especially sugars. About 2% of the fossil teeth from Paleolithic era foraging cultures contain small and shallow caries of the pit and fissure types and these are found mostly on the occlusal (top) surface of teeth. However, after cultures turned to farming the incidence of dental decay increased dramatically. Even so, it wasn't until the widespread use of refined carbohydrates during the last few hundred years that human dental decay reached epidemic proportions. One study, conducted in 1900 of workers in England, revealed that 70% of their teeth contained caries. More important, most of the dental caries occurred in between their teeth, locations associated almost entirely with post-agricultural diets containing high levels of sugar.

Examinations of preserved human feces, or coprolites, are another valuable source of information about our prehistoric ancestors. Coprolites are ideal because they contain the indigestible remains, such as fiber, bones, seeds, and leaves of foods that were actually eaten. In recent years, the scientific study of coprolites has provided valuable clues about the diets, health and nutrition of Paleolithic foraging peoples and those living in early farming communities.

Anthropologist Kristin Sobolik of the University of Maine has spent most of her career examining human coprolites found in prehistoric sites of the arid American Southwest. She has found that ancient foragers ate diets composed mostly of nutritious plant foods that are high in fiber such as sunflower seeds, ground mesquite and cactus seeds, acorns, walnuts, pecans, persimmons, grapes, berries, the soft basal leaf portion of sotol and agave, and cactus flowers, fruits and pads. These ancient foragers balanced their mostly plant-food diets with about 10–20% meat obtained from small animals such as mice, several types of rat-sized rodents, fishes ranging from minnows to gar, freshwater clams, small lizards, caterpillars and grasshoppers, small birds and bird eggs and, when they were lucky, rabbits and deer.

Karl Reinhard, an anthropologist at the University of Nebraska, is a leading authority on ancient human parasite infection. He notes that intestinal parasites can be debilitating and potentially fatal, especially when they infect a person who is already weakened by episodes of famine or prolonged malnutrition. His examination of human coprolites recovered from Southwestern American Indian sites indicates that hunting and gathering populations were almost totally free of internal parasitic infections. However, once groups turned to farming, they became heavily infected. High population densities, poor sanitation, and the compactness of living spaces in pueblos helped increase infection rates of nearly a dozen types of parasites including pinworms, tapeworms and thorny-headed worms.

Lifestyles

We have learned quite a bit about our most recent ancestors, the first *Homo sapiens sapiens*. They emerged as a distinct group sometime around 35,000–40,000 years ago and became the world's first artists. They also invented the spear-thrower, the bow and arrow, harpoon points, and learned how to make and use razor-thin stones, called blades. In northern climates they made tailored clothes to protect themselves against the cold, and roamed over vast areas of the arctic world following their quarry, mostly large game animals such as the mammoth and wooly rhinoceroses. Men and women were physically fit. They had a lifestyle that was in harmony with our biological design. As a result, they enjoyed longer and healthier lives than their descendants who later turned to farming.

Carbohydrates

Primates, including humans, use plant products as their primary source of energy. Each gram of carbohydrate provides four kilocalories (more commonly called calories) of energy when it is completely digested. There are two main types of carbohydrates, simple and complex. The simple carbohydrates are

sugars. They exist naturally as monosaccharides—different types of single-molecule sugars (glucose or dextrose, fructose, galactose), or as double-molecule sugars (sucrose, maltose, lactose) called disaccharides. Our bodies digest both types and both are found naturally in fruits, flower nectars, and the sap of some plants.

Our taste buds love sweet things. Perhaps this is because our early primate ancestors learned that sweet fruits were good sources of food. Tree fruits are a much sought-after food source by many primates because, ounce for ounce, fruits offer more usable calories than do leaves, bark or stems. In addition, the riper the fruit, the sweeter it becomes as its starch is converted to sugars. The association of sweetness with "good tasting," ready-to-eat, high-calorie-value fruits served the early primates and our Paleolithic ancestors well. It encouraged them to search for these tasty food sources and to avoid most sour and bitter-tasting fruits because that usually indicates fruits are poisonous or not yet ripe.

Our ancestors never ate too much sugar. Except for a small amount of sugar found in fruits, in some other natural foods, and an occasional lucky find of honey, our foraging ancestors, and even early farming peoples, had no access to sugar. No human forager, or early farmer, was ever in danger of overdosing on sugar. Perhaps this is why of the four essential taste sensations (sour, sweet, salty, bitter), humans usually avoid foods that are too sour, too salty, or too bitter, but rarely turn away from foods which are too sweet.

Two events increased the consumption of sugar by recent cultures. First, Columbus carried sugarcane to the New World and found that it grew well in the soils of the Caribbean. Second, the Spanish and Portuguese pioneered the importing of slaves as an inexpensive labor source for their plantations that soon produced tons of sugar at a competitive market price.

In England, the availability of inexpensive sugar reduced the per pound cost from the equivalent of a laborer's yearly salary in 1600, to the equivalent of only a dozen eggs by 1700. Increased sugar consumption accompanied the drop in sugar costs and soon the United States and most European countries mirrored the English's use of sugar.

By 1913 the annual consumption of sugar in the U.S. had reached 75 pounds per person. By 1976, U.S. sugar consumption had reached 125 pounds per person per year. That level of consumption is equivalent to 20% of the daily calories eaten by each American.

Anthropologist Sidney Mintz of Johns Hopkins University believes he knows why U.S., as well as world sugar consumption, continues to climb. He notes that only a small portion of the annual sugar consumption of individuals comes from spoonfuls or cubes of sugar those individuals add to foods or drink. Instead, most is added as "hidden" sugar to what we eat. Bakers add sugar to non-yeast-rising products because it makes cakes, cookies, and breads smoother, softer and whiter, and sugars improve their texture. Manufacturers produce heavily-sugared soft drinks because syrup is smoother and more appealing to the mouth and tongue than is flavored water. Sugar slows staleness in bread, stabilizes the chemical contents of salt, cloaks the acidity of tomatoes in catsup, and when added to bland-tasting meats like fish and poultry, sugar makes them taste much "better."

The complex carbohydrates (mainly starches, pectin, and cellulose) are long chains of linked sugar molecules called polysaccharides. Humans can't digest some types, such as cellulose, so it becomes the "fiber" content of our diets. Other carbohydrates, such as starch, are digestible and can be converted to energy.

Paradoxically, until very recently, too much fiber was often a problem in human diets. Our Paleolithic ancestors used pounding and grinding to process plant foods, techniques that did not reduce their intake of high amounts of fiber. Boyd Eaton and his colleagues at the Emory University School of Medicine calculate that our foraging ancestors probably consumed about 150 grams of fiber each day as compared to most modern Americans who only eat an average of 20 grams daily.

The coprolite evidence supports Dr. Eaton's finding. My coprolite studies of pre-agricultural groups living in North and South America reveal diets that were very high in fiber. In many instances, I find that one-half to three-fourths of the total weight of a coprolite consists of indigested fiber.

Our digestive system still needs lots of fiber. Fiber speeds the passage of food through our small intestines, adds needed bulk to our large intestine, stimulates peristalsis necessary for the excretion process, and minimizes the effects of ingested carcinogens which might otherwise cause the DNA in digestive tract cells to mutate into cancers. Low fiber diets are also a factor in the occurrence of disorders such as spastic colon, diverticulosis, hiatal hernia, and hemorrhoids.

Animal Protein

Anthropologist Richard Lee of the University of Toronto has spent a lifetime studying the diets of contemporary foraging societies. He estimates that most of today's foraging societies obtain only about 33% of their calories from animal sources, with the other 66% coming from plant foods. These estimates are considered reliable for most temperate and tropical regions, but some groups living in the arctic eat diets composed almost exclusively of animal products. Lee also notes that among contemporary foragers a significant percentage of their meat often comes from small reptiles, birds, and mammals. My coprolite evidence confirms that such a pattern seems to be ancient and that it may extend back in time to the beginning of the Paleolithic era.

Humans need a constant supply of protein because, unlike fats and carbohydrates, our body cannot store protein as protein. Instead, we store excess protein as fat. Raw meat from animals, fish, and fowl contains from 15–40% protein by weight and is called "a complete protein source." By contrast, most plant foods often contain no more than 2–10% protein and are termed "incomplete" because most lack at least one essential amino acid needed by humans. How much protein do we need? Nutritionists say about 10–20% of our diets should come from protein, a percentage that is within the current range eaten by most non-poverty-level Americans. For many of the contemporary foraging societies, about one-third of their daily calories comes from animal sources and most of that is protein. Nevertheless, some of our Paleolithic ancestors, especially ones we call the "big game hunters," probably relied on meat for as much as 50–60% of their total dietary calories.

We need protein because it provides the amino acids used by our bodies to build new tissues such as muscles, tendons, ligaments and the walls of blood vessels. All of our growth from birth to death, as well as all repairs to our body, depends upon the amino acids we obtain from protein sources. Finally, skin, hair, and nails cannot be formed properly without the correct amount and mixture of amino acids.

Fats

Throughout most of our prehistory human diets have been low in fat. Fats are found in some plant foods, such as seeds and nuts, and in the meat of animals. In prehistoric times fats were a hard-to-find food source because most land-dwelling animals have lean bodies with less than 4% fat. By contrast, more than 30% of the total carcass weights of most American cattle and pigs are fat.

Most fats are composed of long chains of triglyceride molecules, each containing three fatty acids and one glycerol. Cholesterol, often discussed with fats, is needed to produce numerous hormones and bile acids, but it is not really a fat. Instead, cholesterol is a complicated substance composed of molecule rings that reacts more like a wax than a true fat.

There are many types of fatty acids found in nature. Some are *saturated* fats, others are **unsaturated** fats, and the unsaturated group is divided into *mono* or *poly* depending on whether they are linked with one, or more, double bonds of a carbon. The chemistry of fatty acids is complex and, for most of us, knowing why the human body needs them is more important.

Some polyunsaturated fats are called structural fats because our bodies use them to build and repair nearly all cell membranes. We also need these fats to build various types of hormones that regulate our body functions. When digested, our bodies extract nine calories of energy from each gram of fat.

Most saturated fatty acids are called storage or adipose fat because excess amounts can be stored for later use. Some subcutaneous tissues in animals contain storage fat because it provides thermal insulation. However, the majority of saturated fats are stored in other body locations, such as the abdominal cavity and within muscle tissue.

The meat of wild animals provides more protein than fat. Wild animals do have small amounts of fat and it is usually distributed uniformly throughout the body. Also, except for a few species of marine mammals, most fat on wild animals is the unsaturated, structural type. The domestic animals we raise for slaughter, and many of the animals we overfeed as pets or keep in zoos, all have one thing in common, the fact that their meat contains more fat than protein and most of their fat are saturated, storage fat.

Of the foods Americans like most, the majority contain fats. It is unfortunate that we enjoy eating fats and that fats will satisfy our hunger pangs quicker than either protein or carbohydrates. Maybe its nature's way of encouraging us to eat this essential food item. If so, it may have served our foraging ancestors well, but it has become a liability for many of us today. What is worse for many of today's overweight people, our intestines are very efficient at digesting fats, generally allowing no more than 5% to escape before being absorbed. This digestive advantage provided an essential source of calories for our prehistoric ancestors, but it is one of the factors that contributes to making more than 50% of the people in the U.S. overweight.

A direct comparison between the types and amounts of fats eaten by us today and by our hunting and gathering ancestors is revealing. During Paleolithic times a pound of meat from wild game contained one-sixth the amount of total fat, and one-tenth the amount of saturated fat found in a pound of supermarket beef. What's worse, the U.S. Department of Agriculture still grades beef according to the amount of fat it contains. The most expensive grade, called prime beef, must contain at least 46% fat by weight.

It is the amount of saturated fat in our diet that should be cause for alarm. The U.S. Senate's Select Committee on Nutrition and Human Needs reports that the typical American diet consists of 42% fat and that the ratio of polyunsaturated to saturated fat is an alarming 7:16. By comparison, our Paleolithic ancestors ate meat with a fat ratio of 7:5 and their total calories from fat were no more than 20–25%.

It is both the total amount of fat, and the high percentage of saturated fats, that makes many modern diets unhealthy. Specifically, Dr. Edward Giovannucci of the Harvard University School of Medicine reports that a diet high in saturated fats is now considered a causative factor in some forms of prostate cancer. This supports earlier research by others that found a correlation between some forms of breast and colon cancer and diets rich in fats, especially saturated fats.

Dr. Boyd Eaton writes in *The Paleolithic Prescription* that he doubts our Paleolithic ancestors ever had to worry about coronary heart disease, one of today's major killers in the world's more developed countries. High levels of serum cholesterol, diet, age, sex and genetics are all potential contributors to coronary atherosclerosis; yet, of these, we can potentially control only one, our diet.

Many people mistakenly believe that their serum cholesterol level is directly linked to the amount of cholesterol they eat. Ironically, a high cholesterol diet usually only slightly raises a person's serum cholesterol level. For example, the Masai tribe of east Africa drink large amounts of milk and their daily intake of cholesterol often exceeds 1,000–2,000 mg. However, Masai warriors have low serum cholesterol levels of only 115–145 mg/dl.

Like the Masai, our Paleolithic ancestors probably had low serum cholesterol levels even though we suspect they consumed an estimated 300–1,000+ mg of cholesterol daily, depending on their meat supply. Recent research confirms that high fat diets—especially ones high in saturated fat—have a greater influence on raising serum cholesterol levels than does the amount of cholesterol a person eats.

Salt

Mammals normally consume more potassium than sodium (salt is about 40% sodium). Dr. Henry Blackburn, a professor of physiology at the University of Minnesota's Medical School, points out that the mammalian kidney is a marvelous organ for maintaining the delicate balance between sodium and potassium in the human body. However, he also notes that our kidneys were originally designed to **re-tain**, not **excrete** sodium.

One of the greatest changes in human diets of prehistoric times to the present has been the switch from ancient diets rich in potassium and low in sodium, to modern diets containing nearly twice as much sodium as potassium. A typical prehistoric diet of 3,000 calories, coming 60% from fresh plant foods (leaves, nuts, tubers, berries, fruits) and 40% from meat (ungulates, birds, fish, eggs, reptiles) would contain about 7,000 mg of potassium and 900 mg of sodium. By comparison, the U.S. National Academy of Sciences Food and Nutrition Board reports that the average human requirement for sodium is no more than 250 mg per day even though most people in the U.S. are now consuming 6–18 g of salt per day (about 2,400–7,200 mg of sodium) and eating diets that are low in potassium.

Medical researchers believe that high sodium use, especially among people who have a genetic predisposition to retain much of the sodium they ingest, is a primary cause of hypertension. Years ago some believed that the high levels of salt use in our diets resulted from a physiological craving for sodium. Today, most medical doctors believe that our high salt diets are based strictly on an acquired taste, not on a physiological need. Additional evidence linking hypertension with high levels of salt use comes from worldwide statistics that note that the incidence of hypertension is greatest in countries with the highest per capita consumption of salt. Likewise, hypertension does not seem to exist among cultures with traditional low sodium/high potassium diets, such as the Yanomami of Venezuela, the Eskimo of the Arctic, the San of the African Kalahari, and some of the Polynesians still living throughout the South Pacific. As do medical researchers, we believe our Paleolithic ancestors also were free from hypertension because their estimated daily intake of sodium was no more than 600–1,000 mg.

Exercise

Hunting and gathering are activities that require strength and stamina. Hunters tracking game generally have to walk long distances before killing it. Then, they, along with the women and children, would carry the meat back to camp. Gatherers have to dig up large tubers, carry children, gather other foods, find water, and collect firewood before carrying everything back to camp. Studies of modern foraging groups reveal that daily activities of these types ensure that individuals will remain strong and will retain great stamina even into their old age.

Like modern foragers, our pre-agricultural ancestors also had strength and stamina; the evidence is seen in their skeletons. Their weight-bearing leg bones are thick and have pronounced rough areas where muscles and tendons attached.

Human skeletons dating from the early farming era begin to lose these robust features, and by modern times these features are almost gone in the skeletons of people from the industrialized regions of the world. These skeletal changes suggest that even though early farmers worked longer hours, their efforts no longer required the levels of physical stamina and endurance common in the lives of foraging cultures. Finally, after the Industrial Revolution, human strength was replaced by machines. Many people, especially those of the affluent class, could now enjoy a life requiring little physical stamina or strength.

During the 1960s, muscular strength and endurance testing of high school and college-age Americans revealed they were considerably weaker than earlier generations at their same age. I saw evidence of this in 1976 when I directed the excavation of a large archaeological site in southwest Texas that was located halfway up the side of a canyon. Of the 21 college-age students who participated, 13 lacked the strength and stamina to make the climb to the site without the aid of ropes and ladders. As we later discovered, the site had been occupied for nearly 9,000 years by many generations of foragers whose men, women and children probably made the climb from the canyon bottom to the site dozens of times each day unaided by anything more than their strength and endurance.

The Future

Our Paleolithic ancestors were remarkable humans. They beat the odds and survived for more than two million years before being replaced by farmers and herders. Most lived the "perfect" lifestyle and ate the "perfect" diet for which our bodies were designed. And, when we compare ourselves to them, we notice some stark differences.

As a group, our ancestors were slim and trim because they relied upon their physical strength and stamina for survival. They ate less than half the amount of fat eaten by today's Americans and the fat they ate was mostly of the less harmful, polyunsaturated type. The Paleolithic peoples ate large amounts of complex carbohydrates and very few simple carbohydrates. On average, they ate five, ten, or even fifteen times more fiber than most Americans eat today, and their foods were bulky and filling, not the calorie-rich and highly refined types we eat today. Our ancestors ate foods rich in potassium and low in sodium, and their foods probably contained more than twice the amount of calcium Americans consume today.

Rather than be depressed by these chilling comparisons, we ought to use this information to our advantage. We can adopt essential elements from the lives of our foraging ancestors and use them to improve the *quality* of our own lives. The change from nomadic hunters and gatherers to urbanites has brought mixed blessings. Yes, our problems are many; we have overcrowded cities, pollution, new diseases, wars, famine, and poverty. Nevertheless, these are offset by our many achievements in art, literature, science, and medicine. And, in many Western nations, life expectancy is now more than double what it was just 200 years ago.

It is this very aspect, increased longevity, that should concern each of us the most. In many Western societies the healthiness of individuals is fairly constant until their mid 20s. After that, with each increasing decade, the gap widens between those who are still in excellent health and those who are not.

Until recently, medical professionals believed the degenerative process, seen in many of our elderly, was a normal part of the aging process. However, growing evidence suggests that many of the degenerative processes seen in the aged are caused more by their lifestyles and diets than by fundamental changes in their natural physiology.

Each of us can invest in our own future. Our challenge is to make informed choices. We don't have to give up the blessings of civilization, but we do need to live in harmony with our body's physiology. By selecting a diet that approximates the proportions of fats, fiber, protein and complex carbohydrates eaten by our Paleolithic ancestors, and by reducing our intake of sugar and sodium, we can benefit from eating a near "perfect" diet. Then, by adding regular exercise we should be able to maintain reasonable levels of strength and stamina as we age, and continue to enjoy many aspects of the "perfect" lifestyle for which our bodies were designed.

Today, our greatest advantage is an ability to choose our destiny, something our Paleolithic ancestors could not do. If, as individuals, we are willing to make the needed lifestyle changes now, then we will not be included in that unfortunate group who, during the last decade or more of their lives, will suffer from a host of degenerative conditions that are the consequence of a lifetime of eating an improper diet and being unfit and unhealthy.

15

STRINGS ATTACHED[1]

Lee Cronk

Reciprocity or gift-giving is important in non-state societies as a means of exchange and as a way of cementing social relationships. Lee Cronk explores the ways in which gifts create future obligations. Under some circumstances, gift-giving can become a form of competition in which the goal is to demonstrate one's wealth and generosity in public. As Cronk shows, even gifts given in our own society often come with strings attached.

During a trek through the Rockies in the 1830s, Captain Benjamin Louis E. de Bonneville received a gift of a fine young horse from a Nez Percé chief. According to Washington Irving's account of the incident, the American explorer was aware that "a parting pledge was necessary on his own part, to prove that this friendship was reciprocated." Accordingly, he "placed a handsome rifle in the hands of the venerable chief; whose benevolent heart was evidently touched and gratified by this outward and visible sign of amity."

Even the earliest white settlers in New England understood that presents from natives required reciprocity, and by 1764 "Indian gift" was so common a phrase that the Massachusetts colonial historian Thomas Hutchinson

identified it as "a proverbial expression signifying a present for which an equivalent return is expected." Then, over time, the custom's meaning was lost. Indeed, the phrase now is used derisively, to refer to one who demands the return of a gift. How this cross-cultural misunderstanding occurred is unclear, but the poet Lewis Hyde, in his book *The Gift,* has imagined a scenario that probably approaches the truth.

Say that an Englishman newly arrived in America is welcomed to an Indian lodge with the present of a pipe. Thinking the pipe a wonderful artifact, he takes it home and sets it on his mantelpiece. When he later learns that the Indians expect to have the pipe back, as a gesture of goodwill, he is shocked by

[1]This article is reprinted by permission of *The Sciences* and is from the May/June 1989 issue. Individual subscriptions are $28 per year. Write to: *The Sciences*, 2 East 63rd Street, New York, NY 10021.

what he views as their short-lived generosity. The newcomer did not realize that, to the natives, the point of the gift was not to provide an interesting trinket but to inaugurate a friendly relationship that would be maintained through a series of mutual exchanges. Thus, his failure to reciprocate appeared not only rude and thoughtless but downright hostile. "White man keeping" was as offensive to native Americans as "Indian giving" was to settlers.

In fact, the Indians' tradition of gift giving is much more common than our own. Like our European ancestors, we think that presents ought to be offered freely, without strings attached. But through most of the world, the strings themselves are the main consideration. In some societies, gift giving is a tie between friends, a way of maintaining good relationships, whereas in others it has developed into an elaborate, expensive, and antagonistic ritual designed to humiliate rivals by showering them with wealth and obligating them to give more in return.

In truth, the dichotomy between the two traditions of gift giving is less behavioral than rhetorical: our generosity is not as unconditional as we would like to believe. Like European colonists, most modern Westerners are blind to the purpose of reciprocal gift giving, not only in non-Western societies but also, to some extent, in our own. Public declarations to the contrary, we, too, use gifts to nurture long-term relationships of mutual obligation, as well as to embarrass our rivals and to foster feelings of indebtedness. And this ethic touches all aspects of contemporary life, from the behavior of scientists in research networks to superpower diplomacy. Failing to acknowledge this fact, especially as we give money, machines, and technical advice to peoples around the world, we run the risk of being misinterpreted and, worse, of causing harm.

Much of what we know about the ethics of gift giving comes from the attempts of anthropologists to give things to the people they are studying. Richard Lee, of the University of Toronto, learned a difficult lesson from the !Kung hunter-gatherers, of the Kalahari desert, when, as a token of goodwill, he gave them an ox to slaughter at Christmas. Expecting gratitude, he was shocked when the !Kung complained about having to make do with such a scrawny "bag of bones." Only later did Lee learn, with relief, that the !Kung belittle all gifts. In their eyes, no act is completely generous, or free of calculation; ridiculing gifts is their way of diminishing the expected return and of enforcing humility on those who would use gifts to raise their own status within the group.

Rada Dyson-Hudson, of Cornell University, had a similar experience among the Turkana, a pastoral people of northwestern Kenya. To compensate her informants for their help, Dyson-Hudson gave away pots, maize meal, tobacco, and other items. The Turkana reaction was less than heartwarming. A typical response to a gift of a pot, for example, might be, "Where is the maize meal to go in this pot?" or, "Don't you have a bigger one to give me?" To the Turkana, these are legitimate and expected questions.

The Mukogodo, another group of Kenyan natives, responded in a similar way to gifts Beth Leech and I presented to them during our fieldwork in 1986. Clothing was never nice enough, containers never big enough, tobacco and candies never plentiful enough. Every gift horse was examined carefully, in the mouth and elsewhere. Like the !Kung, the Mukogodo believe that all gifts have an element of calculation, and they were right to think that ours were no exception. We needed their help, and their efforts to diminish our expectations and lessen their obligations to repay were as fair as our attempts to get on their good side.

The idea that gifts carry obligations is instilled early in life. When we gave Mukogodo children candies after visiting their villages, their mothers reminded them of the tie: "Remember these white people? They are the ones who gave you candy." They also reinforced the notion that gifts are meant to circulate, by asking their children to part with their precious candies, already in their mouths. Most of the youngsters reluctantly surrendered their sweets, only to have them immediately returned. A mother might take, at most, a symbolic nibble from her child's candy, just to drive home the lesson.

The way food, utensils, and other goods are received in many societies is only the first stage of the behavior surrounding gift giving. Although repayment is expected, it is crucial that it

be deferred. To reciprocate at once indicates a desire to end the relationship, to cut the strings; delayed repayment makes the strings longer and stronger. This is especially clear on the Truk Islands, of Micronesia, where a special word—*niffag*—is used to designate objects moving through the island's exchange network. From the Trukese viewpoint, to return niffag on the same day it is received alters its nature from that of a gift to that of a sale, in which all that matters is material gain.

After deciding the proper time for response, a recipient must consider how to make repayment, and that is dictated largely by the motive behind the gift. Some exchange customs are designed solely to preserve a relationship. The !Kung have a system, called *hxaro*, in which little attention is paid to whether the items exchanged are equivalent. Richard Lee's informant !Xoma explained to him that "Hxaro is when I take a thing of value and give it to you. Later, much later, when you find some good thing, you give it back to me. When I find something good I will give it to you, and so we will pass the years together." When Lee tried to determine the exact exchange values of various items (Is a spear worth three strings of beads, two strings, or one?), !Xoma explained that any return would be all right: "You see, we don't trade with things, we trade with people!"

One of the most elaborate systems of reciprocal gift giving, known as *kula*, exists in a ring of islands off New Guinea. Kula gifts are limited largely to shell necklaces, called *soulava*, and armbands, called *mwali*. A necklace given at one time is answered months or years later with an armband, the necklaces usually circulating clockwise, and the armbands counterclockwise, through the archipelago. Kula shells vary in quality and value, and men gain fame and prestige by having their names associated with noteworthy necklaces or armbands. The shells also gain value from their association with famous and successful kula partners.

Although the act of giving gifts seems intrinsically benevolent, a gift's power to embarrass the recipient and to force repayment has, in some societies, made it attractive as a weapon. Such antagonistic generosity reached its most elaborate expression, during the late nineteenth century, among the Kwakiutl, of British Columbia.

The Kwakiutl were acutely conscious of status, and every tribal division, clan, and individual had a specific rank. Disputes about status were resolved by means of enormous ceremonies (which outsiders usually refer to by the Chinook Indian term *potlatch*), at which rivals competed for the honor and prestige of giving away the greatest amount of property. Although nearly everything of value was fair game—blankets, canoes, food, pots, and, until the mid-nineteenth century, even slaves—the most highly prized items were decorated sheets of beaten copper, shaped like shields and etched with designs in the distinctive style of the Northwest Coast Indians.

As with the kula necklaces and armbands, the value of a copper sheet was determined by its history—by where it had been and who had owned it—and a single sheet could be worth thousands of blankets, a fact often reflected in its name. One was called "Drawing All Property from the House," and another "About Whose Possession All Are Quarreling." After the Kwakiutl began to acquire trade goods from the Hudson's Bay Company's Fort Rupert post, in 1849 the potlatches underwent a period of extreme inflation, and by the 1920s, when items of exchange included sewing machines and pool tables, tens of thousands of Hudson's Bay blankets might be given away during a single ceremony.

In the 1880s, after the Canadian government began to suppress warfare between tribes, potlatching also became a substitute for battle. As a Kwakiutl man once said to the anthropologist Franz Boas, "The time of fighting is past. . . . We do not fight now with weapons: we fight with property." The usual Kwakiutl word for potlatch was *p!Esa*, meaning to flatten (as when one flattens a rival under a pile of blankets), and the prospect of being given a large gift engendered real fear. Still, the Kwakiutl seemed to prefer the new "war of wealth" to the old "war of blood."

Gift giving has served as a substitute for war in other societies, as well. Among the Siuai, of the Solomon Islands, guests at feasts are referred to as attackers, while hosts are defenders, and invitations to feasts are given on short notice in the manner of "surprise attacks." And like the Kwakiutl of British Columbia, the Mount Hagen tribes of New Guinea use a system of gift giving called *moka* as a way of gaining prestige and shaming rivals. The goal is to become a tribal leader, a "big-man." One moka gift in the 1970s consisted of several hundred pigs, thousands of dollars in cash, some cows and wild birds, a truck, and a motorbike. The donor, quite pleased with himself, said to the recipient, "I have won. I have knocked you down by giving so much."

Although we tend not to recognize it as such, the ethic of reciprocal gift giving manifests itself throughout our own society, as well. We, too, often expect something, even if only gratitude and a sense of indebtedness, in exchange for gifts, and we use gifts to establish friendships and to manipulate our positions in society. As in non-Western societies, gift giving in America sometimes takes a benevolent and helpful form; at other times, the power of gifts to create obligations is used in a hostile way.

The Duke University anthropologist Carol Stack found a robust tradition of benevolent exchange in an Illinois ghetto known as the Flats, where poor blacks engage in a practice called swapping. Among residents of the Flats, wealth comes in spurts; hard times are frequent and unpredictable. Swapping, of clothes, food, furniture, and the like, is a way of guaranteeing security, of making sure that someone will be there to help out when one is in need and that

one will get a share of any windfalls that come along.

Such networks of exchange are not limited to the poor, nor do they always involve objects. Just as the exchange of clothes creates a gift community in the Flats, so the swapping of knowledge may create one among scientists. Warren Hagstrom, a sociologist at the University of Wisconsin, in Madison, has pointed out that papers submitted to scientific journals often are called contributions, and, because no payment is received for them, they truly are gifts. In contrast, articles written for profit—such as this one—often are held in low esteem: scientific status can be achieved only through *giving* gifts of knowledge.

Recognition also can be traded upon, with scientists building up their gift-giving networks by paying careful attention to citations and acknowledgments. Like participants in kula exchange, they try to associate themselves with renowned and prestigious articles, books, and institutions. A desire for recognition, however, cannot be openly acknowledged as a motivation for research, and it is a rare scientist who is able to discuss such desires candidly. Hagstrom was able to find just one mathematician (whom he described as "something of a social isolate") to confirm that "junior mathematicians want recognition from big shots and, consequently, work in areas prized by them."

Hagstrom also points out that the inability of scientists to acknowledge a desire for recognition does not mean that such recognition is not expected by those who offer gifts of knowledge, any more than a kula trader believes it is all right if his trading partner does not answer his gift of a necklace with an armband. While failure to reciprocate in New Guinean society might once have meant warfare, among scientists it may cause factionalism and the creation of rivalries.

Whether in the Flats of Illinois or in the halls of academia, swapping is, for the most part, benign. But manipulative gift giving exists in modern societies, too—particularly in paternalistic government practices. The technique is to offer a present that cannot be repaid, coupled with a claim of beneficence and omniscience. The Johns Hopkins University anthropologist Grace Goodell documented one example in Iran's Khuzestan Province, which, because it contains most of the country's oil fields and is next door to Iraq, is a strategically sensitive area. Goodell focused on the World Bank-funded Dez irrigation project, a showpiece of the shah's ambitious "white revolution" development plan. The scheme involved the irrigation of tens of thousands of acres and the forced relocation of people from their villages to new, model towns. According to Goodell, the purpose behind dismantling local institutions was to enhance central government control of the region. Before development, each Khuzestani village had been a miniature city-state, managing its own internal affairs and determining its own relations with outsiders. In the new settlements, decisions were made by government bureaucrats, not townsmen, whose autonomy was crushed under the weight of a large and strategically placed gift.

On a global scale, both the benevolent and aggressive dimensions of gift giving are at work in superpower diplomacy. Just as the Kwakiutl were left only with blankets with which to fight after warfare was banned, the United States and the Soviet Union now find, with war out of the question, that they are left only with gifts—called concessions—with which to do battle. Offers of military cutbacks are easy ways to score points in the public arena of international opinion and to shame rivals, and failure either to accept such offers or to respond with even more extreme proposals may be seen as cowardice or as bellicosity. Mikhail Gorbachev is a virtuoso, a master potlatcher, in this new kind of competition, and, predictably, Americans often see his offers of disarmament and openness as gifts with long strings attached. One reason U.S. officials were buoyed last December, when, for the first time since the Second World War, the Soviet Union accepted American assistance, in the aftermath of the Armenian earthquake, is that it seemed to signal a wish for reciprocity rather than dominance—an unspoken understanding of the power of gifts to bind people together.

Japan, faced with a similar desire to expand its influence, also has begun to exploit gift giving in its international relations. In 1989, it will spend more than ten billion dollars on foreign aid, putting it ahead of the United States for the second consecutive year as the world's greatest donor nation. Although this move was publicly welcome in the United States as the sharing of a burden, fears, too, were expressed that the resultant blow to American prestige might cause a further slip in our international status. Third World leaders also have complained that too much Japanese aid is targeted at countries in which Japan has an economic stake and that too much is restricted to the purchase of Japanese goods—that Japan's generosity has less to do with addressing the problems of underdeveloped countries than with exploiting those problems to its own advantage.

The danger in all of this is that wealthy nations may be competing for the prestige that comes from giving gifts at the expense of Third World nations. With assistance sometimes being given with more regard to the donors' status than to the recipients' welfare, it is no surprise that, in recent years, development aid often has been more effective in creating relationships of dependency, as in the case of Iran's Khuzestan irrigation scheme, than in producing real development. Nor that, given the fine line between donation and domination, offers of help are sometimes met with resistance, apprehension and, in extreme cases, such as the Iranian revolution, even violence.

The Indians understood a gift's ambivalent power to unify, antagonize, or subjugate. We, too, would do well to remember that a present can be a surprisingly potent thing, as dangerous in the hands of the ignorant as it is useful in the hands of the wise.

16

PRYING INTO YANOMAMÖ SECRETS[1]

Napoleon Chagnon

Sometimes the most innocent questions cause the most trouble. While studying the Yanomamö, Chagnon thought that genealogical studies would be an obvious way to learn the language and develop rapport. As this article shows, he greatly misjudged the significance of one's ancestors in the Venezuelan rainforest..

My purpose in living among the Yanomamö was to collect information on their genealogies, reproduction, marriage practices, kinship, settlement pattern, migrations, and politics. The most fundamental of the data was genealogical—who was the parent of whom, with such connections traced as far back as Yanomamö memory permitted. Like most primitive societies, the Yanomamö society is largely organized by kinship relationships, and figuring out this social organization essentially meant collecting extensive data on genealogies, marriage, and reproduction.

It turned out to be a staggering and frustrating problem. I could not have deliberately picked a more difficult people to work with in this regard, because of their very stringent taboos against mentioning the names of prominent living people or of deceased friends and relatives. They attempt to choose names for people so that when the person dies, and they can no longer use his or her name, the loss of the word from their language is not inconvenient. Hence, they name people for highly specific and minute parts of things, such as "toenail of sloth," "whisker of howler monkey," and so on, thereby being able to retain the words "toenail" and "whisker" but somewhat handicapped when they need to refer to these anatomical parts of sloths and monkeys. The name taboo even applies to the living, for one mark of a person's prestige is the courtesy others show by *not* using that person's name publicly. This is particularly true for the men, who are much more competitive for status than the

[1]Excerpts from *Yanomamö: The Last Days of Eden* by Napoleon Chagnon. Copyright © 1992 by Harcourt Brace & Company, reprinted by permission of the publisher.

women are, and it is fascinating to watch boys, as they grow into young men, demanding to be called in public either by a kinship term or by some such reference as "brother of Himotoma" or "nephew of Ushubiriwä." The more effective they are at getting others to avoid using their names, the greater is the public acknowledgment of their esteem and social standing. Helena Valero, a Brazilian woman who was captured as a child by a Yanomamö raiding party, was married for many years to a Yanomamö headman before she discovered what his name was. The sanctions behind the taboo are more complex than just fear: they involve a combination of fear, respect, admiration, political deference, and honor.

At first I tried to use kinship terms alone to collect my genealogies, but Yanomamö kinship terms, like those in all systems, tend to become ambiguous at the point where they include many possible relatives—as the terms "uncle" and "cousin" do in our own kinship system. In a community like Bisaasi-teri, where someone might have thirty cousins, you cannot get the right person simply by saying, "Call my cousin for me." Also, the system of kin classification merges many relatives that we normally separate by using different terms: the Yanomamö call both the actual father and the father's brother by a single term, whereas we call one "father" and the other "uncle." I was forced, therefore, to resort to personal names to collect unambiguous genealogies or pedigrees.

The villagers quickly grasped what I was up to, that I was determined to learn everyone's true name. This amounted to an invasion of their system of prestige and etiquette, if not a flagrant violation of it, and their reaction was brilliant but devastating. They invented *false names* for everybody in the village, systematically learned them, and freely revealed them to me. I smugly thought I had cracked the system and enthusiastically spent some five months constructing elaborate genealogies.

Since they enjoyed watching me work on the names and kinship relationships, I naively assumed that I was getting the most truthful information by working in public. This set the stage for converting my serious project into a hilarious game of the grandest proportions. Each informant would try to outdo his peers by inventing a name more preposterous or ridiculous than one I had been given earlier, the explanation for discrepancies being "Well, he has two names, and this is the other one." They even fabricated devilishly improbable genealogical relationships, such as someone being married to his grandmother or, worse yet, his mother-in-law, a–grotesque and horrifying prospect to the Yanomamö. My practice was to have the informant whisper a person's name softly into my ear, noting that he or she was the parent of such and such or the child of such and such. The eager watchers would then insist that I repeat the name aloud, roaring in hysterical laughter as I clumsily pronounced it, sometimes laughing until tears streamed down their faces. The person named would usually react with annoyance and hiss some untranslatable epithet at me, which only served to reassure me that I indeed had the person's true name. Conscientiously checking and rechecking the names and relationships with multiple informants, I was pleased to see the inconsistencies disappear as my genealogy sheets filled with thousands of those desirable little triangles and circles.

My anthropological bubble burst when, some five months after I had begun collecting the genealogies, I visited a village about ten hours' walk to the southwest of Bisaasi-teri. In talking with the headman of this village, I casually dropped the name of the wife of the Bisaasi-teri headman, to show off a bit and demonstrate my growing command of the language and of who was who. A stunned silence followed, and then a villagewide roar of uncontrollable laughter, choking, gasping, and howling. It seems that I thought the Bisaasi-teri headman was married to a woman named "hairy cunt." It also came out that I was calling the headman "long dong," his brother "eagle shit," one of his sons "asshole," and a daughter "fart breath."

Blood welled in my temples as I realized that I had nothing but nonsense to show for my five months of dedicated genealogical effort and that I would have to throw out almost all the information I had collected on this, the most basic set of data I had come to get. Now I understood why the Bisaasi-teri had laughed so hard when they made me repeat the names they had given me, and

why the person named had reacted with such anger and annoyance.

I would have to devise a new research strategy—an understatement to describe this serious setback to my work. The first change was to begin working in private with my informants, eliminating the horseplay and distractions that had attended the public sessions. The informants, who did not know what others were telling me, now began to agree with each other, and I managed to learn real names, starting with the children and gradually moving on to the adult women and then, cautiously, the adult men, a sequence that reflected the relative degree of intransigence at revealing the names. As I built up a core of accurate genealogies and relationships—which the various informants verified repetitiously—I could test any new informant by soliciting his or her knowledge about these core people whose names and relationships I was sure of. In this fashion, I was able to immediately weed out the mischievous informants who persisted in trying to deceive me. Still, I had great difficulty getting the names of dead kinsmen, the only accurate way to extend the genealogies back in time. Even my best informants continued to falsify the names of the deceased, especially if they were closely related. But the falsifications were not serious at this point and proved to be readily corrected as my interviewing methods improved. Most of the deceptions were of the sort where the informant would give me the name of a living man as the father of a child whose actual father was dead, enabling the informant to avoid using the name of a deceased kinsman or friend.

But the name taboo prevented me from making any substantial progress in tracing the present population back through several generations, without which data I could not, for example, document marriage patterns and interfamilial alliances over time. I had to rely on older informants for such information, and they were the most reluctant informants of all. Even as I became more proficient in the language and more skilled at detecting fabrications, my informants became better at deception. One old man, particularly cunning and persuasive, followed Mark Twain's theory that the most effective lie is a sincere lie. He made quite a ceremony out of giving me false names for dead ancestors. He would look around nervously to make sure nobody was listening outside my hut, would enjoin me never to mention the name again, and would act anxious and spooky as he grabbed me by the head and whispered a secret name into my ear. I was always elated after a session with him, because I would have added several generations of ancestors for particular members of the village, information others steadfastly refused to give me. To show my gratitude, I paid him quadruple the rate that I had been paying the others. When word got around that I had increased the pay for genealogical and demographic information, volunteers began pouring into my hut to work for me, assuring me they had changed their ways and had a keen desire to divest themselves of their version of the truth.

Enter Rerebawä: Inmarried Tough Guy

It was quite by accident that I discovered the old man had been lying. A club fight broke out in the village one day, the result of a dispute over the possession of a woman. The woman had been promised to a young man of the village, a particularly aggressive man named Rerebawä. He had inmarried—that is, he was from another village and had married into the village of Bisaasi-teri—and was doing his bride service period of several years during which he had to provide game and wild foods for his wife's father and mother and help them with certain gardening and other tasks. Rerebawä had already been given one of the daughters in marriage and had been promised her younger sister as his second wife. He became enraged when the younger sister, then about sixteen years old, openly began an affair with another young man of the village, Bäkotawä, and he challenged Bäkotawä to a club fight.

Rerebawä swaggered boisterously out to the duel carrying a ten-foot-long club, a roof pole he had impulsively cut from a house, as is the usual procedure. He hurled insult after insult at both Bäkotawä and his father, trying to goad them into a fight. They tolerated the hitter and nasty insults for a few moments, but Rerebawä's biting words soon provoked them to rage. They stormed angrily out of their hammocks and ripped off their own roof poles, returning the insults verbally, and rushed to the village clearing, where they took up positions some ten feet away from Rerebawä. He continued his insults, trying to goad them into striking him on the head with their equally long clubs. Had either of them struck his head, which he held forward prominently for them to swing at, he would have had the right to retaliate on their heads with his club. But his opponents, intimidated by his fury, backed down, refusing to strike him, and the argument ended. All three then retired pompously to their respective hammocks, exchanging nasty insults as they went. Rerebawä had won the showdown and thereafter swaggered around the village, insulting the two men behind their backs at every opportunity, so genuinely angry that he called the older man by the name of his long-deceased father.

As soon as I heard that name, which was not the same as the one I had recorded, I asked Rerebawä to repeat it, which he did willingly and contemptuously. Quickly seizing on the incident as an opportunity to correct my data, I confidentially asked Rerebawä to tell me more about his adversary's ancestors. He had been particularly brusque with me until now, but we soon became warm friends and staunch allies, partly because we were both outsiders in Bisaasi-teri. Like all inmarried Yanomamö sons-in-law, he had to put up with a considerable amount of pointed teasing and scorn from the locals. With almost devilish glee he gave me the information I wanted about his adversary's deceased ancestors.

I asked about the dead ancestors of other people in the village and got equally prompt and unequivocal answers—he seemed to be angry at everyone in the village. When I compared his answers to those of the old man, it was obvious that one of them was lying. I challenged Rerebawä, and he explained, in a sort of "you damned fool, don't you know better?" tone, that everyone in the village knew that the old man was lying to me and that they were gloating over it when I was out of earshot. The names the old man had given me were those of the dead ancestors of people in a village, so far away that he thought I would never be able to check them authoritatively. As it turned out, Rerebawä knew most of the people in that distant village and recognized the names and also knew enough about recently deceased Bisaasi-teri to be sure that the old man had been lying.

I went over with Rerebawä all the Bisaasi-teri genealogies that I had presumed were close to their final form and had to revise them all because of the numerous lies and falsifications, many of them provided by the sly old man. Once again, after months of work, I had to recheck everything, but with Rerebawä's aid this time. Only the information about living members of nuclear families turned out to be accurate; that about deceased ancestors was mostly fabrication.

Discouraging as it was to know I had to recheck everything yet again, it proved to be a major turning point in my fieldwork. From then on I took advantage of local arguments and animosities in selecting my informants and made more extensive use of informants who had married into the village in the recent past. I also began to travel more regularly to other villages to check on genealogies, seeking out villages whose members were on strained terms with the people about whom I wanted information. I would then return to my base in Bisaasi-teri and check the accuracy of the new information with local informants.

I learned to be scrupulous about selecting local informants so that I was not inquiring about their closely related kin. For each local informant, I had to keep a list of the deceased people that I dared not name in his or her presence. Even so, I would occasionally hit a new name that would send an informant into a rage or a sulk, such as that of a dead "brother" or "sister" (the Yanomamö classify many cousins as brothers and sisters) whose relationship I had not been aware of. That usually terminated the day's work with the informant; he or she would be too upset to continue, and I would be reluctant to risk the accidental discovery of another dead kinsman.

The Larger Society and Rules

It takes many months of living with a people like the Yanomamö to learn the abstract rules and principles they follow in their social interactions. And it is difficult to say precisely how an anthropological fieldworker learns them, except that it is a gradual process, much like the way we learn the rules of our own culture. Most of us cannot, for ex-

ample, explain precisely how or when we came to know that having sex with a sister or brother is bad, but we do know it. Anthropologists are aware, however, that tribal societies have rules about proper behavior and that these rules are usually expressed in the context of (a) kinship, (b) descent, or (c) marriage. So at least we know where to start.

Take one such rule, about who should marry whom. It was difficult to get the Yanomamö to state this as a general principle, and so I tried to establish it indirectly, by asking individuals such questions as "Can you marry so-and-so?" The answers, when pieced together, allowed me to formulate a general rule so self-evident to them that they could not imagine anyone not knowing it. Answers to the question might take the form of: "What? No, I can't marry so-and-so. She is my *yuhaya* [the daughter of my child or sister, or my granddaughter]." Or; "No, she is my *taaya* [my daughter or my brother's daughter]." But eventually, I learned all the kinship terms that both the men and the women used for their kin and which of these terms indicated a prohibited spouse. In this fashion, I also learned that men could marry only those women they put into the kinship category *suaböya* and, by reciprocal extension, that women could marry only the men they put into the category *hearoya*. By collecting genealogies that showed exactly how one person was related to another, I was able to specify a man's "nonmarriageable" and "marriageable" female kin. As it turned out, a man (woman) could marry only those women (men) who fell into the category of kin we call cross-cousins. For a man, these are the daughters of his mother's brother and the daughters of his father's sister.

By contrast, parallel cousins are a person's mother's sister's children or father's brother's children. The sex of the linking kinsmen is parallel; that is, the father and the father's brother are the same sex. The Yanomamö call parallel cousins by kinship terms that mean brother or sister, and, quite understandably, they forbid marriages between these cousins. The biblical discussions of the levirate may help clarify this—the rule that says a man should marry his dead brother's widow. In such a case, the woman's children by her dead husband would call her new husband "father." The Yanomamö simply institutionalize this by calling both men—the father and the father's brother—by the term meaning father, whether or not both men have married the mother. They do the same on the mother's side: the mother and the mother's sister are called by the word meaning mother, and a woman can marry her dead sister's husband. The rule is called the sororate, the mirror image of the levirate. It is quite logical to the Yanomamö that parallel cousins should be classified as brothers and sisters.

The rule, therefore, is that the Yanomamö marry bilateral (from both the father's and the mother's side of the family) cross-cousins. In their words, the rule is: "Men should marry their suaböya." In a sense, it is like saying, "We marry our wives," for the men call their wives *and* their female cross-cousins

suaböya. Thus, to ask them the general question "Whom do you marry?" strikes them as peculiar. They marry their wives, as everyone does.

It is important to note that this marriage rule is embedded in the kinship terminology: men marry women they call suaböya. The Yanomamö kinship system literally defines who is and who is not marriageable to whom, and it has no terms that are limited to what we call in-laws. In a word, everyone in the Yanomamö society is called by one or another kinship term that we would translate as the term for a blood relative. To be sure, the Yanomamö extend kinship terms to those who are nonkin; Kaobawä calls Rerebawä by a kinship term, although they are not related. One fascinating aspect of their society is that *all* neighbors are some sort of kin, and therefore all their social life takes place in a kinship matrix of real and fictive-kin. Nobody can escape it, not even the anthropologist. Kaobawä calls me *hekamaya* nephew (sister's son), and Rerebawä calls me *aiwä*—older brother. Everyone gets placed in *some* sort of kinship matrix, which, to a large degree, defines how one is expected to behave toward specific categories of one's kin. Both Kaobawä and Rerebawä know that I am not his sister's son or his older brother, respectively, but I must be put into some kinship category in order to establish a general basis of proper social behavior. To be outside the Yanomamö kinship system is, in a very real sense, to be inhuman or nonhuman: all humans are some sort of kin. This is what anthropologists mean when they say that a primitive society is largely organized and regulated by kinship. Remember it when you read a shallow account by some journalist or traveler telling how "the natives liked me so much that they adopted me." The natives were simply putting him or her into a kinship category, whether or not they liked the outsider. And it was probably the most exploitable category, that is, the one that would bring in the most gifts for the largest number of people. It is exactly what the Yanomamö did to me.

Here are two humorous examples of how kinship dictates expected forms of behavior, both involving the Yanomamö rule that it is very inappropriate for a man to be familiar with the mother of a woman he can marry or has married. Indeed, they describe such behavior as *yawaremou,* or incest. A man should not look into the face of his mother-in-law, say her name, go near her, touch or speak to her.

On one occasion, I was mapping an empty village with the help of two young men. As we proceeded around the village, we came to a hearth. One of the young men walked out to the middle of the village, took three or four steps in the direction we were headed, and came back and stood on the other side of the abandoned hearth. When I asked why he was acting in such a strange way, the other man whispered in embarrassment, "His mother-in-law lives there." Then both of them blushed.

Some time later, I decided to have a little fun with this taboo. The Yanomamö term for mother-in-law is *yaya,* but the same kinship term also applies to one's father's sister or one's grandmother, women who need not be avoided to the same degree. While visiting my wife's family in northern Michigan one year, I had a photograph taken of me hugging my wife's mother and kissing her on the cheek. On my next field trip, I brought along this photo and many others of my family and my wife's family to show to Kaobawä's people, who were fascinated by them. When we got to the photo of me hugging my mother-in-law, they recognized me and asked, "Who are you hugging?" I responded, "My *yaya.*" Chuckles and giggles followed. Then one of them asked, "Is she your father's mother?" "No," I replied casually. (It is all right to be somewhat familiar with a grandmother.) "Ahh. She must be your mother's mother." Again I nonchalantly said, "No." Murmurs and whispers followed, and their smiles changed to looks of apprehension—there was only one legitimate choice left. "Ahh. She is your father's sister." I paused, to extend the suspense, and then I said offhandedly, "No, she's my wife's mother." Embarrassed laughter and protests exploded from the group. They were incredulous at my audacity and my flagrant violation of the incest avoidance prohibition—the more so because I was carrying around photographic evidence of the misdeed. For several years afterward, visitors from distant villages would come to my hut and beg to see the photograph of me "committing incest" with my wife's mother, as if it were something pornographic. They even blushed as they looked at it.

The discovery of one principle often leads to the identification of others. I knew, for example, that the Yanomamö men held a warm affection for the men they called by the term *shoriwä*. These men, it turned out, are the brothers of the woman a man has married, will marry, or could marry—they are his male cross-cousins. Similarly, the obviously warm relationship between a man and his mother's brother is quite comprehensible in terms of the marriage rule: the man can marry the older man's daughter.

These general rules or principles also exist for notions of descent from remote, long-deceased ancestors, and the anthropologist discovers them in essentially the same way as kinship rules. For the Yanomamö descent through the male line is more important than descent through the female line, especially with regard to general principles of marriage.   Patrilineal descent defines as the members of a group—called a patrilineage—all those individuals who can trace their descent back to some male ancestor using only the male genealogical connections.

An easy way to grasp this is to relate it to the way in which our traditional American culture passes on family names to our descendants. If you are a man named Jefferson, your children are also Jeffersons, including your daughter. If she marries, say, a Washington, her children will be Washingtons. But your son's children will continue to be Jeffersons. Those who have the family name of Jefferson would be a patrilineage, distinct from the patrilineage of the Washingtons.

For the moment, let us assume that an entire village has only Washingtons and Jeffersons in it. The general Yanomamö rule about marriage, insofar as it can be phrased in terms of a descent rule, is that everyone *must* marry outside his or her patrilineal group: if you are a Jefferson, you should marry a Washington, and vice versa. This descent rule, plus the rule of marriage with cross-cousins, can be summarized in the form of a structuralist model of Yanomamö social organization, as shown in the diagram entitled "Ideal Model of the Yanomamö Social Structure." This model shows patrilineal descent and patrilineage exogamy (everyone must marry outside his or her group). Marriage with a cross-cousin is unavoidable if everyone follows these rules: all male Jeffersons have to marry female Washingtons who are approximately their own age, and all male Washingtons have to marry female Jeffersons, as the diagram shows. Over time, every Washington would be marrying a cross-cousin named Jefferson, as Joe Washington's marriage with Hilda Jefferson illustrates. Trace out the relationships for yourself: Joe's father is A and his father's sister is B. Hilda, the daughter of B, is therefore Joe's father's sister's daughter (FZD). Joe's mother is D and his mother's brother is C. Hilda, being also the daughter of C, is Joe's mother's brother's daughter (MBD) as well.

Structural anthropologists, such as Claude Levi-Strauss, are fascinated by the ideal models they can draw to represent, in shorthand fashion, the social structure of a society like this one, using as the basis of the model abstract rules or principles of the sort just described: the society's rules about kinship, descent, and marriage. These are the nice, symmetrical shells I spoke of earlier.

But the real world is much less tidy, and people do not always follow their rules to the letter—usually because they cannot. The ideal model assumes something of a demographic paradise in which each parent has two and only two children, one a son and the other a daughter, the children all live to reproduce, there is no divorce, a brother always gives his sister to a man who gives his sister in return, and so on and on. In the real world, people die, get divorced, have five sons and no daughters, marry several spouses, give their sisters to someone they shouldn't, et cetera. These are the demographic realities that individuals have to contend with. They result in a statistical outcome very different from the one implied in the ideal model—the amorphous creature that is unpleasant to deal with.

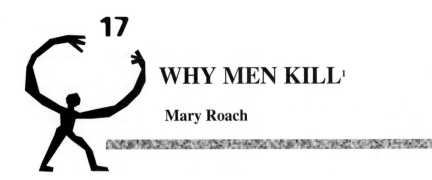

17

WHY MEN KILL[1]

Mary Roach

Although many band and tribal societies are quite peaceful, for the Achuar of the Ecuadorian Amazon, warfare is a way of life. In this article, Mary Roach describes the research of anthropologist John Patton on the causes of Achuar violence. It seems that, despite the high costs of failure in warfare, the benefits to a man who gains a reputation as a good warrior can be considerable.

There are many reasons to be nervous in the village of Conambo in the Ecuadoran Amazon. You can be nervous about crossing a large swift river in a tiny wobbling canoe. You can be nervous about the sand flies that carry *Leishmania* parasites, which bore through your sinuses and eat out your brain. You can be nervous about the giardia in the manioc beer that can wreak havoc with your bowels, the tarantula in the outhouse, the vampire bats in the schoolhouse.

The Achuar people of Conambo are not especially nervous about any of these things. The Achuar are nervous about the Achuar. The Achuar hold the dubious distinction of having had, in recent generations, one of the highest murder rates on Earth. In 1993 a poll of villagers revealed that 50 percent of their immediate male ancestors had died from shotgun blasts. (The traditional Achuar greeting is *Pujamik*—"Are you living?")

If you weren't born here, you for damn sure wouldn't live here. Unless you were John Q. Patton. Patton, an anthropologist at the University of Colorado and the Center for Evolutionary Psychology at the University of California at Santa Barbara, studies the roots of war and killing. He takes a biological approach to human behavior, which is to say he expects Darwinian theory to explain it. And from that evolutionary perspective, war is something of a problem, because it appears to be an altruistic act: you are risking your life for the good of the community. Taking chances with one's life does not, at first glance, appear to be a good way for a young man to pass on his genes. As Patton puts it, "You die, and then where are you reproductively?"

---

[1]**Originally published in *Discover* (December 1998). Reprinted with permission from the publisher.**

Patton was drawn to the Achuar for a couple of reasons, the first being the insights they may offer into early human society. For hundreds of thousands of years, our ancestors lived in small bands that got their food by hunting or gathering, and it was during this time that evolution may have fixed much of our underlying psychology. Unlike our own culture, in which millions of people live within a tangle of political structures, the Achuar live in small villages without any central leadership, and they still get a lot of their food by hunting.

Another reason Patton chose to study the Achuar is that they defy the most commonly accepted reason for war among tribal people: food. According to the "protein hypothesis," tribes fight against each other to gain new territory because there isn't enough to eat in their own. Patton doesn't think the truth is that simple. The rain forest where the Achuar live is sparsely inhabited and teeming with game. According to data collected in the early 1980s, the average Conambo adult consumes 104 grams of protein a day (the U.S. recommended daily allowance is 30 grams). They often eat 4,000 calories a day. The Achuar clearly don't have to fight for their dinner - yet they most certainly do fight.

We are sitting in the Conambo schoolhouse, which serves as Patton's base. Besides the meeting hall, the school, and the church (a former helicopter repair shed built by an oil company), the town is no more than a scatter of thatch-roofed homes, linked by muddy jungle footpaths.

While we talk, Patton fills Ziploc bags with everyday medical supplies, which he will distribute to each household we'll visit today to interview subjects. To compensate villagers for their help, Patton serves as de facto medic. By decree of the Human Subject Review, a sort of Miss Manners for the field-research set, Patton is obligated to provide a net benefit to the community over the course of his stay. "So I held a meeting when I came in," recalls Patton. "'You can help me or not,' I told them. 'But everyone will get medical treatment.'" To barter my welcome (and room and board), Patton hooked me up with Direct Relief International and had me bring in medical supplies: Vermox dewormer for 500.

"Altruism is the conundrum of Darwinian theory," Patton is saying as he opens up boxes of petal pink worm pills. A small crowd has gathered to watch. (It's not hard to be fascinating in Conambo: Wear contact lenses! Have red hair! Eat a Power Bar!) The way most anthropologists have made sense of altruistic acts on the battlefield, Patton continues, has been to think in terms of the survival of the behavioral trait, not the man. The concept is known as kin selection. You'll do something for others if you're closely related; the capacity for altruism gets replicated not by your passing it along to your offspring but by your saving the lives of others who share it.

Kin selection may work as an explanation for war in patrilocal societies, which are centered on fathers and sons and brothers who stay together even when they marry. But it doesn't work for the Achuar. Theirs is a matrilocal society: the men move into the homes and villages of their wives. They fight and die for their fathers-in-law, though they share no blood.

Patton thinks something else is going on. "When people use the term *altruism*, what they usually mean is behaviors that appear to be altruistic but are really some form of enlightened self-interest." The academic term is *reciprocal altruism*: tit for tat masquerading as altruism. Patton has theorized that warriors fight and kill in exchange for a boost in status—and that boost in status sets them up for certain evolutionary perks.

Work done among the Yanomamö of Venezuela and Brazil by Patton's adviser, Napoleon Chagnon of the University of California at Santa Barbara, seems to support this. Chagnon demonstrated that a certain class of accomplished killers, called *unokai*, have on average two and a half times the number of wives and more than three times the offspring of their meeker compatriots. Critics of Chagnon, however, have pointed out that virtually all *unokai* are tribal headmen and that their higher status could have derived from that title and not from their conquests at war. "Chagnon demonstrated that men who had killed had higher reproductive success," says Patton. "Elsewhere, people had demonstrated that high status leads to more children. The missing link in the causal order was some correlation between warriorship and status to connect the two."

That's where Patton comes in. His method is straightforward: he asks each man to rank his fellow men, first by status in the community, then by warrior-

ship. Patton's only tools are a stack of Polaroids, a pencil, and a waterproof field notebook.

It's a simple task made grueling by the demands of rain forest canvassing. We've been on the trails 40 minutes, looking for a house with a man inside. Most of the Achuar men are spending this day hunting, and they don't have Day Timers where they pencil you in. So you slog and sweat and backtrack and try someone else. "This is how it goes here," says Patton. "If you think it'll take an hour, it typically takes two or three."

A man named Ushpa lives on the riverbank. Two hundred yards down the trail, Patton issues a high-pitched *"Hoooo!"* (You don't want to sneak up on an Achuar man unless you plan to fire the first shot.) We find Ushpa sitting in the front yard, weaving a string bag. He holds the bottom of the bag with his big toe, a bigger big toe than most. People here use their bodies like tools: Ushpa's wife has notches in her front teeth where she runs palm frond fibers through to strip them down to make string. Patton exchanges pleasantries, and then he launches into his medical demonstration, drawing stick figures to show the proper dosages.

Ushpa's wife approaches, bearing ceramic bowls of an eggnog-hued drink. The bowls contain *chicha*, a manioc beer whose fermentation is speeded by the saliva of the women preparing it. They don't spit directly in the drink, but chew up the manioc and spit that in: small consolation when you're facing a drinking bowl the size of a riding helmet. To set down the bowl is almost as rude as refusing it. Patton manages to hold his steady in one hand while demonstrating how to open a Tylenol child-safety cap with the other. (Cultural anthropology breeds singular talents. Here is a man from urban Los Angeles who can smoke tapir meat, pick a bat out of the rafters with a blowgun, and hold his own at *chicha* drinking contests.)

From his backpack, Patton extracts his deck of Polaroids. With a schoolboy translating Spanish into Achuar (Conambo children learn Spanish at the government school), Patton explains that he wants Ushpa to arrange the Polaroids according to who is the most *juunt*—an Achuar word that translates loosely as "big." He arrived at the term by talking to villagers. "I'd say to them, 'Some people, when they talk, people don't pay attention. But others, when they talk, people always listen. Is there a name for someone like that?'"

We are joined by a visitor, Mirunzhi, one of Conambo's most formidable males and an Achuar dead ringer for Willem Dafoe. You wouldn't want to bend this man's fender. A love-at-first-sight situation develops between Mirunzhi and Patton's backpack, a nifty purple rubber river-running pack that could carry a lot of monkey meat.

"Quien es mas juunt?" begins Patton, holding aloft a pair of snapshots. Ushpa chats quietly with Mirunzhi. The translator presents the answer: "How much you pay for that bag?"

Patton is used to this sort of thing. Thus far this summer, he has promised his tent to a man in exchange for a blowgun and traded a wristwatch for an anaconda tooth. (Casio digital watches are a status item among Conambo men, even though few know how to read them and even fewer have reason to.) "Three hundred thousand sucres," Patton answers. Ushpa spits manioc pulp on the floor. Mirunzhi looks depressed.

Eventually Patton gets the men to focus on the task at hand, and soon Ushpa has the Polaroids laid out on the floor, a photographic hopscotch of intense, unsmiling faces. After noting the order of the photographs, Patton gathers them up for round two: warriorship. *"Quien es mas achima?"* *Achima* is the Achuar word for "warrior." "If a war was to break out and there was a battle, who would prove himself to be the best?"

Patton has been asking the Achuar this question since 1992, and his results are striking. When he lines up the rankings Achuar men give for both qualities, warriorship accounts for as much as 78 percent of the variation in men's status. The better a warrior you are, the more status you apparently earn. To Patton, this is the first step toward understanding how war persists in human societies—tracing the effect of being a good warrior on your success in society, and ultimately in passing on your genes.

The Achuar concept of warriorship encompasses not only strategy and skill but also valor, willingness, and lack of hesitation. As Patton puts it, "There's a big difference between hitting the target and hitting the target when the target is trying to hit you." Wisdom also plays a part. "In talking to people about this, one of the things that kept coming up was that a good warrior was *mas pensativo*—he's more thoughtful." A good warrior knows when to fight and when not to, whom to pick on and whom not. This notion of wisdom in warriorship helps explain how Patton can get Achuar men to rank their peers even though many of them haven't seen war during their lifetime. "In a society where in the past half the men got killed, you assume that a man who reaches old age must be doing something right." A Polaroid of an older man invariably places higher on the warriorship ranking than those of the town's youngest men, regardless of the size of their biceps or the fierceness of their gaze.

A third visitor has arrived, a shaman from a nearby village. He carries a shotgun, and you get the sense it's not for monkeys. There was a time, during the 1950s, when the Achuar and their enemies the Shuar didn't set down their guns until they went to sleep. Populations were decimated not just by intertribal raids but by fierce feuding within communities. Making matters worse, deaths by natural causes were often attributed to shamanic foul play. A man would die of, say, a stroke. His son, seeing no outward cause of death, would visit the local shaman to find out if someone had put a curse on his father. The shaman would go into a hallucinogenic trance and very often come out of it with the source of the curse. A revenge assassination invariably followed.

These days, with the help of outside arbitrators called in to settle feuds, things have quieted down. Raids between the Shuar and the Achuar have all but disappeared, supplanted by trading between the two. The last murder here occurred around 1988. Though it's also true that just a few weeks back, members of the community were talking about killing a man who misspent community funds on prostitutes in Puyo.

With intertribal raids and revenge murders becoming less common, will warriorship still confer status among the Achuar, or will something else take its place? Patton concedes that other skills-- speaking Spanish, for example--will factor into a man's overall status. Spanish enables a man to travel and earn money outside the community and to be involved in rain forest politics. "But will it or something else replace warriorship? I suspect not. Yes, the ability to interact with the outside is important, but guess what? You do these rankings and who are the high-ranking men? They're Mirunzhi. They're Kaiyashi. These men don't speak any Spanish at all. They're high-ranking warrior guys."

Even in our society, where status is tied to income and address, wartime exploits will carry a man a long way. "I have this slide that I use in lectures that was the cover of the *National Enquirer*," comments Patton. "It says STORMIN' NORMAN SCHWARZKOPF, SEXIEST MAN IN AMERICA. We still have this tribal psychology about our warriors."

Ushpa is finishing up the warriorship task, but Patton has a new line of questions for him: "If a conflict arose here in Conambo, who would side with whom?" Patton is aware that the town's social alliances can skew the men's rankings of one another. There's a natural tendency to underrate the status of men who aren't part of one's clique. But in mapping the social structure of Conambo,

Patton is also measuring a phenomenon called triadic awareness: the ability to triangulate political loyalties and make informed decisions about the likely consequences of violence. The men of Conambo have a keen sense of whom they can and can't trust in the event of conflict. Patton would argue that this is an evolved trait. "There's a strong selective pressure to be able to make good who-to-trust decisions: you're wrong, you're dead."

Here, according to Patton, are the forces that were behind the origin of human social structures. You want to be part of a group that's big enough to beat the other guys, or at least be a threat to them, yet not so big that you can't keep everyone fed. Friendships are forged according to who can offer whom what, as a sort of insurance policy. "I think that's the natural state," says Patton. He cites the example of chimpanzees: since they have no weapons, their power is based on physical strength. In some cases the apes other apes want as friends are the strongest ones. In other cases the chimps make a strategic alliance: two weaker ones will join up because together they can defeat a stronger chimp.

When you've got weapons, it's warriorship, not brute strength, that counts. Patton has mapped Conambo's social organization along two dimensions: status, on the vertical, and alliances, on the horizontal. He sees little guys attaching themselves to big guys and big guys gaining advantage by having lots of little guys in their fold.

In this sense, Patton sees a strong parallel between Amazonian tribes and inner-city gangs in the United States. "In

a gang, just as here, there's no question that you choose your friends in terms of who you think is going to back you up and who might be an important person to have on your side." Gangs also serve to demonstrate the link between status and warriorship. Prospective members assume they're probably not going to earn their status by getting a graduate degree and landing a prestige job. "They realize they're not part of the wider social network, so they create their own, with its own social hierarchy." As in the Amazon, it's a hierarchy based on violence. "Killing and warfare are one of the few ways," says Patton, "that men can distinguish themselves and compete for status."

Even among law-abiding Westerners, you can sometimes encounter signs of the Conambo-style social contract. "Next time you pass some guy on the corner with a tin cup and a sign that says HOMELESS VETERAN," Patton says, "what he's telling you is, 'I took the risk, but you didn't give me the benefit.' The feeling of guilt that we have comes from this idea that we had a social contract with this man and we broke it. I definitely think those psychological mechanisms are still there."

Patton packs the coveted purple backpack and bids his adieus. A toddler waves good-bye. She is teething on a plastic bottle of pinkeye medication. The next house on the agenda belongs to a youngish man named Robert. (Some men go by their Achuar names, others by names they picked up from missionaries.) Robert stands out among the Polaroids, not for his status or warriorship—both on the low side—but for his outfit. He chose to put on his Sunday best, a pink-and-red-flowered Hawaiian shirt.

Robert in person is more soft-spoken than his clothes. He lives with his wife and children and a rangy black dog that you do not want to pet. A pot is boiling on a wood fire, and termites are streaming out of one of the logs.

Robert puts the Polaroid of Robert at the top of the layout. He is doing something more commonly associated with camping mattresses and life jackets: in Patton's words, he's self-inflating. What Patton means is that Robert has placed his Polaroid considerably higher in the warrior hierarchy than his exploits or reputation would merit. Robert thinks he's boss of the beach. This is the kind of guy you want to watch out for. A man at the bottom of the heap has the most to gain and the least to lose. He's more likely to make a rash grab for power. He's also more likely to lose should the conflict turn violent. Which is where good bluffing tactics come in.

Richard Wrangham, a Harvard primatologist who helped formulate current ideas about violence in human evolution, has a theory called military incompetence. It explains why a man like Robert would blunder forth into battle when any fool can see the odds are stacked against him. Evolution should have put a stop to this sort of behavior, but it hasn't. Wrangham and Patton argue that self-deceit facilitates it. A strong bluff can deter an enemy, even an enemy who'd most likely win. And the most effective bluffers are the ones who don't think they're bluffing. It's possible to elevate your status and enjoy the perks of being a mighty warrior without even going into battle. Eventually your number is bound to come up, but in the meantime you've sired a pack of bluffers to carry on the trait.

So it is that ultimately suicidal violent traits can turn out to be evolutionarily successful. Take the case of despots and dictators. Here are men who live with enormous risks every day of their lives. When the risk-taking pays off, it pays off big.

"Remember that the despotic individual is really only a vehicle for the trait," says Patton. "Let's say we have 10 individuals with the psychology to be despotic. Nine get wiped out; they push it too far. One of them succeeds and gets 20 wives. Overall, it's still a good reproductive payout." Patton cites the example of a man from Conambo named Basilio, whose grandfather was a warrior of wide repute. Eventually someone killed him, but in the interim he amassed ten wives and several dozen children. "The salmon who stays out at sea instead of struggling upstream may live a long life," says Patton, "but he doesn't reproduce. From an evolutionary perspective, he might as well be dead."

Two women are ladling *chicha* from a vast ceramic urn. Patton wipes termites off his pants leg and leans back against the porch: "It's Miller time!" Robert's daughter sets down a plate of yams the color of Barney. We eat nine. When steamed tapir fetus may be waiting around the bend, you make the most of purple yams.

Late one evening, we are sitting on the schoolhouse veranda, watching moths suck minerals from a sweat-infused T-shirt that hangs on the line. A man appears out of the darkness and speaks to Patton in hushed, urgent tones. A woman named Suitiar has fallen ill on the trail near the house of a man named Kaiyashi. The suddenness and severity of the illness has led her family to suspect witchcraft, and a shaman—the man we saw earlier today carrying a shotgun—is about to perform a ritual to remove a *tsentsak*, a supernatural psychic dart blown by another shaman, often at someone else's behest. As a backup, they want Patton there, with his bag of Western pills and ointments. And so we make our way to Kaiyashi's house on the far side of the river. It's rush hour in the jungle. Leaf-cutting ants cross the airstrip in columns six inches wide. Frogs make sounds that are way too big for them. Overhead, shooting stars and fireflies flash, and it's sometimes hard to tell which is which.

Kaiyashi's home is lit by candles, but even with electric light the scene would make your hair stand on end. Valerio, the shaman, has taken a hallucinogen that will enable him to divine the sender of the *tsentsak*. This he follows up with mouthfuls of tobacco juice, which will facilitate the woman's cure. He bends over Suitiar and inhales dramatically, as if to suck out the dart. Then he leans back, stands, and commences an affront of gruesome gargling, followed by a godawful hawking retch and a splat of tobacco juice that lands loudly in Kaiyashi's front room.

Patton is uneasy. The situation has an ominous background and could easily turn violent. Suitiar, the woman who fell sick, is Ushpa's wife. Barely three weeks ago, Ushpa and Suitiar lost a daughter, who died inexplicably on the trail. (Patton suspects the cause was dehydration from dysentery.) The dead girl's mother-in-law, Piricinda, took *mai-kua*, an atropine drug that nonshamans take to divine the source of a *tsentsak* on their own. In her trance, she saw Conambo's shaman. The shaman denied the charge and fingered a second shaman, who he said had taken his own form. The second shaman left town soon after. Smart move, inasmuch as Piricinda's husband Mirunzhi was primed for revenge. Should Ushpa's wife die tonight, so close on the heels of his daughter's death, the shaman might find himself the victim of an assassination.

We head back to the schoolhouse. A pair of nylon shorts has dropped from the line while we were gone, interrupting a work party of leaf-cutting ants who apparently took it for a floppy blue leaf and set about cutting up the leg. "Did I tell you," says Patton, shaking off the ants, "my theory about revenge and the origins of religion?"

Patton has no data to back up his theory and assumes it will anger certain anthropologists who don't like his Darwinian approach. He tells me anyway. When you spend this much time among the Achuar, you can't get too worked up about the wrath of indignant academics.

It goes like this: When humans enter into a social contract for mutual defense, they agree to back each other up. What happens when one of them dies? The social contract ends. Unless there's the threat of revenge. What is revenge?

The extension of that social contract to the afterlife: Even though he's dead, you still need to honor that contract. How do you do that cognitively? Spirits—your friend's spirit will not rest until you avenge his death. And it is a belief in spirits that all religions have in common. "So there you have it," says Patton. "The evolution of the concept of spirit may be a simple cognitive solution to the extension of a social contract for mutual defense. These shorts are wrecked."

At breakfast the next morning at the house of an Achuar named Isaac, Valerio, the shaman, reports that Suitiar is feeling better. He says it was a boa constrictor that sent the *tsentsak*. (Certain animals are believed to have the power to send the psychic darts. The darts can even strike by accident, ricocheting off shamans' shields and hitting innocent bystanders.) The local shaman is off the hook. Peace in Conambo continues its shaky course.

Ushpa is over for a bowl of *chicha*, still weaving his bag. Children are taking turns trying to hit a piece of fruit with a blowgun. Isaac's wife serves bowls of rodent soup. I get a lower leg,

foot intact. People here seem kind and friendly. It's hard to imagine them raising shotguns at each other. "There's a phrase," says Patton, spitting out toenails. "'An armed society is a polite society.' When you don't have institutions like police and any conflict can escalate to something serious, you have to be very careful." Besides, he adds, he's not making the case that the Achuar are violent by nature.

"We're not talking about a gene for violence here. We're talking about the evolution of the strategic use of violence: knowing when to push it and when not to. The biggest mistake people make about the kind of anthropology I do is that they assume that what we're talking about is these simple, knee-jerk instincts. When in fact these instincts are complex, evolved strategies. What drives violence is: When do the costs and benefits favor it, and when do they favor peace? I have no problem saying warfare is a product of our biology. I also say that doesn't mean it's a biological inevitability."

Good. Then no one will shoot me if I give my rodent ankle to the dog.

18

SEX IN HISTORY[1]

Laura Betzig

Although scandals involving men in high political office have been big news lately, there may be nothing really new about them at all. As Laura Betzig suggests, sexual access to many women may have been a perquisite of the politically powerful for thousands of years.

Civilized Practices

Have you heard the one about JFK? FDR? Nelson A. Rockefeller? For some reason, powerful people seem to lie seamy side up, out-of-doors, at around high noon. By which I mean to say: We are obsessed with the private lives of public men. We always have been—for at least the last few thousand years. We interrogate them; we investigate them; we libel them; we slander them—though it isn't always clear to the interrogators, investigators, slanderers or libelers why we should care.

Where to begin? We could begin with civilization, nearly 6,000 years ago at Sumer. New years in Sumer are supposed to have started with a sacred rite. The king played Damuzi (a.k.a. Tammuz), the fertility god, opposite Inanna (a.k.a. Ishtar), the fertility goddess. He wore splendid headgear; she wore two gold finger rings, two silver earrings, six ivory breast ornaments, one

"golden vulva" (I quote the authority, H.W.F. Saggs) and so on. They had sex in a temple, and made the land fertile. Purely apocryphal, probably. But Mesopotamian kings at Sumer, and later at Assyria and Babylon, are guessed to have had sexual access to wives, concubines and hundreds—maybe even thousands—of slaves.

A little later, in Egypt, Amenophis III, father of Akhenaten, started a harem with Tiy, his one Great Wife. He added two Syrian princesses, two Babylonian princesses, one Arzawa princess, "droves" of Egyptian women, and two princesses from Mitanni, one of whom alone brought along 317 ladies-in-waiting. Egyptian kings, like other kings, are said —by Donald Redford— to have made a "constant demand" of provincial governors for more beautiful servant girls.

Women—particularly beautiful women—have probably been requisitioned as tribute wherever tribute has

---

[1]Originally published in *Michigan Today* 26(1): 1-3 (March, 1994). Reprinted by permission of the author.

been requisitioned. Descriptions tend to be rough, but uniform. Take, for instance, R.H. van Gulik's survey, *Sexual Life in China.* He says that by the 8th century BC, kings kept one queen *(hou),* three consorts *(fu-jen),* nine wives of second rank *(pin),* 27 wives of third rank *(shih-fu),* and 81 concubines *(yu-chi).* That was the tip of the iceberg: imperial harems numbered in the thousands. Lesser men kept fewer women. Great princes kept hundreds; minor princes, members of the nobility and generals kept upwards of 30; upper middle-class men might have six to 12; middle-class men might have three or four. Van Gulik is explicit about how women were picked, cared for and copulated with. By T'ang times, kings had meticulous books kept on the hour of every insemination, the date of every menstruation and the first signs of every conception.

I could go on. In India, a *Jataka* (an account of the Buddha's birth) estimates the size of the royal seraglio at 16,000 in the 5th century BC; that's the recordholder as far as I'm aware. Big harems were common until remarkably recently. According to his friend and eyewitness, Diwan Jarmani Dass, His Highness Maharaja Sir Bhupinder Singh, friend to Mussolini and George V, died with a harem of 332 women— and liked to float them on ice blocks in transparent clothes. As in the Old World, so in the New. In Mexico, according to Franciscans who wrote about Aztecs after the conquest, Montezuma II, who met Cortes, kept 4,000 "concubines"; every member of the Aztec nobility is supposed to have had as many consorts as he could afford—counted by the scores among lesser, by the hundreds among greater lords. And in Peru, according to Garcilaso de la Vega—who was born of a Spanish governor and an Incan princess—kings kept "houses of virgins," with 1,500 women in each, in every principal province.

Politics as Sex

Fresh out of two failed careers, at Edinburgh and Cambridge, first as a family doctor, second as a clergyman, Charles Darwin set sail as naturalist aboard H.M.S. Beagle, at the age of 22, in 1831. In five years he watched, among other things: Galapagos Islands finches, Pacific atolls and lots of "primitive" people. In the late 19th century, authorities like J. F. McLennan, Lewis Henry Morgan and Friedrich Engels pushed a theory of "primitive promiscuity." As far as they were concerned, access to women—like access to everything else—was once communally held. Darwin demurred. As he put it in 1871, in *The Descent of Man,* "The licentiousness of many savages is no doubt astonishing," but as a rule "the strongest and most vigorous men ... would succeed in rearing a greater average number of offspring" —taking privileged, if not exclusive, sexual access to "the most attractive women."

Darwin was vindicated, in part, in Edward Westermarck's *History of Human Marriage* 20 years later; he's been more or less vindicated ever since. Power paralleled polygyny, once. Good hunters on the Kalahari got two or three, not just one, wife. In the Amazon, headmen had as many as 10 "wives"— more than anybody else. In Polynesia— on Fiji, Samoa, Tahiti—chiefs typically kept on the order of a hundred women. And in "pristine" states like Sumer, Egypt, India, China, Aztec Mexico and Inca Peru—as in secondary states from Africa to Asia to the Americas—kings' harems numbered in the thousands. The correlations are consistent—and statistically significant—any way I've cut them.

But why? Because if Darwin was right about natural (and sexual) selection, the whole point of competition is reproduction. To put it plainly, the point of politics is sex. Why do red deer have big antlers? Why are elephant seals so fat? Why do jungle fowl wear spurs on their heels? The better to butt/shove/jab you, my dear; the better to take a harem myself. Why is every man with a big harem a despot? Because collecting women— like tribute, like labor, like homage—tends to require force. People (red deer, elephant seals, jungle fowl and so on) tend to cede favors on two accounts. One is, they get a favor back; the other is, they get beat up if they don't. There are, in short, positive and negative sanctions. Negative sanctions appear to have been necessary, often.

I don't want to bore you with the grisly history of human politics, but I'll offer a few examples. At Sumer, about which we know relatively little, we know at least that kings derived power from Enlil, who symbolized compulsion by force. In India and China, punishment by torture was highly refined, and systematically biased to exempt the rich. In Aztec Mexico, kings killed singers who sang out of tune, as well as anybody guilty of "insubordination"—always broadly defined. In Inca Peru, Garcilaso, a sympathetic observer, says the death penalty could follow most infractions; and in particular, for violating any woman in a nobleman's harem, the guilty man's wife, children, servants, kin, friends and flocks were killed, his village was pulled down, and the site strewn with stones. As another sympathizer, Poma de Ayala, put it: "All was truth and good and justice and law."

From Depotism to Democracy

We live by another law now. Once every state was a polygynous despotism. Now most seem to be relatively monogamous democracies. When, where and why did things change? That is, I think, a critical question. Answering it has become an obsession. I'll tell you what I've found.

I've found that things change, roughly, with the rise of industry. Karl Marx was convinced that from around the 16th century, the division of labor and spread of capital greatly increased the exploitation of the subordinate class. In, for instance, his notes on *Pre-Capitalist Economic Formations*, he wrote:

It is of course easy to imagine a powerful, physically superior person who first captures animals and then captures men in order to make them catch animals for him; in brief, one who uses man as a naturally occurring condition for his reproduction like any other living thing; his own labour being exhausted in the act of domination. But such a view is stupid, though it may be correct from the point of view of a given tribal or communal entity; for it takes the isolated man as its starting-point. But man is only individualized through the process of history.

It is this "stupid view" that I back. And I would argue that the switch that began around the 16th century—with the division of labor and the mobility of a money economy - was less a switch from primitive communism to exploitation, than from despotism to democracy.

But, as everybody knows, Europeans have been strictly monogamous—and fairly democratic—for millennia. Maybe yes; maybe no. Peter Garnsey, author of *Social Status and Legal Privilege in the Roman Empire*, showed that bias in Roman law codes, as in legal texts since Hammurabi's Babylon of the 18th century BC, was systematically graded according to status. In Rome, lowly offenders got aggravated forms of the death penalty—exposure to wild beasts, crucifixion, burning alive. Exalted offenders got exile and expulsion from office.

But the grisliest evidence of Roman despotism comes straight from the Latins. Suetonius says Augustus, the first emperor, did in a Roman knight for "taking too close an interest" in one of his speeches; drove a consul-elect to suicide after a "spiteful comment" provoked his threats; and had a praetor tortured and sentenced to death for hiding writing tablets under his toga. Later emperors were even nastier.

If not strictly democratic, then, Romans were surely monogamous. Sure, they married—like most despots did—strictly monogamously. But they seem to have mated—like most despots did—strictly polygynously. I'll pick up with the Latins, again. According to Suetonius, Augustus's "friends used to behave like Toranius, the slave-dealer, in arranging his pleasures for him—they would strip mothers of families, or grown girls of their clothes and inspect them as though they were for sale." According to Tacitus, Tiberius's "former absorption in state affairs ended. Instead he spent his time in secret orgies" when he retired to Capri. And according to Cassius Dio, Caligula liked to say he'd copulated with the moon; "he made this a pretext for seducing numerous women," including his sisters.

This sort of gossip tends to get more malicious as time goes on. Fabulous stories are told about Commodus, Marcus Aurelius's successor and son. According to the infamous *Scriptores Historiae Augustae*, he "rioted" in the palace, at banquets and in the baths, "along with 300 concubines gathered together for their beauty and chosen from both matrons and harlots, and with minions, also 300 in number, whom he had collected by force and by purchase indiscriminately from the common people and nobles solely on the basis of bodily beauty." This would be absolutely incredible to me—as it has been to most credible historians—if it weren't so consistent with the gossip told about so many other emperors in so many other empires.

It's consistent, too, with evidence in connection with Roman slavery. Estimates suggest slaves made up about two-fifths of the population of Italy alone in the third century BC, and maybe one-fifth of the population of the whole Roman empire in the first century AD. Few historians have suggested, however, that owners might have been their fathers. But sexual access to slave women was taken for granted by masters - Latin literature, art and architecture is full of such allusions - and taken at risk by other men. Most compellingly, masters provided *vernae*, the "homeborn" slaves those women bore, with: wet nurses (some *vernae*, called *collacteri*, were nursed together with legitimate daughters and sons); *pedagogi* and *educatores*, childminders and teachers (some of whom, again, minded and tutored legitimate children); a *peculium*, or allowance (legally indistinguishable from the one allotted to legitimate sons); early manumission, or freedom; substantial legacies or, in default of a legitimate heir, even the bulk of an estate; high positions; terms of affection; and a place for their remains— and for their children's and their children's children's remains—in the masters' family tombs.

Rude Bishops

The medieval evidence is sketchier. But to me it paints a similar picture. Gregory of Tours starts his 6th-century *History of the Franks*: "I recount for you . . . the holy deeds of the Saints and the way in which whole races of people were butchered." Among other things, King Guntram is said to have killed his second wife's half-brothers for making "hateful and abominable remarks" about the queen; and King Chilperic, having levied "extremely heavy" taxes, is supposed to have punished people who plotted to kill the collector by "having them tortured and even put to death out of hand." In England, William of Malmesbury's 12th-century *Chronicle of the Kings of England* tells more horrible stories. Hardecanute, in the 11th century, reputedly ordered Worcester plundered and burned because two of his tax collectors were killed there; and Henry I, in the 12th century, punished transgressions among his court "by a heavy pecuniary fine, or loss of life."

Bishops, of whom Gregory of Tours was one, were no better—particularly to those who opposed them. Gregory describes two, Salonius and Sagittarius, who were "no sooner raised to the episcopate than their new power went to their heads." Gregory says they sent a mob to attack another bishop having a birthday party; they beat their own congregations with sticks; and, overall, "with a sort of insane fury they began to disgrace themselves in peculation, physical assaults, murders, adultery and every crime in the calendar."

Medieval polygyny? Certainly not. Everybody, even the most eminent of medieval historians, knows that polygyny was stopped by the Catholic Church. I don't think so. I think Jack Goody, who wrote a famous book called *The Development of the Family and Marriage in Europe*, was right: I think the quarrel between church and state in the Middle Ages was about marriage (which has to do with things like inheritance and succession), *not* about mating (which has to do with sex). I think the sketchy evidence suggests medieval priests and lords, cardinals and kings, quibbled about marriage, and went about their merry polygynous ways.

According to a cleric named Lambert, whose *Historia comitum Ghisnensium* is a 13th-century account of his benefactor, Count Baudouin: "From the beginning of adolescence until his old age, his loins were stirred by the intemperance of an impatient *libidoe* . . .; very young girls, and especially virgins, aroused his desire." Baudouin's bedchamber, in the most inaccessible part of his castle, had direct access to his servant girls' quarters, to the rooms of adolescent girls upstairs and to the nursery—which Lambert's 20th-century resurrector, the French historian Georges Duby, calls "a veritable incubator for the

suckling infants." Baudouin was buried with 23 bastards in attendance, besides 10 living legitimate daughters and sons; these are likely, as Duby says, to have been fruits of just the family tree's primary limbs.

Literary sources raise the possibility that young women were kept apart in *gynaecea* or *chambres des dames*—women's quarters or ladies' chambers—where they entertained the lord of the house (and no one else) and made shirts. Even census records suggest, as the eminent medievalist David Herlihy put it, that "women tended to congregate in the households of the powerful, even on monastic estates." Down to the nitty-gritty level, if parish records from late-medieval Tuscany and England are right, rich men's houses held more women and children than poor men's houses.

Upstairs Went Downstairs

It was as late as 1840 when Alexis de Tocqueville, in *Democracy in America*, wrote: "I go back from age to age up to the remotest antiquity, but I find no parallel to what is occurring before my eyes." He meant, of course, the fall of kings and rise of the common man. I won't chronicle the rise of democracy in modern England - to tell you the truth, I haven't got that far. But I'll hint that polygyny might have declined, nice and gradually, at about the same time.

William of Malmesbury's *Chronicle* is full of the usual epithets—like "polluted by his lusts," "abused the beauty of his person in illicit intercourse," and "wholly given up to wine and women." Kings and princes have always been (still are) notorious for affairs with high-ranking women; many owned up to having got high-ranking bastards by them. But if affairs in early modern England were like they've been everywhere else, then peers and gentry should have had sex with, and probably got bastards by, lower-ranking, less well-remembered women as well. In Rome, many of those women may have been slaves. In England, many of those women may have been maids.

Lawrence Stone, the world's authority on the sex lives of the British upper class, scrutinized six early modern diaries. They leave the distinct impression that sex was easy to get. Respectable married women may have been relatively hard to come by, but actresses were accessible; so were "shirt and ruffle makers," high-class whores, women in brothels and women on the street. Last, but not least, "there were the poor amateurs, the ubiquitous maids, waiting on masters and guests in lodgings, in the home, in inns; young girls whose virtue was always uncertain and was constantly under attack." Stone adds: "These last were the most exploited, and most defenseless, of the various kinds of women whose sexual services might be obtained by a man of quality."

If he's right, then polygyny in early modern England—as in other places and times—should roughly have paralleled household size. Life-cycle service—by which young men and women spent the flower of their youth in relatively wealthy households—was a long-standing pattern in Britain. Domestic servants, in particular, tended to be young, unmarried and *female*. More than half the population aged 15-24 was "in service." Most "productive" servants - in apprenticeships or on farms— were boys, while most domestic servants - at work in their masters' homes— were girls. Over the last few centuries, British domestic servant staffs shrank. Dramatically. In the early 16th century, for instance, men like the Earl of Northumberland, or Cardinal Wolsey, had several hundred—as many as 400— domestic servants on their main estates. Numbers stayed high—in the hundreds—to the late 16th-early 17th century. Then they started to drop. By the mid-17th century, most large estate staffs were down to 30 to 50. In Gregory King's *Scheme of the Income and Expense of the Several Families of England* for 1688, maximum mean household size ranged from just 8 for gentlemen, 10 for esquires, 13 for knights and up to 40 for temporal lords. By the mid-20th century, servants had all but been wiped out. According to Richard Wall who—along with an army of volunteers and academics at the Cambridge Group for the History of Population and Social Structure—has analyzed hundreds of parish records, there were 61 servants per hundred households in England in the late 17th century, 51 in the late 18th century, from 14 (urban) to 33 (rural) in the mid-

19th century, 2 in 1947, and zero in 1970. If my guess is right, those shrinking staffs meant shrinking sexual access—read, polygyny—by the British aristocracy.

What About Us?

What about us? Has the United States been, from the beginning, a two-strictly-monogamous-parents-plus-kids populist democracy? Not really. In the debate over the US Constitution, for instance, Alexander Hamilton—future secretary of the treasury—said, according to James Madison's *Notes*: "Let one branch of the Legislature hold their places for life, or at least during good behavior. Let the Executive also be for life." Even moderates like Madison in *The Federalist Papers* said things like: "Liberty may be endangered by the abuses of liberty as well as by the abuses of power ...; the former, rather than the latter, is apparently most to be apprehended by the United States."

In 1787, at ratification, voting rights were determined by state—and limited in most by sex, race and wealth. In Virginia, suffrage was given to white men over 21 who owned 50 acres of improved land, or a town lot, or were employed as artisans in Richmond or Williamsburg; in South Carolina, voters were white men over 21 worth at least five hundred pounds worth of land. Property qualifications were gone within about a generation. But not until nearly a hundred years later, in 1870, did the 15th Amendment let men vote regardless of "race, color or previous conditions of servitude"; 50 years after that, in 1920, the 19th Amendment extended suffrage to women.

Loath as I am to spread slander about our forefathers, let me suggest that membership in the early American aristocracy may have had its sexual privileges, too. Well-to-do pre-abolition US households hired servants or owned slaves. There was gossip about miscegenation. Charles Lyell, for instance, noticed in his *Travels in the United States* that "the anxiety of parents for their sons, and a constant fear of their licentious intercourse with slaves, is painfully great"; and a sister of Madison is said by Arthur Calhoun to have remarked, "We southern ladies are complimented with the name of wives, but we are only the mistresses of seraglios." After abolition, the household staffs of American aristocrats—like those of English aristocrats—shrank. Rich men might have had to leave home more often, at least.

Which reminds me. Have you heard the one about Thomas Jefferson? Ben Franklin? George Washington? Apocryphal stories never end.

19

TO KISS: WHY WE KISS UNDER THE MISTLETOE AT CHRISTMAS[1]

Vaughn M. Bryant, Jr., and Sylvia Grider

Have you ever wondered why many of us kiss under the mistletoe at Christmas, or why we knock on wood for good luck? Where did this odd habit begin and what original significance did it have? These are just a few of the questions that Drs. Bryant and Grider explore in this examination of fact and folklore associated with kissing, Christmas, and mistletoe.

While growing up in Texas we were intrigued by a boast, often made by the citizens of Goldthwaite, a small town in west central Texas. On the outskirts of this town is a large sign proclaiming it the Mistletoe Capital of the World. Most Texans like to boast, but this claim, we thought, had to be a joke. Yet, it may be true. Each Christmas season a company in Goldthwaite collects and ships more than one million packages of mistletoe to cities all over North America.

Mentioning this boast often brought laughter from the students in our introductory folklore classes at Texas A&M in College Station. But when the laughter stopped, students wondered why this small, parasitic plant had become the basis of a million-dollar commercial industry in our society. Stu-

dents were even more curious about why we kiss under the mistletoe at Christmas.

We had no ready answer. Thus we began our odyssey searching not only for the origins of man's fascination with mistletoe, but also asking why this plant is associated with Christmas and why we traditionally use it as an excuse to steal a kiss.

Part of this tradition dates back to the Celts, who dominated Europe from the fifth to the first centuries B.C. Among these aggressive and warlike people an influential priestly caste, called Druids, acted as judges and conducted religious activities. Romans such as Julius Caesar, Pomponius Mela, Tacitus, and Pliny the Elder wrote extensively about both the Celts and the Druid rites, and it was among these

---

[1]This article appeared in the December 1991 issue and is reprinted with permission from *The World & I*, a publication of The Washington Times Corporation, copyright © 1991..

writings that we found our first clues about the importance of mistletoe.

The early writings of Pliny the Elder were most useful. He notes that the Druids revered the oak as the most sacred of trees and that no Druid was ever seen without an oak twig hanging from his apparel. It is because of the Druids' reverence for the oak, and the powerful spirits they believed resided inside its wood, that we still "knock on wood" for good luck. Druids often tapped on oak trees to awaken the sleeping spirits and ask for good luck.

Roman historians noted that each year, around November, the Druids presided over the winter celebration of Samhain, which has evolved into our Halloween. By then, the sacred oaks were barren except for the green boughs of mistletoe growing from their branches, a sign, the Druids believed, of eternal fertility. With time, the mistletoe became even more revered than the sacred oak.

The Celts believed mistletoe could heal diseases, make poisons harmless, bring fertility to childless women, protect against evil spells, and bring the blessings of the gods. Thus, they customarily carried a sprig of it or placed a bough above the door of their houses. So sacred was the mistletoe that enemies were banned from fighting beneath it, and when Celts met under the mistletoe they were required to greet each other in friendship. Even after they had been conquered by the Roman legions and, later, after their conversion to Christianity, the Celts retained their winter custom of suspending mistletoe above a doorway, as a token of love and peace. Today, the belief in mistletoe's magical powers has spread to many regions, but it is still strongest among the modern descendants of the Celtic peoples. But, as we discovered from the Roman records, the Celts never kissed beneath the mistletoe. The Celts, like most other early European cultures, likely knew nothing about kissing, and there is no recorded evidence that it was ever part of their culture.

Today, most of us accept the Christmastime custom of kissing under the mistletoe, and kissing in general, as one of the niceties of our culture. We practice it, we enjoy it, we write about it, we associate it with love and happiness, and most believe that kissing is as universal in human culture as lovemaking. Yet, our research revealed that kissing is a fairly recent phenomenon, and that kissing under the mistletoe did not become common until long after the original Celts had disappeared.

If the Celts didn't invent kissing, who did? Maybe the ancient Neanderthals kissed, or at least our more recent predecessors of the last ice age. If so, we may never know. These cultures left no written records, no cave paintings of kissing, and no archaeological records of lovers embracing in a kiss. Even later, when the first towns were settled and the first farmers planted crops of barley and wheat, there was no hint of kissing

The first cities and the earliest writing date to around 3500 B.C. Archaeologists have pieced together the story of our urban beginnings and have deciphered the meanings of the earliest written records. What they found were recipes for making wine and beer, records of crop yields and taxation, and versions of early laws. Yet, among these earliest texts there are no references to kissing, perhaps suggesting that it was still unknown and unpracticed.

This situation changed around 1500 B.C., when the Vedic Sanskrit texts of India were written. In the four major texts of Vedic literature we found references to rituals, spells, and sacred charms, all of which were important to these early Indo-European cultures. Also buried in the verses of the Vedic literature and the accompanying sutra texts are references to the custom of rubbing and pressing noses together. This practice, it is recorded, was a sign of affection, especially between lovers. This is not kissing as we know it today, but we believe it may have been its earliest beginning.

The epic *Mahabharata,* written about five hundred to one thousand years later, relates the Vedic priests' attempt to institutionalize the beliefs and practices of their culture. It contains references suggesting that affection was being expressed by lip kissing. By the early fifth century A.D., Vatsyayana had recorded many of the oral verses of the ancient Vedic period in the *Kama Sutra,* a classic text on erotica and other forms of human pleasure. In it, he faithfully records many examples of erotic kissing and even techniques on how to kiss. Among the many examples are detailed instructions on how one should kiss, what parts of the human body should be kissed, and special kissing techniques one should use when dating and after marriage.

This information leads us to believe that erotic kissing became part of Indo-European culture between the writing of the early Vedic texts, around 1500 B.C., and the consolidation of Indian culture during the next one thousand years. From India, the custom of kissing seems to have spread slowly westward with other Indo-European cultural traits such as the use of horses.

The Greeks were the first Europeans to help the spread of kissing. In 326 B.C. the armies of Alexander the Great conquered parts of India as far eastward as Delhi. During Alexander's campaign, Strabo, Arrian, and other historians chronicled the influences and impressions that Indian culture had on the Greek armies. Although we have not found a specific mention of kissing in the writings about the Greek conquest of India, we believe this is where the Greeks encountered literary references to kissing. Later, when the link between the Greeks and India was strengthened by the formation of the Seleucid Empire in Iran, there was a stronger merging of cultural traits, probably including kissing.

After Alexander's death, his empire collapsed. During the subsequent Hellenistic period the remnants of his armies established new empires throughout the eastern Mediterranean region. Although mentioned in the chronicles of these cultures, kissing does not seem to have become an important practice in the eastern Mediterranean region until the Roman era. We are not certain, but we believe that there must have been resistance to the acceptance of kissing by the conquered peoples of the eastern Mediterranean region, even though it remained popular among the Greek rulers of those new empires.

Despite the Greek contribution, the Romans should be credited with popularizing kissing throughout the Mediterranean and Europe. But even after the conquering legions first introduced the practice to the Celts, kissing was not immediately linked to mistletoe.

The Romans had different kinds of kisses. Their *osculum* was a kiss of friendship, most often delivered as a peck on the cheek. It was not a kiss of passion; rather, it was an affectionate way of greeting a friend. So popular did this form of kissing become, that in ancient Rome it was said that one could hardly go anywhere without giving and receiving friendship kisses. In later years, the members of the Roman senate would exchange this type of affectionate kiss at the opening of each session, and nonsenators often kissed a senator's toga as a sign of respect for the person and his office.

Today most Western cultures still use the osculum. In the United States, affectionate kisses are bestowed on the cheeks of close relatives or friends, and our custom dictates that males don't kiss males. In some Western cultures, however, such as the Greek, French, and Russian, it is still proper and expected, as it was in Roman times, for males to kiss each other on the cheeks, or even the lips, as a sign of friendship.

Roman and Erotic Kissing

During the first century B.C. another Roman word for kissing began to take on new meaning. In the writings of the poet Catullus we find frequent reference to a more passionate type of kiss called the *basium.* For example, Catullus writes of his loving mistress Lesbia, and asks affectionately about the number of kisses he needs: "as many as the grains of sand in the Libyan deserts, or as the stars that look down, in the silent watches of the night, on the stolen loves of men."

It is from this Latin word for passionate kissing that most of the later Romance languages took their word for kissing. In Spanish it is *besar,* and in Italian, *baciare.* In French, however, the verb *baiser,* once used only for kissing, has taken on the specialized meaning of intercourse. The colloquial English word *buss* came into the language originally as *bass,* and both connote noisy, wet, smacking kissing. The present English word *kiss* is from a Germanic word root.

Not content with two words for kissing, the Romans added another, *savium,* and its diminutive, preferred by poets like Catullus, *saviolum,* a kiss "sweeter than sweet ambrosia." This was their kiss of wild passion, the ultimate kiss, the one Americans now call the "soul kiss," or "French kiss." In *Amores,* Ovid refers to such "kisses of the tongue" as "shameful," "voluptuous," and "lewdly taught."

Kissing became so much a part of Roman culture that laws were passed proclaiming a young woman's right to a man's hand in marriage if he kissed her passionately in public. This was, however, in response to the prevailing custom that placed a greater emphasis on the couple's engagement than on their marriage. When a young couple was ready for marriage, a ceremonial party was held in their honor. At the appropriate time, they would seal their formal engagement with a passionate kiss in view of all those attending. Later, in a simple and quiet civil ceremony, the couple paid a fee for a license and were then considered married.

Holy Kiss of Peace

Centuries later, Christians shifted the recognition of marriage away from the engagement party to the marriage ceremony. This guaranteed the influence of the church in the important rites of passage in the lives of the faithful. After that, no marriage in the Christian world was considered accepted, in the eyes of God, without the ritual and consent of the church. The public and passionate kiss at the end of the wedding ceremony sealed the eternal bond of love between the bride and groom.

In the early Christian period, kissing was not restricted to weddings. However, early codes of behavior regulating many activities, including sexual freedom and kissing, soon became part of established church doctrine.

Christianity, the principal religion of Western culture, arose in Judea, one of the eastern provinces governed by Rome, and the people of the region had accepted many Roman customs, including kissing. This is evident in Paul's epistle to the Romans, where he writes, "Salute one another with a holy kiss." The gospel according to Luke tells how a prostitute paid homage to Christ by washing his feet with tears, "and did wipe them with the hairs of her head, and kissed his feet." Both references reveal how Roman customs of kissing were adapted for Christian purposes.

In the first reference, the "affectionate kiss" of the Romans becomes the "holy kiss" signifying Christ's affection and blessing to all of humankind, as administered by his representatives, the priests. The "holy kiss," or "kiss of peace," as it was also known, thus becomes an important Christian ritual because it is a visual reinforcement of God's love administered during rites ranging from baptism and confession to marriage and the ordination of priests. Lastly, the celebration of Christ's birth also followed Roman customs of that time. Roman law prescribed that the birth dates of Roman rulers should be celebrated by holidays and festive activities. However, it wasn't until the rule of Constantine I (A.D. 312–37) that the celebration of Christmas, on December 25, was introduced as a special feast day in the Roman Empire. The other kiss, as mentioned by Luke, is also borrowed from a Roman custom: kissing as a visual sign of submission and respect. Throughout the Roman Empire, subjects kissed the robes or signet rings of Roman generals and governors as a sign of respect. Subjects also kissed the statues of Roman gods and other symbols of Roman power and authority to signify their submission and respect. From the beginning of Christianity, the kiss has been an important ritual carried out by faithful Christians and their clergy. Even today it is commonplace to see some Christians kiss the altar, cross, vestments, Bibles, statues, and relics of religious importance.

Although accepted by Christians as an important ritual of faith, by the late Middle Ages certain kinds of kissing were becoming too erotic for many stoic watchers of the faith. During the fourteenth century, in an attempt to regulate kissing, the church took stern action. At the Council of Vienna in 1311–12, the church passed laws stating that Christians who kissed one another while thinking of fornication were guilty of committing a mortal sin, regardless of their subsequent conduct. The new law also stated that Christians who kissed solely for carnal delight were guilty of committing a venial sin, a less serious offense.

Another attempt to stop erotic kissing was the introduction of the *osculatorum,* a metal disk on a handle with ornate engravings depicting images of Christ or various saints. During church services the osculatorium was passed among the congregation, and the faithful would kiss the disk rather than kissing each other as had become the custom. However, by the Middle Ages, kissing had become so much a part of Western culture that even these efforts to limit kissing met with little success.

We suspect that by the Middle Ages it was difficult to prevent the holiday practice of kissing under the mistletoe. Yet, exactly when Christians began kissing under the mistletoe remains a mystery. Even so, based on our research we have developed some intriguing hypotheses. All indications suggest that the earliest practice of kissing under the mistletoe began during the early medieval period in areas of Europe where the influence of ancient Celtic customs remained strong, even after the Roman conquest. This hypothesis is strengthened by the earliest recorded observances of this practice, which reveal a blend of three cultural beliefs: the Celtic belief in the magic powers of the mistletoe, the Roman custom of kissing to seal a betrothal, and the Christian custom of marriage being more important than the betrothal. It was believed that a kiss under the mistletoe was a serious commitment and not to be taken lightly. Such kisses were seen as the physical expression of an eternal love to one another, and more importantly, a promise of marriage. Thus, the couple who sealed their engagement with a kiss under the mistletoe, and then followed through with a church marriage, would be assured of good fortune, fertility, and a long and happy married life together.

From this original linking of kissing with the mistletoe, and the strong commitments it assumed, came a slow relaxing of the implied commitments and a view of mistletoe kisses as simply part of the joyous celebration of the Christmas season. This relaxing of custom probably occurred after the Middle Ages, when a renaissance of frivolity became associated with all forms of kissing after the long period of clerical repression.

This Christmas season, when you are kissed under a sprig of mistletoe, you may want to tell your "kisser" of the serious commitment and binding pledge that have been evoked. If, on the other hand, kissing frivolity is your goal, at least you will know that the mistletoe, the celebration of Christ's birth, and kissing each originated from different cultural sources yet became forever bonded into one of our favorite Christmas traditions.

20

WHEN BROTHERS SHARE A WIFE[1]

Melvyn C. Goldstein

Melvyn Goldstein explores why many Tibetan cultures prefer fraternal polyandry marriages—several brothers sharing one wife. Is it because there is a scarcity of females, or is it necessary to keep population levels low in a barren and bleak environment? He also shows why fraternal polyandry insures its participants of living the "good life" and why the custom is self-perpetuating.

Eager to reach home, Dorje drives his yaks hard over the 17,000-foot mountain pass, stopping only once to rest. He and his two older brothers, Pema and Sonam, are jointly marrying a woman from the next village in a few weeks, and he has to help with the preparations.

Dorje, Pema, and Sonam are Tibetans living in Limi, a 200-square-mile area in the northwest corner of Nepal, across the border from Tibet. The form of marriage they are about to enter— fraternal polyandry in anthropological parlance—is one of the world's rarest forms of marriage but is not uncommon in Tibetan society, where it has been practiced from time immemorial. For many Tibetan social strata, it tradition-ally represented the ideal form of marriage and family.

The mechanics of fraternal polyandry are simple. Two, three, four, or more brothers jointly take a wife, who leaves her home to come and live with them. Traditionally, marriage was arranged by parents, with children, particularly females, having little or no say. This is changing somewhat nowadays, but it is still unusual for children to marry without their parents' consent. Marriage ceremonies vary by income and region and range from all the brothers sitting together as grooms to only the eldest one formally doing so.

The age of the brothers plays an important role in determining this: very young brothers almost never participate in actual marriage ceremonies, although

---

they typically join the marriage when they reach their midteens.

The eldest brother is normally dominant in terms of authority, that is, in managing the household, but all the brothers share the work and participate as sexual partners. Tibetan males and females do not find the sexual aspect of sharing a spouse the least bit unusual, repulsive, or scandalous, and the norm is for the wife to treat all the brothers the same.

Offspring are treated similarly. There is no attempt to link children biologically to particular brothers, and a brother shows no favoritism toward his child even if he knows he is the real father because, for example, his older brothers were away at the time the wife became pregnant. The children, in turn, consider all of the brothers as their fathers and treat them equally, even if they also know who is their real father. In some regions children use the term "father" for the eldest brother and "father's brother" for the others, while in other areas they call all the brothers by one term, modifying this by the use of "elder" and "younger."

Unlike our own society, where monogamy is the only form of marriage permitted, Tibetan society allows a variety of marriage types, including monogamy, fraternal polyandry, and polygyny. Fraternal polyandry and monogamy are the most common forms of marriage, while polygyny typically occurs in cases where the first wife is barren. The widespread practice of fraternal polyandry, therefore, is not the outcome of a law requiring brothers to marry jointly. There is choice, and in fact, divorce traditionally was relatively simple in Tibetan society. If a brother in a polyandrous marriage became dissatisfied and wanted to separate, he simply left the main house and set up his own household. In such cases, all the children stayed in the main household with the remaining brother(s), even if the departing brother was known to be the real father of one or more of the children.

The Tibetans' own explanation for choosing fraternal polyandry is materialistic. For example, when I asked Dorje why he decided to marry with his two brothers rather than take his own wife, he thought for a moment, then said it prevented the division of his family's farm (and animals) and thus facilitated all of them achieving a higher standard of living. And when I later asked Dorje's bride whether it wasn't difficult for her to cope with three brothers as husbands, she laughed and echoed that rationale of avoiding fragmentation of the family land, adding that she expected to be better off economically, since she would have three husbands working for her and her children.

Exotic as it may seem to Westerners, Tibetan fraternal polyandry is thus in many ways analogous to the way primogeniture functioned in nineteenth-century England. Primogeniture dictated that the eldest son inherited the family estate, while younger sons had to leave home and seek their own employment—for example, in the military or the clergy. Primogeniture maintained family estates intact over generations by permitting only one heir per generation. Fraternal polyandry also accomplishes this but does so by keeping all the brothers together with just one wife so that there is only one set of heirs per generation.

While Tibetans believe that in this way fraternal polyandry reduces the risk of family fission, monogamous marriages among brothers need not necessarily precipitate the division of the family estate: brothers could continue to live together, and the family land could continue to be worked jointly. When I asked Tibetans about this, however, they invariably responded that such joint families are unstable because each wife is primarily oriented to her own children and interested in their success and well-being over that of the children of other wives. For example, if the youngest brother's wife had three sons while the eldest brother's wife had only one daughter, the wife of the youngest brother might begin to demand more resources for her children since, as males, they represent the future of the family. Thus, the children from different wives in the same generation are competing sets of heirs, and this makes such families inherently unstable. Tibetans perceive that conflict will spread from the wives to their husbands and consider this likely to cause family fission. Consequently, it is almost never done.

Although Tibetans see an economic advantage to fraternal polyandry, they do not value the sharing of a wife as an end in itself. On the contrary, they articulate a number of problems inherent in the practice. For example, because authority is customarily exercised by the eldest brother, his younger male siblings have to subordinate themselves with little hope of changing their status within the family. When these younger brothers are aggressive and individualistic, tensions and difficulties often occur despite there being only one set of heirs.

In addition, tension and conflict may arise in polyandrous families because of sexual favoritism. The bride normally sleeps with the eldest brother, and the two have the responsibility to see to it that the other males have opportunities for sexual access. Since the Tibetan subsistence economy requires males to travel a lot, the temporary absence of one or more brothers facilitates this, but there are also other rotation practices. The cultural ideal unambiguously calls for the wife to show equal affection and sexuality to each of the brothers (and vice versa), but deviations from this ideal occur, especially when there is a sizable difference in age between partners in the marriage.

Dorje's family represents just such a potential situation. He is fifteen years old and his two older brothers are twenty-five and twenty-two years old. The new bride is twenty-three years old, eight years Dorje's senior. Sometimes such a bride finds the youngest husband immature and adolescent and does not treat him with equal affection; alternatively, she may find his youth attractive and lavish special attention on him. Apart from this consideration, when a younger male like Dorje grows up, he may consider his wife "ancient" and prefer the company of a woman his own age or younger. Consequently, although men and women do not find the idea of sharing a bride or a bridegroom repulsive, individual likes and dislikes can cause familial discord.

Two reasons have commonly been offered for the perpetuation of fraternal polyandry in Tibet: that Tibetans practice female infanticide and therefore have to marry polyandrously, owing to a shortage of females; and that Tibet, lying at extremely high altitudes, is so barren and bleak that Tibetans would starve without resort to this mechanism. A Jesuit who lived in Tibet in the eighteenth century articulated this second view: "One reason for this most odious custom is the sterility of the soil, and the small amount of land that can be cultivated owing to the lack of water. The crops may suffice if the brothers all live together, but if they form separate families they would be reduced to beggary."

Both explanations are wrong, however. Not only has there never been institutionalized female infanticide in Tibet, but Tibetan society gives females considerable rights, including inheriting the family estate in the absence of brothers. In such cases, the woman takes a bridegroom who comes to live in her family and adopts her family's name and identity. Moreover, there is no demographic evidence of a shortage of females. In Limi, for example, there were (in 1974) sixty females and fifty-three males in the fifteen- to thirty-five-year age category, and many adult females were unmarried.

The second reason is also incorrect. The climate in Tibet is extremely harsh, and ecological factors do play a major role perpetuating polyandry, but polyandry is not a means of preventing starvation. It is characteristic, not of the poorest segments of the society, but rather of the peasant landowning families.

In the old society, the landless poor could not realistically aspire to prosperity, but they did not fear starvation. There was a persistent labor shortage throughout Tibet, and very poor families with little or no land and few animals could subsist through agricultural labor, tenant farming, craft occupations such as carpentry, or by working as servants. Although the per person family income could increase somewhat if brothers married polyandrously and pooled their wages, in the absence of inheritable land, the advantage of fraternal polyandry was not generally sufficient to prevent them from setting up their own households. A more skilled or energetic younger brother could do as well or better alone, since he would completely control his income and would not have to share it with his siblings. Consequently, while there was and is some polyandry among the poor, it is much less frequent and more prone to result in divorce and family fission.

An alternative reason for the persistence of fraternal polyandry is that it reduces population growth (and thereby reduces the pressure on resources) by relegating some females to lifetime spinsterhood. Fraternal polyandrous marriages in Limi (in 1974) averaged 2.35 men per woman, and not surprisingly, 31 percent of the females of child-bearing age (twenty to forty-nine) were unmarried. These spinsters either continued to live at home, set up their own households, or worked as servants for other families. They could also become Buddhist nuns. Being unmarried is not synonymous with exclusion from the reproductive pool. Discreet extramarital relationships are tolerated, and actually half of the adult unmarried women in Limi had one or more children. They raised these children as single mothers, working for wages or weaving cloth and blankets for sale. As a group, however, the unmarried women had far fewer offspring than the married women, averaging only 0.7 children per woman, compared with 3.3 for married women, whether polyandrous, monogamous, or polygynous. While polyandry helps regulate population, this function of polyandry is not consciously perceived by Tibetans and is not the reason they consistently choose it.

If neither a shortage of females nor the fear of starvation perpetuates fraternal polyandry, what motivates brothers, particularly younger brothers, to opt for this system of marriage? From the perspective of the younger brother in a landholding family, the main incentive is the attainment or maintenance of the good life. With polyandry, he can expect a more secure and higher standard of living, with access not only to his family's land and animals, but also to its inherited collection of clothes, jewelry, rugs, saddles, and horses. In addition, he will experience less work pressure and much greater security because all responsibility does not fall on one "father." For Tibetan brothers, the question is whether to trade off the greater personal freedom inherent in monogamy for the real or potential economic security, affluence, and social prestige associated with life in a larger, labor-rich polyandrous family.

A brother thinking of separating from his polyandrous marriage and taking his own wife would face various disadvantages. Although in the majority of Tibetan regions all brothers theoretically have rights to their family's estate, in reality Tibetans are reluctant to divide their land into small fragments. Generally, a younger brother who insists on leaving the family will receive only a small plot of land, if that. Because of its power and wealth, the rest of the family usually can block any attempt of the younger brother to increase his share of land through litigation. Moreover, a younger brother may not even get a house and cannot expect to receive much above the minimum in terms of movable possessions, such as furniture, pots, and pans. Thus, a brother contemplating going it on his own must plan on achieving economic security and the good life not through inheritance but through his own work.

The obvious solution for younger brothers—creating new fields from virgin land—is generally not a feasible option. Most Tibetan populations live at high altitudes (above 12,000 feet), where arable land is extremely scarce. For example, in Dorje's village, agriculture ranges only from about 12,900 feet, the lowest point in the area, to 13,300 feet. Above that altitude, early frost and snow destroy the staple barley crop. Furthermore, because of the low rainfall caused by the Himalayan rain shadow, many areas in Tibet and northern Nepal that are within appropriate altitude range for agriculture have no reliable sources of irrigation. In the end, although there is plenty of unused land in such areas, most of it is either too high or too arid.

Even where unused land capable of being farmed exists, clearing the land and building the substantial terraces necessary for irrigation constitute a great undertaking. Each plot has to be completely dug out to a depth of two to two and a half feet so that the large rocks and boulders can be removed. At best, a man might be able to bring a few new fields under cultivation in the first years after separating from his brothers, but he could not expect to acquire substantial amounts of arable land this way.

In addition, because of the limited farmland, the Tibetan subsistence economy characteristically includes a strong emphasis on animal husbandry. Tibetan farmers regularly maintain cattle, yaks, goats, and sheep, grazing them in the areas too high for agriculture. These herds produce wool, milk, cheese, butter, meat, and skins. To obtain these resources, however, shepherds must accompany the animals on a daily basis. When first setting up a monogamous household, a younger brother like Dorje would find it difficult to both farm and manage animals.

In traditional Tibetan society, there was an even more critical factor that operated to perpetuate fraternal polyandry—a form of hereditary servitude somewhat analogous to serfdom in Europe. Peasants were tied to large estates held by aristocrats, monasteries, and the Lhasa government. They were allowed the use of some farmland to produce their own subsistence but were required to provide taxes in kind and corvée (free labor) to their lords. The corvée was a substantial hardship, since a peasant household was in many cases required to furnish the lord with one laborer daily for most of the year and more on specific occasions such as the harvest. This enforced labor, along with the lack of new land and the ecological pressure to pursue both agriculture and animal husbandry, made polyandrous families particularly beneficial. The polyandrous family allowed an internal division of adult labor, maximizing economic advantage. For example, while the wife worked the family fields, one brother could perform the lord's corvée, another could look after the animals, and a third could engage in trade.

Although social scientists often discount other people's explanations of why they do things, in the case of Tibetan fraternal polyandry, such explanations are very close to the truth. The custom, however, is very sensitive to changes in its political and economic milieu and, not surprisingly, is in decline in most Tibetan areas. Made less important by the elimination of the traditional serf-based economy, it is disparaged by the dominant non-Tibetan leaders of India, China, and Nepal. New opportunities for economic and social mobility in these countries, such as the tourist trade and government employment, are also eroding the rationale for polyandry, and so it may vanish within the next generation.

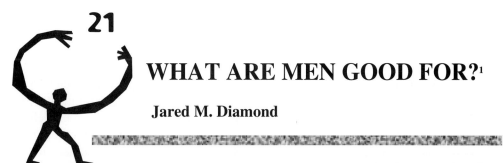

21

WHAT ARE MEN GOOD FOR?[1]

Jared M. Diamond

Are men really needed anymore? Any woman can buy sperm at a sperm bank and have children without the need for a man. Yet, is there still a vital role played by men in our society? Jared Diamond looks at this question and argues that men still do have a role in society, but it isn't for the reasons many of us believe.

When I first began to work in the New Guinea highlands, I often became enraged when I saw how grossly women were abused. Along jungle trails I encountered married couples, the woman typically bent under a huge load of firewood and vegetables, carrying an infant, while her husband sauntered along, bearing nothing more than his bow and arrow. Men's hunting trips seemed to be little more than male-bonding opportunities, yielding only a few prey animals consumed on the spot by the hunters. Wives were bought, sold, and discarded without their consent.

Later, when I had children of my own and shepherded my family on walks, I felt I could better understand the New Guinea men striding beside their families. The men were functioning as lookouts and protectors, keeping their hands free so that they could quickly deploy their bows and arrows in the event of an ambush by men of another tribe. But the men's hunting trips and the sale of women as wives continue to trouble me.

The question "What are men good for?" may sound like a flip one-liner, but it touches a raw nerve in our society. Women are becoming intolerant of men's self-ascribed status and are criticizing those men who provide better for themselves than they do for their wives and children. The question is also a theoretical problem for anthropologists. In terms of services offered to mates and children, males of most animal species are good for nothing but injecting sperm. They part from the female after copulation, leaving her to bear the entire effort of feeding, protecting, and training the offspring. But human males differ by (usually) remaining with mates and offspring. A

[1]Reprinted with pemrission from *Natural History* 5/93. Copyright © 1993 American Museum of natural History.

widespread assumption among anthropologists is that men's familial roles contributed crucially to the evolution of our species' most distinctive features. The reasoning is as follows.

Men's and women's economic roles differ in all surviving hunter-gatherer societies, a category that encompassed all human societies until the rise of agriculture 10,000 years ago. Men invariably spend more time hunting large animals, while women spend more time gathering plant foods, trapping small animals, and caring for children. Anthropologists traditionally argue that this division of labor arose because it promoted the nuclear family's joint interests and thereby represented a sound, cooperative strategy. Men are much better able than women to track and kill big animals, for the obvious reason that men don't have to carry infants around to nurse them. In the view of most anthropologists, men hunt in order to provide meat for their wives and children.

A similar division of labor persists to some degree in modern industrial societies, since most women still devote more time to child care than men do. While hunting is no longer an important male occupation and women now work outside the home, men still provide for their spouses and children by holding paying jobs. Thus, the expression "bringing home the bacon" has a profound and ancient meaning.

Meat provisioning is considered a distinctive function of human males, shared with only a few other mammal species, such as wolves and African hunting dogs. Like many other primate males, men protect their mates and their offspring, but that service is viewed as less of a net contribution by men to society than is hunting, since men defend their families mainly from other men. Meat provisioning is assumed to be linked to other uniquely human features, in particular the continued association of men and women in nuclear families after copulation and the ability of human children (unlike young apes) to obtain their own food for many years after weaning.

From this theory, the correctness which is generally taken for granted, allow two straightforward predictions about men's hunting: First, if the main purpose of hunting is to bring meat to the hunter's family, men should pursue the hunting strategy that reliably yields the most meat. Hence the presumed explanation for men hunting big animals is that they thereby bag, on average, more pounds of meat per day than by hunting small animals. Second, a hunter should be expected to bring his kill to his wife and children, or at least to share it with them preferentially. But do the two predictions square with reality?

Surprisingly, neither assumption has been much tested. Less surprisingly, perhaps, a woman anthropologist has taken the lead in testing them. Kristen Hawkes of the University of Utah, has studied Paraguay's Northern Aché Indians, measuring their foraging yields in a study carried out jointly with Kim Hill, A. Madalena Hurtado, and H. Kaplan. In collaboration with Nicholas Blurton Jones and James O'Connell, Hawkes conducted other tests based on the practices of Tanzania's Hadza people.

The Northern Aché used to be full-time hunter-gatherers, and they continued to spend much time foraging in the forest even after they began to settle at missionary agricultural settlements in the 1970s. Aché men hunt large mammals, such as peccaries and deer, and also collect masses of honey from bees' nests. Women process starch from palm trees, gather fruits and insect larvae, and care for children. The contents of an Aché man's hunting can vary greatly from day to day. He brings home enough food for many people if he kills a peccary or finds a beehive, but he gets nothing at all on one-quarter of all days spent hunting. In contrast, women's returns vary little from day to day because palms are abundant: how much starch a woman gets depends mainly on how much time she spends pounding it. A woman can always count on getting enough for herself and her children, but she can never reap a bonanza big enough to feed many others.

The first shock resulting from the studies by Hawkes and her colleagues concerned the difference between the returns achieved by men's and women's strategies. Peak yields were, of course, much higher for men than for women, since a man's daily bag topped 40,000 calories when he was lucky enough to kill a peccary. However, such glorious days are greatly outnumbered by the humiliating days when he returns empty-handed. A man's average daily return of 9,634 calories per day proved to be lower than that of a woman

(10,356), and a man's median return (4,663 calories per day) was even lower.

Thus, Aché men would do better in the long run by sticking to the unheroic "women's job" of pounding palms than by devoting themselves to the excitement of the chase. Since they are stronger than women, men could, if they chose to, pound even more daily calories from palm starch than can women. In going for high but very unpredictable returns, Aché men can be compared with gamblers who aim for the jackpot, even though in the long run the gamblers would do much better by putting their money in the bank and collecting the boringly predictable interest.

The other shock was that successful hunters do not bring meat or honey home mainly for their wives and children, but share it widely. Women share also, but not so widely as men. As a result, three-quarters of all food that an Aché consumes is acquired by someone outside the consumer's nuclear family.

These findings suggest that something other than the best interests of his wife and children lies behind an Aché man's preference for big-game hunting. As Kristen Hawkes described these paradoxes to me, I began to develop an awful foreboding that the true explanation might prove less noble than the necessity of bringing home the bacon. I began to feel defensive about my fellow men and searched for explanations that might restore my faith in the nobility of our strategy.

My first objection was that Kristen Hawkes' calculations of hunting returns were measured in calories. In reality, any nutritionally aware modern reader knows that not all calories are equal. Perhaps the purpose of big-game hunting lies in fulfilling our need for protein and fat, which are more valuable to us nutritionally than are the humble carbohydrates of palm starch. However, Aché men target not only protein-rich meat but also honey, whose carbohydrates are every bit as humble as those of palm starch. While Kalahari San men (Bushmen) are hunting big game, San women are gathering and preparing mongongo nuts, an excellent protein source. While lowland New Guinea hunters are wasting their days in the usually futile search for kangaroos, their wives and children are predictably acquiring protein in the form of fish, rats, grubs, and spiders. Why don't San and New Guinea men emulate their wives?

I next began to wonder whether Aché men might be unusually ineffective hunters, a modern aberration among hunter-gatherers. Undoubtedly, the hunting skills of Eskimo and Arctic Indian men are indispensable, especially in winter, when little food other than big game is available. Tanzania's Hadza men, unlike the Aché, achieve higher average returns by hunting big game more than small game. But New Guinea men, like the Aché, persist in hunting even though yields are very low. And Hadza hunters persist in the face of enormous odds, since on most hunting days they bag nothing at all. A Hadza family could starve while waiting for the husband/father to win his gamble of bringing down a giraffe. In any case,

from the family's point of view, it is an academic question whether big-game hunting yields higher or lower returns than alternative strategies, since all the meat occasionally bagged by a Hadza or Aché hunter isn't reserved for the family.

Still seeking to defend my fellow men, I then wondered: Does widespread sharing of meat and honey smooth out hunting yields, constituting a form of reciprocal altruism? That is, I expect to kill a giraffe only every twenty-ninth day, and so does each of my hunter friends, but we all go off in different directions, and each of us is likely to kill our giraffe on different days. If successful hunters agree to share meat with the rest of the social group, most people will have full bellies most of the time. According to this scenario, hunters would share their catch with the best other hunters, those from whom they are most likely to receive meat in return.

In reality, though, successful Aché and Hadza hunters share their catch with anyone, regardless of whether he's a good or hopeless hunter. That raises the question of why an Aché or Hadza man should bother to hunt at all, since he can claim a share of meat even if he never bags anything himself. Conversely, why should he hunt when any animal that he kills is shared widely? Why doesn't he just gather nuts and rats, which he can bring to his family exclusively?

As my last defense (objection?) I hypothesized that wide sharing of meat helps the hunter's whole tribe, which is likely to flourish or perish together. It's not enough to concentrate on nourishing your own family if the rest of your tribe is starving and can't fend off an attack by tribal enemies. But that line of reasoning brought me back to the original paradox: The best way for the whole Aché tribe to become well nourished is for all to humble themselves, by pounding good old reliable palm starch and collecting fruit or insect larvae. The men shouldn't waste their time gambling on the occasional peccary.

Thus collapsed all four of my efforts to defend Aché big-game hunting as a sensible way for men to contribute nobly to the best interests of their wives and children. Kristen Hawkes then drove home some painful truths, reminding me that the Aché man himself (and not his wife and children) gets big benefits from his kills.

To begin with, among the Aché, as among most other peoples, extramarital sex is not unknown. Dozens of Aché women, asked to name the possible fathers (sex partners at the time of conception) of sixty-six of their children, named an average of 2.1 men per child. (Before you condemn Aché women as exceptionally loose, reflect that genetic markers show that 5 percent to 40 percent of American and British babies have been sired by a man other than the mother's spouse. And these numbers underestimate the frequency of adultery, because not every bout of adultery results in conception.) When asked about a sample of twenty-eight Aché men, women named good hunters more often than poor hunters as their lovers, and named good hunters as possible fathers of more of their children.

To understand the biological significance of adultery, recall that the facts of reproductive biology introduce a fundamental asymmetry into the interests of men and women. Multiple sex partners contribute nothing directly to a woman's reproductive output. Once a woman has had an ovum fertilized by a man, having sex with another man cannot lead to another baby for at least nine months, and probably for at least several years under hunter-gatherer conditions of extended lactational amenorrhea. In a few adulterous minutes, though, a married man may increase his total number of children. Now compare the reproductive outputs of two hypothetical men pursuing the two different hunting strategies that Hawkes terms the "provider" strategy and the "showoff" strategy. The provider brings home foods such as palm starch and rats, yielding moderate but predictable returns. The showoff instead hunts for big animals, aiming at occasional bonanzas instead of higher mean returns. The provider obtains on the average the most food for his wife and children, although he never gets enough of a surplus to feed anyone else. The showoff usually brings less food to his wife and children, but does occasionally get lots of meat to share with others.

Obviously, if a woman gauges her genetic interests by the number of children she can rear to maturity, which is, in turn, a function of how much food she can provide them, she is better off marrying a provider. But she is further well served by having showoffs as neighbors, with whom she can trade occasional sex in return for extra meat for herself and her offspring. The whole tribe also likes a showoff because of the occasional bonanzas that he brings home for sharing.

In terms of advancing his own genetic interests, the showoff gains advantages as well as disadvantages when compared with the provider. One advantage is the extra offspring sired adulterously, as I've already explained. But the showoff also gains prestige in his tribe's eyes. Others in the tribe want him as a neighbor because of his gifts of meat, and they may reward him with their daughters as wives. For the same reason, the tribe is likely to give favored treatment to the showoff's children. Disadvantages are that the showoff's less reliable provisioning of his own family may mean that he may have fewer legitimate children reaching maturity. The showoff's wife may also philander, so some of her children may not be his. Is the showoff better off giving up the provider's certainty of fathering of a few children in return for the possibility of fathering many children?

The answer depends on several numbers, such as the extra number of legitimate children that a provider's wife can rear, the percentage of a provider's wife's children that are legitimate, and the potential extra survivorship that a showoff's offspring may gain from their favored status. The answer may differ among tribes, depending on the local ecology. For the Aché, Hawkes esti-

mates that over a wide range of likely conditions, showoffs can expect to pass on their genes to more surviving children than can providers. This fact, rather than the traditionally accepted view of bringing home the bacon to wife and children, may be the motive reason behind big-game hunting. Aché men thereby do good for themselves rather than for their families.

Thus, men hunters and women gatherers don't always constitute a division of labor whereby the family unit most effectively promotes its joint interest. They also don't constitute an arrangement in which the work force is selectively deployed for the good of the group. Instead, the hunter-gatherer lifestyle involves a classic conflict of interest, in which what's best for a man isn't necessarily best for a woman and vice versa. Spouses share interests but also have divergent interests. A woman is better off married to a provider, but a man is not better off being a provider.

Biological studies in recent decades have demonstrated many such conflicts of interest in animals and humans: not only conflicts between husbands and wives (or between mated animals) but also between parents and children and among siblings. While biologists explain the conflicts theoretically, all of us recognize them from experience, without doing any calculations of genetics and foraging ecology. Conflicts of interest between spouses and close relatives are the commonest, most gut-wrenching tragedies of our lives.

How generally can these findings be applied? The conclusions of

Hawkes and her colleagues await testing for other hunter-gatherers. The answers are likely to vary among tribes and even among individuals. From my experience in New Guinea, Hawkes' conclusions are likely to apply even more strongly there. New Guinea has few large animals, hunting yields are low, and empty bags are frequent. Men consume much of their catch while they are off in the jungle; and when big animals are brought home, the meat is shared widely. New Guinea hunting is hard to defend economically, but it brings obvious payoffs in status to successful hunters.

What about the relevance to our own society? Perhaps you're already livid because you foresaw that I'd raise that question, and you're expecting me to conclude that American men aren't good for much. Of course that's not what I conclude. I acknowledge that many (most? by far the majority of?) American men are devoted husbands, work hard to increase their income, devote that income to their wives and children, do much child care, and don't philander.

But, alas, the Aché findings are relevant to at least some men in our society. Some American men do desert their wives and children. The proportion of divorced men who renege on their legally stipulated child support is scandalously high, so that even our government is proposing to do something about it. Single parents outnumber co-parents in the United States, and most of those single parents are women.

Among those men who remain married, all of us know some who take better care of themselves than of their wives and children, and who devote inordinate time, money, and energy to philandering and to male status symbols and activities, such as cars, sports, and alcohol consumption. Much bacon isn't brought home. I don't claim to have measured what percentage of American men rate as showoffs rather than providers, but the percentage of showoffs appears not to be negligible.

Even among devoted working couples, time budget studies show that American working women spend on the average twice as many hours on their responsibilities (defined as job plus children plus household) as do their husbands, yet women receive on the average less pay for the same jobs. When American husbands are asked to estimate the number of hours that they and their wives each devote to children and household, the same time-budget studies show that men tend to overestimate their hours and to underestimate their wives' hours. It's my impression that men's household and child-care contributions are on the average still lower in some other industrialized countries, such as Australia, Japan, Germany, France, and Poland, to mention a few with which I happen to be familiar. That's why the question "What are men good for?" continues to be debated within our societies, as well as among anthropologists.

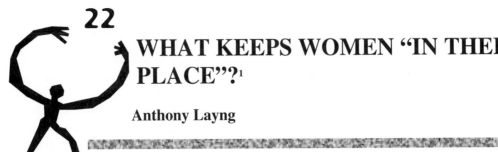

22

WHAT KEEPS WOMEN "IN THEIR PLACE"?[1]

Anthony Layng

Anthony Layng explores the history of how gender-oriented economic roles developed. These are traditionally: man the hunter and provider, women the gatherer and child guardian. He points out why these conceptions are archaic and how gender roles are still reinforced in modern cultures. Finally, he explores what changes need to be carried out before true gender equality becomes a reality.

" . . . Sexual equality will not be achieved until we face up to the fact that inequality is a product of our own behavior and attitudes."

During the decade of the 1970's, women in numerous nations called for the elimination of sexual discrimination. In the U.S., this latest feminist resurgence ambitiously attempted to end all inequalities between the sexes—including those involving employment, political participation, property rights, recreation, language, and education—and some reforms were achieved. An increasing number of women began to act like they were socially equal to men; there has been much talk about teaching girls to be more assertive; and there is now considerable confusion about what constitutes appropriate sex roles. Yet, judging by the fact that the Equal Rights Amendment did not pass and that it presently shows little promise of being resuscitated in the near future, many seem to have concluded that most American women are, by and large, content to remain where they are in relation to men. Further, since women in other industrialized nations have remained essentially "in their place," it appears that there are other formidable obstacles to overcome if we are to bring about such fundamental social change.

Why do sexual inequalities persist in the face of concerted feminist challenges? Is there any realistic basis for us to hope that sexual discrimination ever will be eliminated? What must be done to bring about full emancipation of

[1]Reprinted from *USA Today Magazine*, May 1989, pp. 89-91. Society for the Advancement of Education. Reprinted by permission of the publisher.

women? What is it that keeps women "in their place"?

To understand fully how women have been kept "in their place," we first must learn how they came to be there. This requires consideration of the course of human evolution. Prior to 4,000,000 years ago, there was probably little social differentiation based on gender, because the two sexes were not economically interdependent; one could survive quite well without assistance from the other. It is likely that economic interdependence developed only after the evolving human brain reached a size that necessitated earlier birth, before the cranium of an infant was too large to pass through the birth canal. Giving birth earlier meant that the babies were less mature and would be more dependent on their mothers for a longer period of time. Prolonged helplessness of infants eventually created a need for mothers to depend on others for food and protection.

At the same time, more evolved brains enabled us to invent and use tools that resulted in our becoming effective hunters, in addition to being scavengers. Females with helpless infants still could gather and scavenge a variety of foods, but they were likely to be relatively handicapped hunters and so came to depend on males to provide them with a more reliable source of meat.

Increasing brain size and improved hunting skills also meant that some of our ancestors could begin to occupy northern regions where successful hunting was necessary for survival, since those foods that could be gathered were insufficient during some seasons. In such an environment, females with infants would not live long without food provided by others. Under these circumstances, a sexual division of labor made very good sense.

Although biological factors created the especially long dependency of human infants, the solution to this problem may have been entirely cultural. There is little evidence to suggest that any instinct developed at this time which led females to restrict their economic activities to gathering roots and fruits and men to go off in search of game, but doing so was sound strategy. Such specialization—encouraging females to learn and concentrate on gathering, and teaching only males to be hunters—was an efficient and realistic adaptation requiring only a change in our ancestors' learned behavior and attitudes.

So, a sexual division of labor emerged, but what about sexual inequality? The subordination of females was not brought about by this economic change alone, for, although economic specialization by sex made women dependent on men, it also made men dependent on women. Where human populations subsist entirely by what can be hunted or gathered, most of the food consumed is provided by the gatherers—women. Meat acquired by hunters may be given a higher social value than nuts and berries and the like; but, if the technology employed in hunting is very primitive, meat is difficult to acquire and frequently absent from the menu. Thus, when men began to concentrate on hunting, an interdependence between the sexes emerged, each relying on the other to provide food that made survival possible.

Beliefs and Customs

The development of a sexual division of labor may have preceded and even facilitated social inequality, but it did not create male dominance. Although male dominance would be very difficult to achieve in the absence of a sexual division of labor, it takes firm beliefs and customs as well to retain a higher status for men. The following examples illustrate how societies in various parts of the world have directed the socialization of their children to assure that women will be kept "in their place."

• *Mythology which justifies maintaining female subordination.* Mythology and folklore are used in tribal societies to explain and justify the social *status quo.* The story of Adam and Eve illustrates how sexist myths can be, but some are even less subtle than Genesis in rationalizing male preeminence. Frequently found tales of Amazons or an era when our ancestors lived in matriarchal communities may be functionally equivalent to the Adam and Eve account; although they serve as inspiring models for some women, they may be far more instrumental in reminding men why they must be ever-vigilant in protecting their favored status. So, such tales become an important part of the conservative social learning of children.

• *Seclusion based on the concept of pollution.* In many horticultural societies, women must retire to a special hut during menstruation, since it is believed that their condition magically would jeopardize the well-being of the community. Their economic inactivity during these and other periods of seclusion serves to indicate symbolically that their economic contributions are of secondary importance. This subconsciously may suggest to children in the community that the labor of men is too important to be so restricted by taboos.

• *Segregation of male domains.* Many tribal societies have a men's house in the center of each village in which nearly all important political and ritual plans are made. Women are not allowed to enter this house, under the threat of severe punitive sanctions such as gang rape. Since this form of segregation effectively precludes the participation of women in the political arena, they are not likely to develop any political aspirations while growing up.

• *Exclusion from sacred public rituals.* Tribal societies customarily devote much energy to elaborate religious events, believing that the health of the community depends on these. With very few exceptions, men direct these rituals and play all the key roles; commonly, women merely are observers or participate only in a support capacity. A primary function of these public rituals is to reinforce social values. Since they even attract the full attention of young children, tribal members learn early that men are more important than women, for they are the ones charged with magically protecting the people.

• *Exclusion from military combat.* As in the case of religious ritual in tribal societies, war is considered necessary to insure the survival of the community and almost always is conducted exclusively by men. Success as a warrior brings conspicuous prestige and admiration from women and children alike. Here again, the socialization process, instilling norms and attitudes of correct conduct, leads easily and inevitably to the conclusion that everyone's welfare depends on the performance of the men, and that the women should be suitably grateful.

• *Exclusion from high-status economic roles.* Women in most tribal societies are important producers and consumers, but their economic role is restricted largely to domestic concerns, producing food and goods for kinsmen. When it comes to regulating the exchange of goods between kin groups or with outsiders, men usually dominate such activities. This division of economic roles is fully consistent with the assumption that men are more important socially and more skillful politically. Given such an assumption, the economic differences between the behavior of men and women are likely to seem both proper and inevitable.

• *Veneration of female virginity.* If the religious, political, and economic activities of women are of secondary importance, then what, besides producing children, is their real value? One might be tempted to speculate that, because children in primitive societies are taught to venerate female virginity, this indicates that the status of women is not so lowly as might otherwise be assumed. However, it seems far more likely that this concern with virginity is an extension of the double standard and a reflection of the belief that the major value of women is their sexuality and fertility, their unexalted role as wife and mother.

• *Preference for male children.* When parents usually prefer that their next child will be a boy, this attitude may be considered as both a consequence of and contributor to the higher status of men. Before young children are mature enough to appreciate that one sex socially outranks the other, they can understand that their parents hope to have a boy next time. Impending childbirth in a home is given much attention and takes on real importance; this often may be the earliest opportunity for children to learn that males are more valued than females.

• *Sexist humor and ridicule* are used as important socialization methods in all societies and lend themselves quite effectively to maintaining a sexual hierarchy. Girls who behave like boys, and boys who behave like girls, almost inevitably inspire ridicule. Sexist jokes, particularly when they are considered to be good-natured, are especially effective in this regard. Women who take offense or fail to find such jokes amusing are accused of having no sense of humor, thus largely neutralizing their defense against this social control mechanism.

• *Sexual stereotyping.* Stereotypes of any sort are likely to be of little use in teaching social attitudes to children unless they are accepted by the children as true images of nature. To believe that women and men behave differently because it is the way they were created helps to prevent misgivings from arising about the social inequality of men and women. To the extent that such status differences are believed to be imposed by human nature, the cultural supports of such inequality are not likely to be recognized and, therefore, will not be questioned.

Do Women Accept Subjugation?

A society which effectively keeps women "in their place" need not employ all of the above techniques to do so; just a few will suffice, so long as there is general agreement throughout the population that the *status quo* of sexual inequality is both appropriate and natural. It is just as necessary that women accept this view as it is for men. Although some reformist writers argue that the subjugation of women was instigated by a male chauvinist plot forced upon unwilling victims, it seems amply evident that these social control mechanisms could not work effectively without the willing cooperation of women. They, too, must believe that they were designed by their creator to be subordinate; religious, political, and economic leadership are less suitable for them; and they have their own domains and should not be so immodest as to attempt to interfere where they do not belong. They, too, must consider military exploits as unsuitable for themselves.

Is this asking too much? Do not women value their virginity and that of their daughters as much as men do? Do they not condemn promiscuous women and at the same time tolerate promiscuous men? Is it not common for women to hope to have male children, in preference to daughters? Most women accept sexual stereotypes as an accurate reflection of nature to some degree, and they continue to encourage sexist humor by their laughter.

It seems clear that the "lowly" status of women was not brought about by a conspiracy, nor is it perpetuated only by men. There is no reason to view the above social controls as sinister or perverse where women willingly, even enthusiastically, teach their sons to be "real" men and their daughters to admire such men without wanting to be like them. In other words, in tribal societies, it is not male suppression which makes women subordinate.

It is only when we assume a missionary mentality, viewing such societies in light of our own society's values, that we think these women long for emancipation. Such an ethnocentric view fails to recognize that inequality, where it is accepted by all concerned as inevitable and proper, can be advantageous to lower-status individuals as well as to those who outrank them. Dominance hierarchies, like pecking orders, establish and maintain social order, a condition which tribal societies understandably prefer to disorder and uncertainty. Women in traditional societies do not contribute to their own subordination because they do not know any better or because they are forced to comply with the wishes of the men; they do so because they are socialized appropriately in an orderly society which is culturally well-adapted to its environment.

In tribal societies, sexual inequality is relatively high and protest against such inequality is relatively low. However, an increasing number of women in other societies are protesting sexual discrimination and their subordinate position. Most of this dissent comes from stratified and heterogeneous populations, where gossip, ridicule, and taboos are relatively ineffectual social control techniques. Social order in these more complex societies tends to be enforced by laws and specialized agencies, rather than depending upon voluntary compliance. Even in such complex societies, most may be wholly supportive of the social *status quo,* in spite of their own lowly status. Nevertheless, most of the discontent about sexual inequality comes from these populations.

In spite of such feminist discontent, sexual hierarchies still survive in even highly modernized societies like our own. American women have gained important rights in recent years, but many Americans continue to find Biblical justification for sexual discrimination. Many still think that our nation's economy appropriately remains under the domination of men, and, although the number of exclusively male domains (athletic teams, lodges, clubs, etc.) have been reduced greatly in recent years, a large number still find general endorsement and remain very much intact. Sexual stereotypes continue to enjoy robust

health, the double standard is far from moribund, and sexist humor and ridicule seem to have recovered from their recent bout with militant feminism in the 1970's.

Today, in spite of a recent Gallup poll indicating that more than half the women in the U.S. consider themselves to be feminists, the most ambitious goals of the feminist movement have not been realized. However, it has grown increasingly difficult to convince American women that it is proper for them to be socially inferior to men, or that they should behave submissively. It seems that those customs and beliefs which deny opportunity to women in America are going to continue to be questioned by some who are very persuasive. Since a sexual division of labor has become largely anachronistic for our technologically advanced society, we may anticipate that efforts to preserve exclusive privileges for either sex will encounter increasing resistance.

Although tribal societies need to depend on a system of ascriptive statuses to maintain an orderly social structure, we do not. Tribal populations are not at risk in assigning economic roles strictly by sex, because not basing such assignments on individual aptitude and inclination is of little importance where the economy requires only a narrow range of tasks. In modern industrial society, however, where much highly skilled specialization is essential, selecting candidates for such positions from a limited talent pool, from only half of the adult population, places such a society at an unnecessary disadvantage, one which shows up very clearly if that society must compete with other nations which do not handicap themselves in this fashion. Also, traditional American values which exalt equality, opportunity, and achievement (matters of relatively little concern in tribal societies) are bound to give us increasing difficulty if we continue to deny equality to women and so restrict their ability to achieve the success that they desire and that our economy requires.

Since men have been politically dominant in all human societies, it is not surprising that many scholars have concluded that it is our nature, not our nurture, that has necessitated this inequality. Still, if sexual inequality is inevitable, given our nature, why must tribal populations resort to so many cultural methods to keep women subordinate and submissive?

Knowing how women have been kept "in their place" so long is essential if attempts to combat sexual inequality are to have some success. Just as the most effective medical cure is based on accurate causal diagnosis of an illness, so must social reform efforts take into account the nature of that which we would alter. If we recognize the various ways that our society uses cultural means to perpetuate differential socialization for boys and girls, we are prepared better to redesign that process to foster equality between the sexes. Similarly, if we are aware of the customary practices which encourage women to be submissive, we are more able to challenge and change such customs effectively. To fully understand how and to what extent women are kept "in their place" in the U.S., it is important that we understand how various societies effectively accomplish stable inequality.

Before all of this can enable us to eradicate male dominance, it may be that we first must learn why our society continues to deny equality of opportunity to women, for it is unlikely that we do so only as a result of cultural inertia. It may be that inequality is socially functional in ways that we do not understand fully.

Nevertheless, if women are to achieve total equality, if such a fundamental change can be brought about, it will require far more than passing the Equal Rights Amendment or changing discriminatory laws piecemeal. Since longstanding customs which encourage inequality thoroughly are ingrained in our culture, sexual equality will not be achieved until we face up to the fact that inequality is a product of our own behavior and attitudes. Only then might we discard this vestige of our tribal heritage.

23

JUDAS TRANSFORMED[1]

June Nash

As Christianity has spread around the world, often by conquerors and colonizers, a common response among indigenous people has been to combine aspects of the new religion with their own traditional religions. Good examples of such syncretic religions can be found among the Mayan Indians of Central America. In this article, June Nash describes the ways in which Mayans have incorporated the biblical figure of Judas Iscariot into their traditions and used him as a way to express their feelings about the dominant culture of the Ladinos.

When I saw Judas last year in Guatemala, he was wearing a sport shirt, jogging pants, running shoes, and a blue hard hat—at least that was how some Maya portrayed this reviled figure. The conquering Spaniards had introduced him as the betrayer of Jesus, a personage in the drama of the Crucifixion. But in the delicate operation of imposing and maintaining the Catholic religion in Mexico and Central America, the priests could not prevent Judas from slipping away and taking on a life, and meaning, of his own.

I first encountered a Maya Judas forty years ago, when I began anthropological fieldwork in Cantel, a township in the western highlands of Guatemala. Inhabited by Quiche-speaking Maya, Cantel was a farming center with a large textile factory. The settlement clustered around the large colonial church that stood atop a high hill. Below flowed the Samala River, which had run red with the blood of the slain in 1524, when the Maya king Tecum-Uman fought and died in battle with the conqueror Pedro de Alvarado.

The Maya still spoke of that battle, and during Carnival they subtly reenacted it. The conquerors had introduced a dance commemorating the Spaniards' struggle with the Moors, which the Maya continued to perform. The dancers dressed in costumes of both roles but, embracing the enemy of the Spaniards as their own race, they mingled brown masks of Tecum-Uman with the black masks of the Moors. In everyday life as well, the Maya remained hostile to those they called Ladinos, those of mixed Indian and Spanish de-

[1]Reprinted with permission from *Natural History* (March, 1994). Copyright © the American Museum of Natural History (1994).

scent who identified with the foreign culture. Their attitude was a result of a long history of exploitation and oppression by Ladinos, who controlled the plantations, markets, and institutions of government.

Judas was one of the effigies paraded about during Holy Week each year, when the priest and the catechists (loyal followers of orthodox Catholicism) stage-managed the Passion of Christ. In 1954 the priest was a young Franciscan, newly arrived in Guatemala after previous service in China. His goal was to rescue Catholicism from the folk traditions that had been shaping religious practices during the previous decades, when communities like Cantel did not have resident priests. His major adversaries were the groups of devotees, known as brotherhoods, that had arisen around various saints. Particularly resistant were the mayordomos, or caretakers of the brotherhood houses, who were responsible for the saints' figures. Even Judas had his own brotherhood, being granted a far less negative role in the folk tradition than by the church.

At times during Holy Week, the two religious factions came into conflict over the ceremonial use of public space. For example, on Holy Saturday, those upholding the folk traditions took the figure of the body of Christ, recumbent in its bower of flowers and pine needles, on a slow march through the town, accompanied by the mournful tune of trumpets and wooden ratchet noisemakers. The priest tried to get them to return the figure while it was still daylight, but the mayordomos insisted on a very slow pace, out of respect. The sacristan was obliged to allow the mayordomos to reenter the church after midnight.

Generally, however, the two groups coordinated their activities, the catechists exerting their control in the church while the mayordomos held sway in the plaza and the brotherhood houses. For example, on Holy Thursday, in dramatizing the biblical scenario, the catechists set the image of Christ bearing the cross in the center of the nave. But outside the church that evening, under the direction of the mayordomos, the folk-traditionalists played the role of "the killers of Christ." The streets filled with the spectators' raucous cries of "the Jews!" as participants ran through the town seeking the one who played the role of Jesus. Often pausing to rekindle their energies in the liquor shops, they continued their search until they discovered "Jesus" and dragged him to an improvised jail in the corner of the plaza.

Judas, a straw figure with a wooden mask, belonged to one of the brotherhoods and was entirely defined by folk tradition. Costumed in a black wool suit, felt hat, and laced shoes, he was a caricature of a Ladino (in those days, Indians typically went barefoot or wore sandals and had straw hats and cotton clothing). Among his devotees were those who wished to gain commercial success or who profited from Indian labor. Some were Ladinos from outside Cantel; most were *de vestido* Indians (Indians "of clothing"), those in transition from their Maya culture.

On Saturday, the brotherhood dedicated to Judas, who was also called San Simón, removed his effigy from the brotherhood house, mounted it on a donkey, and led it around town to visit all the shops, including the liquor stores in the town center. Each shop owner gave Judas a five-dollar donation to insure luck in business. Many also plied him with drinks, pouring *posh*, a distilled cane liquor, through a funnel into his open mouth. The drinks, collected through a tube that extended into a rubber "stomach" bag, were later consumed by his followers.

These offerings were considered an important part of business management. I recall the great anxiety of the druggist, a *de vestido* Indian, when she learned that the image had passed her shop while she was out, and how she ran to catch up with the entourage to make her offering. Although presumably introduced into the local culture as a villain, Judas was welcomed in his peregrination, at least by those engaged in commerce. Perhaps they recognized, in his transaction for thirty pieces of silver, Judas's commitment to commerce at any cost.

The priest frowned on the whole Judas cult and had even ordered the catechists to raid the brotherhood house and destroy the figure. But although the catechists had apparently succeeded on several occasions in burning the straw body and wooden mask, the brotherhood always secreted the "true" mask, tying it to a new straw effigy each year. Except for his appearance during Holy Week, Judas remained safe in an altar in the brotherhood house.

I met Judas in another guise in 1957, when I was assigned to do fieldwork in the Tzeltal-speaking Maya community of Amatenango del Valle. A pottery-making town in the highlands of Chiapas, Mexico, Amatenango was known to outsiders as one of the most hostile of nineteen indigenous communities surrounding the Spanish "royal city" of San Cristóbal de las Casas. Early in my fieldwork, I learned that the homicide rate was high and rising. I also learned that two anthropologists had been ordered to leave there because the community did not appreciate their presence. I found it difficult to start a conversation with any of the Indians. The area priest who served the community confirmed my impression, adding that the hostility of the inhabitants to outsiders made his work easier because it kept away the Protestant missionaries. Despite the proximity of the (as yet unpaved) Pan-American highway, the only Ladino living in town was the schoolteacher, who barricaded himself with his family in the large adobe schoolhouse on the plaza, with an arsenal of rifles for protection.

As might be expected, folk beliefs had made severe inroads on whatever Catholic orthodoxy the community had absorbed. Mariano Lopez Shunton, one of the town elders, gave me a vivid example of this when he told me the story of "How Jesus Gained Control over the World." In ancient times, Mariano said, Judas prevented the corn plants from growing by making them come out with one "arm" and one "leg," so that they fell over. Jesus and Mary outwitted him by enticing Judas, whom Mariano called "the leader of the Jews," to a fiesta. Mary danced with Judas and plied him with liquor so that he forgot the fields. Meanwhile, Jesus guarded the fields of corn so that the plants grew straight and tall. In this role, Jesus was identified with the preconquest deity Cananlum, "caretaker of the earth," while Mary was identified with Me'tikchik, "our grandmother the moon," who was also in charge of crops.

While in this story Christ appeared in a positive light, images of Christ—especially the figure of Christ on the Cross—were regarded with ambivalence. In Amatenango, men who claimed extraordinary powers over life and death without validation as folk healers were killed as witches. Saint Peter the Martyr, whose image in Amatenango showed him with a cleaver imbedded in his skull, was taken to have been a powerful witch, later redeemed by his role as the protector against lightning. Similarly, the crucified Christ could have been viewed as a punished witch, evoking little sympathy.

I spent varying amounts of time in Amatenango over the next decade. During the Holy Week rituals, the Crucifixion was reenacted in the church under the supervision of the Ladino priest, with the assistance of the mayordomos, who manipulated the images like puppets. The participation of the mayordo-

mos in the official drama was welcomed, in contrast to the situation in Cantel, where members of the religious brotherhoods were in conflict with the priest.

Although Judas enjoyed some popularity as a cult figure in Cantel, in Amatenango he was almost universally reviled. The priest referred to him as the King of the Jews and identified him as the "killer of Christ." And on Good Friday, following the enactment of the Crucifixion, the mayordomos hauled the effigy of Judas up the belfry "to show the world that he killed Christ." They jabbed him with long poles, laughing when one well-directed blow landed and someone yelled, "Eunuch!"

As I had observed in Cantel, however, Judas was something more than the betrayer of Christ. In the 1960s, when men of the town universally wore white cotton shirts and large-waisted trousers tied with a red sash, the effigy was costumed in the canvas pants, black jacket, boots, and cowboy hat of a Ladino rancher. And Judas's ride around town on Saturday, reminiscent of the one carried out in Cantel, further identified him as a Ladino, since riding a horse was a prerogative of Ladinos during colonial times. As I watched his image, tied to the saddle and with a cigarette in his mouth, I realized that under cover of the role of Christians outraged by the killing of Christ, the Indians were acting out their own hatred of Ladinos.

The priest did not acknowledge this performance, calling it a "pagan" practice, but as soon as his Volkswagen left the churchyard, the entourage set out. Although in Cantel the merchants had showered Judas with donations, in Amatenango only the folk healers gave money. Perhaps they felt an obligation toward Judas as one source of their power over illnesses caused by witchcraft (I could only speculate, since none of them confirmed this). Following Judas's ride around town, the effigy was dismembered and later burned, the wooden mask being saved to be used the following year. The money that had been collected was used to buy liquor—associated with the water used to bathe the body of Christ—that was served to the mayordomos and their assistants.

Another variation on the theme of Judas was described in a 1965 monograph, *Los Escándalos de Maximón* (The Scandals of Maximón), by anthropologist E. Michael Mendelson. Mendelson reported that among the Atitec-speaking Maya of Santiago Atitlán, one of Guatemala's beautiful lake towns, the figure wore a shirt, pants, and belt similar to those worn by the Indians, but along with them he wore a Ladino-style blue jacket, boots, and a broad-brimmed hat. He had a large cigar placed firmly in his mouth. Despite his role in the Christian Holy Week enactment, everyone (except for the clerics) called him Maximón. The Indians told Mendelson that Maximón was the oldest of the animal spirits; he was also called the Black Magician, patron of those "prayer makers" who, like the curers of Amatenango, divine the cause of illness.

To Mendelson, Maximón seemed to be the incarnation of a traditional fertility spirit. This association was evident in the fruit offerings displayed on his altar and the corncobs hung on the image during the cult celebrations of Holy Week. Christ might have redeemed humanity from original sin, but in the eyes of the Indians—given the Catholic church's identification of sexuality with sin and portrayal of Jesus as an ascetic—he exposed the world to sterility. In one of the myths they recounted to Mendelson, "God cooperated with the ancient kings to sow the world with good things, but something happened and the world has died." Through Maximón, the Maya restored the positive aspects of sex and fertility.

According to one myth of Maximón's origin, the ancient authorities decided to make a talking figure to scare men away from other men's wives, who would otherwise be seduced during their husbands' trips to the plantations or the capital city. Created as a guardian of sexual morality, however, Maximón became the principal transgressor. He would impregnate women, whose children would then resemble him or perhaps show some deformity. Or he would transform himself into a woman and lure men into sexual relations, after which they would die in three days.

Thirty years later, anthropologists Nathaniel Tarn and Martin Prechtel report that the cult of Maximón is still alive and well in Santiago Atitlán. In their research, they identify Maximón with Mam, the Maya god of the under-world, and describe him as "the changing power who maintains the world in movement while changing people's sexual partners."

They point out that Judas–Maximón represents negative, as well as positive, aspects of sexuality. Young men ask the prayer makers to intercede for them with Maximón, viewed as the patron of romantic love. But the Maya of Santiago Atitlán also regard romantic love itself as destabilizing, posing a threat as it does to parental control over the selection of mates. As the deity of unbridled sexuality, according to Tarn and Prechtel, Maximón stimulates both desire and its aftermath, disorder.

Cantel, Amatenango del Valle, Santiago Atitlán, and other Maya communities have all placed their own peculiar stamp on Judas, using the figure to embody different local concerns. (In the 1980s, one anthropologist even found a Judas figure in a guerrilla camp in Guatemala, where Maya were counterattacking the genocidal forces of Gen. Efrain Rios Montt.) Judas has also responded to change over time. The Judas I saw in Amatenango in the 1960s had changed by 1992, as the community itself became more engaged in commerce with the outside world. That year I arrived on Holy Saturday, as the new young priest directed the drama in the church. The effigy of Judas was already hanging over the entrance. Instead of his predecessor's gloomy rancher's clothing, he was dressed in a jogging suit with his feet stuffed into Nike sneakers.

On Sunday a boisterous and jocular group of mayordomos bore the hanged body of Judas on muleback, greeting the householders and asking for offerings. Now, all the people—not just the curers—offered money. Also carried in the procession by the women prayer makers was the church's statue of Our Lady of the Rosary weeping over the recumbent body of the crucified Christ. When I lived in the village in 1965, the priest had not permitted the removal of saints' statues from the church for fiestas, because of the conflicts that often arose between villagers and visiting Ladinos, and women did not play any public role in ceremonies.

The sporty Judas of 1992 was greeted more peacefully than in the past. While before, Ladinos were perceived as dominating the commercial world as marketers and plantation bosses, more Indians now had gained, or hoped to gain, a piece of the action. Many of them owned trucks, and dozens of television aerials poked up from the cement block houses that had replaced many of the old wattle-and-daub dwellings. The women who were active in the saints' associations, and who bore the statue of Our Lady of the Rosary, were full-time potters, some who had good trade networks with national museums and tourist shops.

Holy Week was celebrated more lavishly than ever, with eating and drinking in most of the houses. Even the Judas figure had proliferated, with several families hanging effigies in their own courtyards. As before, the mayordomos cheerfully imbibed the drinks that were their reward for carrying out the fiesta. Most of them preferred the soft drinks that were rapidly replacing the strong, home-brewed liquor.

In the nearby city of San Cristóbal, the custom of hanging Judas in effigy had developed into a competition of Holy Week figures, promoted by the municipal authorities. The offer of a cash prize had generated some lively dioramas, which were displayed under bright lights in the garden of the newly painted gray-and-white municipal building. Drawing from a variety of themes, the tableaux departed widely from the Passion Play. First prize, appropriately in the quincentennial year of Columbus's arrival, went to a local sculptor's depiction of a Spanish conquistador beating an emaciated, Christlike Indian with a sword.

One contestant mounted a multitiered tableau of the class system, showing the rich landlords on top, stamping out the life of the gasping peasants. Another depicted the police evicting families from the San Juan Chamula barrio (this dispute reflected religious differences within the Indian community and a land grab by local elites). Yet another tableau sought to raise people's consciousness about sexual harassment and violence toward women by dramatizing the American prizefighter Mike Tyson's jailing for rape. These new conflicts cut across the division between Indians and Ladinos, which was no longer so keenly felt.

Last year I again made my pilgrimage to Amatenango on Holy Saturday. As the time came on Sunday for Judas's ride around town, at ten in the morning, his hanged effigy was unceremoniously cut down from the belfry and hoisted on the back of a horse. He was still garbed in a gaily colored sport shirt and jogging pants as he had been the year before, but this time, strapped above his flaming pink face was a blue hard hat. When I asked his caretaker what he represented, he said, "A government agent," and his assistant added, "Yes, a forestry agent!" and they both laughed. Judas's identity now centered on a specific Maya conflict with the government. New laws limited the cutting of trees; in addition, I was told, the forestry agents would sometimes solicit bribes from violators or even confiscate the cut wood and sell it for their own profit.

As the Maya gain greater entry into the Ladino world, the animosity is still there, but now it is focused on particular adversaries instead of on the generalized Ladino. This January, a local rebellion gained international attention as a group of indigenous people calling themselves the Zapatista Army of National Liberation attacked the military barracks near San Cristóbal and seized nearby towns. They specifically rejected the North American Free Trade Agreement and the reform act permitting the sale of communal lands. Perhaps this year, Judas will be dressed as a Mexican soldier.

24

ANYTHING BUT QUIET[1]

Samuel Fromartz

Expressive culture comes in many forms, including visual art, dance, and music. This article by Samuel Fromartz describes a form of drumming called taiko. Based on traditional Japanese forms, taiko has recently gained a large following in North America. In addition to the aesthetic appeal of the drumming itself, the story of taiko in North America is also a good example of how people may improvise and innovate in an effort to regain some of their lost ethnic identity and traditions.

Seiichi Tanaka never planned to be a founder of *taiko*—Japanese drumming—in the United States. He actually came to San Francisco from Japan in 1967, at the age of twenty-four, to pursue a martial arts career. But then, at a local spring Cherry Blossom Festival, he was surprised by the absence of the familiar drums, which he remembered playing even as a child. ("The drummers would get drunk and then fall asleep. That's when I would try taiko.") The following year, he borrowed some drums from a Buddhist temple in San Francisco and organized his own contingent of players, at first consisting mostly of Japanese nationals living in the Bay Area. Tanaka's martial arts background helped shape his philosophy and approach, which emphasizes the drummers' intense physical and mental training and their disciplined and graceful movement. His group, San Francisco Taiko Dojo, has since grown and influenced the development of others in the United States and Canada.

The first major gathering marking this three-decade-long movement in North America was held in 1997 and drew nearly 500 people to Little Tokyo, the predominantly Japanese American community of downtown Los Angeles. During one jam session, while others were relying on brute force, Tanaka's drumming seemed effortless, as if it were an afterthought to the fluid movement of his entire body. In a master class he held afterwards—ninety students rotating through the drums—he urged: "You have to totally relax. Let the energy come from your *ki* [center]. Feel the energy come from the mother

[1]Reprinted with permission of *Natural History* (March, 1998). Copyright © the American Museum of Natural History (1998).

earth, from the bottom of your feet." He stressed a kind of loose intensity, in which the mind focuses on the tips of the *bachi*, or drumsticks. And he heartily endorsed the yelps one often hears from performers at taiko concerts. "Screaming is very important! After you scream you feel good."

Taiko rarely strays from an emphasis on percussion instruments. The pulse is maintained by the resonant tones of large and small drums, the clackety-clack that these wood-and-skin instruments make when they are hit on the side, and the shrill sound of the *atarigane* (a bowl-shaped metal instrument struck with deer antlers attached to a bamboo stick). Gongs of various size and shape add musical depth, and a bamboo flute occasionally offers a melody. When the drummers solo, they improvise in response to the rhythms, engaging in a kind of dance with the strong undercurrents.

This music has ancient roots. The drums, which vary in form and use, probably came to Japan from China and Korea beginning around the fifth century, following the paths of Buddhism and theatrical arts. The drums are used in *gagaku*, the traditional Japanese court music that has changed little since the eleventh century. Regional folk styles of taiko have developed throughout Japan, tied to festivals and religious rites. But strictly speaking, the group drumming (*kumi-daiko*) popular today—in which several performers play drums of various sizes, some keeping the beat,

others soloing—is a post-World War II development.

In Japan, the rise of *kumi-daiko* coincided with the late 1960s counterculture movement, which led some young people to reexplore folk arts that had been neglected as a consequence of the rapid modernization and Western bias of the post-war era. Ondekoza and its offspring, Kodo, now among Japan's best-known taiko groups, were established as rural communes in which the participants self-consciously sought to rediscover their roots. Japanese American youth began to explore taiko during the same turbulent times, when they were battling what was viewed as the stiff assimilationist outlook of their parents' generation and the prevalent stereotype of the "quiet Japanese" (taiko is anything but quiet). The 1997 taiko conference was organized by the Japanese American Cultural and Community Center (JACCC) and held at their headquarters in Little Tokyo. Founded in 1980, JACCC is a nonprofit organization whose mission is to preserve and promote Japanese and Japanese American heritage and arts.

Masao Kodani is the minister of the Senshin Buddhist temple in Los Angeles. According to him, before Pearl Harbor, "Every adult was expected to offer something in terms of entertainment, whether it was a poem, singing, or dancing." But the war—and the internment by the United States of 110,000 Japanese Americans in barbed-wire-ringed camps—had a corrosive effect on that tradition. Despite huge economic and emotional losses suffered by Japanese Americans, their overwhelming response to that experience was assimilation. And among the things that got left behind were the small celebrations of the community's cultural spirit.

Kodani took charge of the temple as a young minister in 1968. This gated compound lies in an African American and Latino neighborhood of south-central Los Angeles that had been largely Japanese American until the 1970s. Taiko drums are used in some of the temple ceremonies and festivals, but usually with other instruments and not for the kind of athletic group performances with which they are now associated. After the 1969 Obon Festival (a summertime celebration of the ancestors), Kodani remembers, he and a member of the temple, George Abe, were putting the drums away for another year when they began playing them. They played for about four hours, until they were sweating, their hands bleeding. "George, I think we should do something about this!" Kodani remembers saying. Shortly thereafter (just one year after Tanaka formed his group in San Francisco) Kinnara Taiko was founded. It was the first contemporary taiko group to come directly from the Japanese American community.

Tanaka linked up with Kinnara Taiko and shared knowledge, especially about building drums. Most traditional taiko drums are made by hollowing out a tree trunk and stretching animal skin over the head. Especially in the case of an *odaiko*, or large drum, this can be quite an undertaking. Kinnara Taiko's innovation was to use oak wine barrels. Without this cost-saving resource, taiko probably would not have developed in North America the way that it did. Another difficulty was stretching the skin. The group first used pliers, Kodani said, pulled by the biggest guy in the congregation. Later, with the help of Tanaka, they devised a system with car jacks to stretch the skin. "We had to go through many experiments, breaking jacks and skins," Tanaka says. It's now a standard method.

For someone like Johnny Mori, who grew up in the sixties and was an early member of Kinnara Taiko, the group seemed a natural link to Japanese culture. "Mentally, for me, it was very rewarding to identify with what I thought was a Japanese thing," he says. "But lo and behold, this particular taiko, this Japanese American taiko, had no roots whatsoever in Japan, nothing at all. Basically, we sat around and said, 'Are we making this thing up?' and Reverend Masao said, 'Yeah, we're just making this up.' And I go, 'This has no connection? No other Buddhist group in Japan does this?' And he said, 'Nope.' I go, 'Wow, I always thought I had this connection to Japan—and I don't.' "

At first, this realization bred insecurity, which was compounded by comments from Japanese who told the group they were not playing taiko. But when other Japanese Americans cheered them on, especially the older Issei (first-generation immigrants), they grew more confident. What they were doing, the sounds they made, reflected who they were. It was a uniquely American form.

To be sure, there were missteps along the way. P. J. Hirabayashi, of San Jose Taiko, remembers that young musicians jamming on the taiko drums "had no inkling how to play." Alan Okada, of New York's Soh Daiko, recalls one of their early instructors improvising on saxophone while the group played drums. The question they faced then—and still face—was how to maintain the traditions of taiko and still create music that resonated personally. "We were lucky enough to know there are traditions, and some of those traditions are valuable and need to be maintained," Okada says. "And we were lucky enough to know that you can change things . . . . It's a living folk art, and it evolves."

Today, there are more than one hundred taiko groups—most formed in the eighties and nineties—performing throughout North America, from Calgary and Vancouver to Los Angeles, Honolulu, and Burlington, Vermont. In Japan, there are roughly 5,000 groups, including several major professional troupes. Week-long festivals attract thousands, and groups play for hours; at one festival, a thousand drummers play simultaneously. Kodo, along with a number of other professional groups, has been a force in that evolution in Japan. It tours eight months out of the year, conducts workshops the world over, and holds a percussion festival at its base on Sado Island, off the east coast of Japan. (Last year, groups from Senegal, Trinidad, Indonesia, and Ireland appeared.) Kodo has become so influential that its members bemoan how novice groups in Japan copy its pieces instead of developing their own.

Yoshiaki Oi, a founding member of Kodo and now a teacher in the group, applauds the American style. He says he heard a specific Kodo piece played at the Los Angeles conference. "In Japan, you hear the same melody [played by other groups], but it's the same presentation that we do, with the same sound, but what I heard here was different." He hopes that North American groups will appear more frequently in Japan "to show what creativity is all about."

Kenny Endo, who grew up in Los Angeles and now lives in Hawaii, has probably taken taiko the farthest among Americans. He composes, runs a school, tours regularly, and plays with musicians in Japan and the United States. His interest took him to Japan for ten years in the 1980s, where he studied taiko and *hogaku hayash*—the classical Japanese ensemble for flute and drums found in Noh and Kabuki. He played percussion in the Kabuki theater as a professional and was the first foreigner to earn the distinction of being granted a *natori*, a stage name that is also an informal license to teach. But Endo previously worked in funk, Latin, and jazz bands, even as he studied with the San Francisco Taiko Dojo. All these experiences show up in his work. "I feel a responsibility and a desire to continue the traditional music, whether it's Kabuki music or festival music," Endo says. "But I also feel a desire, for my own expression, to compose and use taiko in other types of contexts with other people." At the conference's concluding concert, Endo introduced a violist and saxophonist to play with his taiko ensemble. He also played a *tsuzumi* (an hourglass-shaped hand drum used in Kabuki) with Tanaka's group.

Perhaps the climactic moment came when drummers lined up to take turns on a three-foot-wide drum nestled horizontally on a wooden stand. Two performers at a time pounded at opposite ends, one as soloist and the other in a back-up role. As the sweat flew off their bodies, which in some cases were clothed only in loin cloths, the drummers unleashed a rhythmic frenzy, summoning up a deep roar with mounting intensity.

Following the concert, conference participants partook of food and drink set out by the JACCC in the open plaza outside the hall. But the milling crowd was still reluctant to disperse.

After a couple of hours, some of the musicians spontaneously struck up a playful, raucous *tankobushi*, a traditional song and dance at Obon festivals, then segued into other taiko dance music. Somebody picked up a bamboo flute, another started to tap on a table, and then a couple homed in on plastic garbage cans and turned them upside down for drumming. Surrounded by deserted office buildings in downtown Los Angeles, the plaza felt like a village in the midst of a valley. The musicians formed a huge circle, couples danced in the center, and even Tanaka boogied into the fray to loud cheers. Everyone clapped and laughed long into the night; it was a celebration of rhythmic spirit as old as the taiko drum itself.

25

COFFE, TEA OR OPIUM?[1]

Samuel M. Wilson

The modern world system has its roots in the expansion of Western European powers that began several hundred years ago. As this article on the opium trade in nineteenth-century China shows, nations at the core of the world system sometimes used surprising means of enhancing their power over nations in the system's periphery and semiperiphery.

In 1839, China's commissioner for foreign trade, Lin Zexu (Lin Tse-hsü), was running out of diplomatic options. Traders from the East India Company and other European enterprises were pressing him ever more forcefully to turn a blind eye to the illegal importation of opium into his country. They were implicitly backed by Britain's heavily armored warships—such as the *Blenheim* and *Wellesley,* carrying seventy-four cannons each—which could crush China's navy and lay waste to her ports. But the opium trade was damaging public health and bleeding China of her wealth. In 1838, the Manchu emperor had given Lin extensive power and ordered him to control the demand of China's people for opium and force the barbarian merchants to cut off the supply.

After his appointment, Lin began to study European culture, looking for clues to barbarian behavior. He obtained a partial translation of Emer de Vattel's 1758 *Le Droit des Gens* ("The Law of Nations"), and he bought and studied the British ship *Cambridge.* Although it was not the largest of the "East Indiamen"—big defended freighters—and although it had been stripped of its guns and its intricate rigging was a mystery to Lin's sailors, the ship was ample evidence that these British were clever at naval warfare.

Lin also visited Macao, the Portuguese trading entrepôt near Canton, and carried out some anthropological fieldwork:

As soon as I entered the wall of Macao, a hundred barbarian soldiers dressed in barbarian military

[1]This article originally appeared in the November, 1993 issue of *Natural History*. It has been reprinted in *The Emperor's Giraffe and Other Stories of Cultures in Contact*, written by Samuel M. Wilson and published by Westview Press of Boulder, Colorado, a member of the Perseus Books Group. It appears here with permission from Perseus Books Group.

uniform, led by the barbarian headman, greeted me. They marched in front of my sedan playing barbarian music and led me into the city.... On this day, everyone, man and woman, came out on the street or leaned from the window to take a look. Unfortunately the barbarian costume was too absurd. The men, their bodies wrapped tightly in short coats and long "legs," resembled in shape foxes and rabbits as impersonated in the plays.... Their beards, with abundant whiskers, were half shaved off and only a piece was kept. Looking at them all of a sudden was frightening. That the Cantonese referred to them as "devils" was indeed not vicious disparagement. [Chang Hsin-pao, *Commissioner Lin and the Opium War* (Cambridge: Harvard University Press, 1964)]

Although the Chinese forbade opium importation, willing trading partners were easily found among the Chinese merchants. And if trade became too difficult for the foreigners in the principal port of Canton, there were a thousand miles of coastline, and thousands of miles more of inland borders, through which opium could be transported. Lin saw that the opium trade was ruining China. Informed by his reading of de Vattel and by his extensive dealings with the British representatives, in early 1839 he appealed to Queen Victoria, attempting to conceal the sense

of superiority that the Chinese rulers felt toward Westerners:

We have heard that in your honorable nation, too, the people are not permitted to smoke [opium], and that offenders in this particular expose themselves to sure punishment.... Though not making use of it one's self, to venture nevertheless to manufacture and sell it, and with it to seduce the simple folk of this land, is to seek one's own livelihood by exposing others to death, to seek one's own advantage by other men's injury. Such acts are bitterly abhorrent to the nature of man and are utterly opposed to the ways of heaven.... We now wish to find, in cooperation with your honorable sovereignty, some means of bringing to a perpetual end this opium, so hurtful to mankind: we in this land forbidding the use of it, and you, in the nations of your dominion, forbidding its manufacture. [Chang Hsin-pao, *Commissioner Lin and the Opium War*]

The British were the biggest traders in China, but merchants from the United States were present too. Lin considered petitioning this other, possibly significant state, but understood that twenty-four chiefs governed the American people, and thought that communicating with them all would be too difficult.

In his letter to Queen Victoria, Lin sought to explain the situation logically. Earlier communications from the Chinese government had not been so diplomatic. The commander of Canton had sent an edict to the Western traders demanding, "Could your various countries stand one day without trading with China?" This threat came in part from the Chinese leaders' delusion that the British would die if deprived of tea, China's largest export (a delusion the British may have shared). The same edict took note that, according to the Western press,

> your motives are to deplete the Middle Kingdom's wealth and destroy the lives of the Chinese people. There is no need to dwell on the topic that the wealth of the Celestial Empire, where all five metals are produced and precious deposits abound, could not be exhausted by such a mere trifle, but for what enmity do you want to kill the Chinese people?

China had withstood barbarian traders without difficulty for two thousand years. But now it was feeling the aftershock of the Western encounter with the Americas and with the closely related expansion of European influence across the globe. The importation of opium reached staggering proportions in the early nineteenth century after the British-run East India Company took control of the drug's production in India. During the trading season of 1816–17,

about forty-six hundred 150-pound chests of opium entered China. This number rose to 22,000 by 1831–32 and 35,000 by 1837–38. That was more than 5.25 million pounds of opium, the carefully collected and dried sap extruded from 4.8 trillion opium poppies.

The period from the seventeenth century to the present could be termed the Age of Addiction, for the international economy and the fortunes of nations depended on trade in addictive or semiaddictive agricultural products. The young United States exported tobacco, the habit for which spread rapidly across Europe, Africa, and Asia. The Spaniards carried the New World practice of tobacco smoking to Europe and the East Indies, and as its popularity spread, the plant came to be widely cultivated throughout the Old World. In their Indonesian colonies the Dutch tried filling their pipes with a combination of opium and tobacco. The Chinese continued to smoke the opium, but left out the tobacco.

The British became addicted to the carefully processed leaves of *Camellia sinensis,* or Chinese tea (originally, China was the only exporter). Caffeine-rich coffee was another drug for which Europeans and others developed a craving. A native plant of Ethiopia, coffee's range of cultivation expanded hand in hand with European colonialism. Perfect growing conditions were found in both the New World and Southeast Asia, giving rise to the exotic names for coffee familiar today: Jamaica

Blue Mountain, Mocha Java, Guatemalan, Sumatran, and Colombian. These and other nonessential but deeply desired plant products—cocaine, chocolate, and marijuana—have captured huge markets.

Addictive substances are wonderful exports for the countries that produce and ship them. They are highly valuable and compact agricultural products that can be exchanged for hard currency, and the demand of addicts is—for physiological reasons—what economists would call highly inelastic. Farmers get much more from their land and effort than they would by growing things for a local market, and middlemen on both sides of the border get rich. The losers in the transaction—apart from the users themselves—are the importing countries, which run up uncontrollable trade deficits.

From the opening of the Silk Road in the Middle Ages, Western countries were eager to obtain Chinese spices, fabrics, and tea, viewing them as superior to European products. The problem for England and other nations was that they had very little that China wanted, so they had to pay in the most respected and accepted international currency, Spanish silver dollars. With good reason, the Chinese thought the British could not live without tea. About all China would take in trade was British woolen and cotton cloth. American merchants, lacking England's textile manufacturing infrastructure, struggled still more to find anything the Chinese would take in trade. They too paid mainly with Spanish silver, but they also brought natural products—sealskins and other furs from the Northwest Coast, aromatic wood, cotton, wild American ginseng—with which to trade.

By capitalizing upon a massive addiction to smoked opium in China—and in substantial measure helping to create it—England and the other Western nations shifted the balance of trade in their favor. As social historian Fernand Braudel put it, "China was now literally being paid in smoke (and what smoke!)." Most of the rest of what England traded was woven cotton, also grown and spun in India. In return, at the time of Commissioner Lin's appeal to Queen Victoria, the Chinese were trading about 60 percent tea, 12 percent silks, and most of the rest about 25 percent, silver and gold.

The opium trade was not the only alarming foreign influence in Lin's day. The barbarians seemed to have designs on Chinese territory. The port of Canton lay thirty miles upriver from the great Gulf of Canton, twenty miles wide and fifty miles long. At the western approach to the bay was the Portuguese trading colony of Macao, which the Chinese had allowed to exist since 1557. On the other side of the gulf lay the island of Hong Kong, which the British sought to turn into a secure headquarters for their trading operations. Even if the Europeans had lacked naval superiority, they could have defended both places from invasion by land or sea. China had always insisted that barbarians of any stripe carry out their trade and then leave, but instead of acting as temporary visitors, the Western traders were staying longer and longer, becoming in effect permanent residents.

Another major grievance was that the foreigners would not submit to Chinese laws when in China. Some European sailors murdered Chinese citizens, but their leaders would not turn over the culprits to the Chinese magistrates. Lin's research revealed that foreigners in England were required to obey British law, but when he confronted the British commanders with this double standard, they merely conceded that he had a case and again refused to turn over British subjects to almost certain execution. Other European and American traders acted similarly.

Despite the barbarian offenses, Lin preferred negotiation and reasoned discussion to fighting a battle that he felt would be difficult to win. In a final, carefully worded letter to Queen Victoria, he wrote:

> Let us suppose that foreigners came from another country, and brought opium into England, and seduced the people of your country to smoke it. Would not you, the sovereign of the said country, look upon such a procedure with anger, and in your just indignation endeavor to get rid of it? Now we have always heard that Your Highness possesses a most kind and benevolent heart. Surely then you are incapable of doing or causing to be done unto another that which you should not wish another to do unto you. [Chang Hsin-pao, *Commissioner Lin and the Opium War*]

Moral persuasion has not, historically, proved very effective in dealing with drug smuggling or rulers who sanction it. Unofficially, the contents of the letter were probably widely known but as with his previous attempts, Lin received no official response. Britain was determined that the opium trade would continue, by force if necessary, and because China had been unwilling to open formal diplomatic channels, the British government would not accept a letter to the queen from a commissioner.

Lin's efforts to rein in the barbarians and subdue the Chinese appetite for opium were ultimately unsuccessful, and the emperor harshly accused him of failing:

> Externally you wanted to stop the trade, but it has not been stopped. Internally you wanted to wipe out the outlaws, but they are not cleared away.... You are just making excuses with empty words. Nothing has been accomplished but many troubles have been created. Thinking of these things I cannot contain my rage. What do you have to say now?

Lin replied that the Chinese should address the threat and fight the British, falling back to the interior and fighting a guerrilla war if necessary. He warned the emperor not to attempt to placate the British: "The more they get the more they demand, and if we do not overcome them by force of arms there will be no end to our troubles. Moreover there is every probability that if the English are not dealt with, other foreigners will soon begin to copy and even outdo them."

In June of 1839, Lin had 20,000 chests of opium destroyed in Canton, and the foreign merchants fell back to Macao. The British sent a fleet of their most powerful warships on a punitive expedition, and they overwhelmed the Chinese fleet whenever they faced it. Among their warships were the "ships-of-the-line," massively armed vessels that demonstrated the advantage of superior technology over superior numbers in modern warfare. In the summer of 1842, China was forced to sign the humiliating Treaty of Nanking, which required $21 million in reparations, opened five ports to British trade (including Canton and Shanghai), and ceded Hong Kong, surrounding islands, and part of the mainland to Queen Victoria. China also agreed that future Chinese-British relations would be on terms of "complete equality." This condition seems ironic, because the terms of the treaty were certainly in the Western merchants' favor. This wording was insisted upon by the British, however, because previously China had dealt with Westerners as barbarian traders, never recognizing them as official representatives of foreign governments. Nowhere did the treaty mention opium, but every-

one knew that the drug had been at the heart of the war.

One hundred fifty years later, China still feels the sting of this defeat. The recently negotiated treaty for the return of Hong Kong in 1997 is viewed as just a fraction of the restitution owed. In 1990, writing in the *Beijing Review,* historian Hu Sheng, president of the Chinese Academy of Social Sciences, lamented the cost of the war in terms of Chinese health, hard currency, and national honor. He also observed that for the next hundred years China was under continuous attack by the West and Japan, but because the emperors were willing to tolerate their presence, the people were unable to rise up and throw out the foreigners. In his view, and in that of many Chinese, "Only the Chinese Communist Party could do this."

For his failure to curb the barbarians, Lin Zexu was demoted and disgraced, and spent the last few years before his death supervising irrigation projects and the repair of dikes. In retrospect, he is regarded as a hero. "The Chinese army, commanded by Lin," writes Hu, "resisted the invaders together with the local people. However, the corrupt Qing court was unable to continue the resistance and succumbed to the invaders."

Commissioner Lin would no doubt feel vindicated, and perhaps even take some pleasure in the way many Western nations are now on the receiving end of the drug policies they helped invent.

26

SECRETS OF THE FOREST[1]

A. C. Roosevelt

It is often thought that development in the tropics is hampered by the poor quality of soils typically found in that region. One of the supports for this view has long been the lack of any evidence of large populations living in tropical rainforests during prehistory. Recent archaeological findings in the Amazon region of Brazil, however, cast doubt on this pessimistic view. As A. C. Roosevelt argues, there is now considerable evidence that the Amazon once supported complex societies with large populations. One possible implication is that more development may be possible in that region than is commonly thought. It may be that the biggest obstacle to development in that region is not the quality of the soils, but rather the laws that regulate land tenure and taxation.

In 1942 Allan R. Holmberg, a doctoral student in anthropology from Yale University, ventured deep into the jungle of Bolivian Amazonia and searched out an isolated band of Siriono Indians. The Siriono, Holmberg later wrote, led a "strikingly backward" existence. Their villages were little more than clusters of thatched huts. Life itself was a perpetual and punishing search for food: some families grew manioc and other starchy crops in small garden plots cleared from the forest, while other tribesmembers scoured the country for small game and promising fishing holes. When local resources became depleted, the tribe moved on. As for technology, Holmberg noted, the Siriono "may be classified among the most handicapped peoples of the world." Other than bows, arrows and crude digging sticks, the only tools the Siriono seemed to possess were "two machetes worn to the size of pocket knives."

Although the lives of the Siriono have changed in the intervening decades, the image of them as Stone Age relics has persisted. Indeed, in many respects the Siriono epitomize the popular conception of life in Amazonia. To casual observers, as well as to influential natural scientists and regional

---

[1]This article is reprinted by permission of *The Sciences* and is from the November/December 1992 issue. Individual subscriptions are $28 per year. Write to: *The Sciences*, 2 East 63rd Street, New York, NY 10021.

planners, the luxuriant forests of Amazonia seem ageless, unconquerable, a habitat totally hostile to human civilization. The apparent simplicity of Indian ways of life has been judged an evolutionary adaptation to forest ecology, living proof that Amazonia could not—and cannot—sustain a more complex society. Archaeological traces of far more elaborate cultures have been dismissed as the ruins of invaders from outside the region, abandoned to decay in the uncompromising tropical environment.

The popular conception of Amazonia and its native residents would be enormously consequential if it were true. But the human history of Amazonia in the past 11,000 years betrays that view as myth. Evidence gathered in recent years from anthropology and archaeology indicates that the region has supported a series of indigenous cultures for eleven millennia; an extensive network of complex societies—some with populations perhaps as large as 100,000 —thrived there for more than 1,000 years before the arrival of Europeans. (Indeed, some contemporary tribes, including the Siriono, still live among the earthworks of earlier cultures.) Far from being evolutionarily retarded, prehistoric Amazonian people developed technologies and cultures that were advanced for their time. If the lives of Indians today seem "primitive," the appearance is not the result of some environmental adaptation or ecological barrier; rather it is a comparatively recent adaptation to centuries of economic and political duress. Investigators who argue otherwise have unwittingly extrapolated the present onto the past.

The evidence for a revised view of Amazonia will take many people by surprise. Ecologists have assumed that tropical ecosystems were shaped entirely by natural forces and they have focused their research on habitats they believe have escaped human influence. But as the University of Florida ecologist Peter Feinsinger has noted, an approach that leaves people out of the equation is no longer tenable. The archaeological evidence shows that the natural history of Amazonia is to a surprising extent tied to the activities of its prehistoric inhabitants.

The realization comes none too soon. This past June political and environmental leaders from across the world met in Rio de Janeiro to discuss how developing countries can advance their economies without destroying their natural resources. The challenge is especially difficult in Amazonia. Because the tropical forest has been depicted as ecologically unfit for large-scale human occupation, some environmentalists have opposed development of any kind. Ironically, one major casualty of that extreme position has been the environment itself. While policy makers struggle to define and implement appropriate legislation, development of the most destructive kind has continued apace over vast areas.

The other major casualty of the "naturalism" of environmental scientists has been the indigenous Amazonians, whose habits of hunting, fishing and slash-and-burn cultivation often have been represented as harmful to the habitat. In the clash between environmentalists and developers, the Indians, whose presence is in fact crucial to the survival of the forest, have suffered the most. The new understanding of the prehistory of Amazonia, however, points toward a middle ground. Archaeology makes clear that with judicious management selected parts of the region could support more people than anyone thought before. The long-buried past, it seems, offers hope for the future.

The first Europeans to venture into the tropical lowlands east of the Andes reported seeing rich and populous towns clustered along the Lower Amazon floodplains. Friar Gaspar de Carvajal, a member of the Spanish expedition led by Francisco de Orellana in 1541, wrote of gazing inland upon "very large cities that glistened white." He marveled at one that "stretched for five leagues without there intervening any space from house to house." The landscape itself, Carvajal explained, "is as good, as fertile as our Spain."

By the middle of the present century, however, such reports were being set aside as apocryphal. Anthropologists began arriving in Amazonia in the 1940s, and the scenes they encountered were not at all like the ones described by the early explorers. There were no signs of the hierarchical societies that Carvajal claimed to have found; no evidence of hundred-mile-long chiefdoms guarded by flotillas of war canoes. Only small bands of nomadic

Indians such as the Siriono were present to greet the twentieth-century explorers. Naturalists in the nineteenth century had noted the existence of ruins of large prehistoric settlements and evidence of a long, indigenous cultural history. But modern scholars, eager to develop standards for their new profession, believed what their eyes told them and dismissed the conclusions of their predecessors as unprofessional and unscientific.

Meanwhile, investigators recruited by the anthropologist Julian H. Steward for a Smithsonian Institution project set about documenting the traditions and ways of life of the existing natives. In 1949 Steward published the conclusions in his *Handbook of South American Indians* and distilled from them his theory of ecological determinism, a theory later championed by the Smithsonian archaeologists Clifford Evans and Betty J. Meggers. Evans and Meggers interpreted the primitive culture of the Indians as an adaptation to the low fertility of tropical soil. Presumably because it had been weathered by rain for many millions of years, the tropical-forest land was thought to be deficient in nutrients essential to crop growth. Such infertile land, Meggers argued in a paper of her own, could never support the agricultural needs of large, dense human populations. As a result, she concluded, indigenous Amazonian cultures could never have evolved beyond the most basic economic level of foraging and slash-and-burn horticulture. The "law of environmental limitation," Meggers wrote, was "insurmountable."

By such reasoning any traces of prehistoric civilization—remains of pottery and stonework, signs of early agriculture, large settlements and earthworks—had to be classified as imports from outside the region. They must have come from more favorable environments, such as the arid, temperate highlands of the Andes and Mesoamerica, where the Incan and Aztec civilizations later developed. So confident were Evans, Meggers and their associates of the truth of the theory that they ignored evidence that did not confirm it. Through archival studies the archaeologist Jose Brochado of the Federal University of Rio Grande do Sul in Brazil has discovered that the Smithsonian laboratory produced radiocarbon dates for early Amazonian cultures but that Evans and Meggers rejected them and fought to prevent investigators with opposing views from working in Amazonia.

Ecological determinism gained some currency, especially among natural scientists who actively supported the preservation of the tropical rain forest. To its credit, the theory fostered interest in the Amazonian region and bolstered the conservation movement there. Nevertheless, in the past dozen years a wide range of research has shown the theory to be fundamentally flawed. The reevaluation has awakened archaeology to the dangers of doggedly pursuing theories at the expense of empirical evidence.

One fault of ecological determinism is that it is based on an inaccurate description of the Amazonian environment. Evans and Meggers noted that the geologically ancient soils of Brazil, Colombia, Venezuela and the Guiana countries—Guyana, Suriname and French Guiana—are acidic and poor in nutrients. Because many of the remaining Indian tribes were (and still are) located in hinterland forests that possess such poor-quality soils, the anthropologists considered the areas the typical environment to which Amazonian Indians had adapted over the ages. But such places are not typical of Amazonia as a whole. The region includes extensive tracts whose geology is dominated by limestone and volcanic rocks that, when weathered under tropical rains, give rise to soils rich in nutrients.

Even to characterize all of Amazonia as a tropical rain forest is misleading. Much of the lowland gets less rain than do true tropical rain forests. Although northwestern Amazonia, in Colombia, can get as much as 150 inches of rain a year, with few or no dry months, other, large areas receive half that amount or less, and they regularly suffer droughts for six months of the year. In such regions the soil tends to hold more nutrients because leaching is less intense there than it is in the true rain forests. I must point out that the seasonally dry tropical forests did not result from a reduction in rainfall caused by recent deforestation. Seeds from characteristic tree species can be found in abundance in archaeological deposits dating back thousands of years, indicating that the seasonal forests are an ancient habitat in Amazonia.

Another distinct Amazonian habitat whose potential often is overlooked is the river floodplains. The floodplains are formed of deep layers of nutrient-rich sediments eroded from the Andes. In the dry season the floodplains support a wide array of plant and animal life; during the rainy season the rivers run high, dumping fresh silt onto the floodplains. Counting the beds of present and prehistoric rivers, the floodplains constitute a substantial soil resource. The fertile land is valued today by commercial ranchers, and floodplain backwaters support productive fisheries.

Given the extensive areas of good soil in Amazonia, there is no reason to think the environment would have hindered cultural development. True, good soil is much less abundant overall than poorer soil, but that is the case in most parts of the world. When archaeologists study the rise of ancient Egypt, they locate the agricultural base of the culture on the fertile Nile floodplain; they certainly do not regard the vast desert sands that surround it as any sort of "insurmountable barrier" to development. Why should investigators in Amazonia proceed any differently? Indeed, there is far more floodplain land along the Amazon than there is along the Nile.

On reexamination, the prehistory of Amazonia attests to a long and complex sequence of human adaptations that show no signs of having been unduly hampered by ecological limits. The first traces of human habitation are located in the Monte Alegre uplands, a region of varied geology that lies alongside the wide floodplains of the Amazon mainstream near the Brazilian city of Santarém. Many contemporary investigators considered the tropical forest impenetrable to early hunters, but the reports of nineteenth-century naturalists led me to the site of Caverna da Pedra Pintada; there, in 1991 and 1992, I uncovered a distinctive culture roughly 11,000 years old, as ancient as the earliest scientifically accepted cultures discovered elsewhere in the Americas. The earliest Amazonians were far from primitive: they created large panels of multicolored rock paintings and made fine knives, chipped spear points and scrapers of yellow flint, siltstones and quartz crystals. The remains of their food indicate they were adapted to the tropical habitat, harvesting fruits from the forest and animals from the nearby streams and lakes.

In the millennia that followed, Amazonians established villages along rivers and lakes and began making pottery. The settlements left behind enormous mounds of shells and fish bones, middens so extensive that some have served as commercial sources of lime for more than 200 years. Nineteenth-century workers were aware of such refuse heaps, but ecological determinists of the twentieth century assumed the sites were no more than 1,000 years old. After learning of one site, Taperinha, from an article by a nineteenth-century geologist, I excavated it in 1987. The pottery shards and associated materials were dated via radiocarbon and thermoluminescent methods and shown to be between 6,000 and 7,500 years old.

My discovery of pottery has surprised many archaeologists, because it marks the earliest known record of pottery making in the western hemisphere. Determinist archaeologists consistently resisted the possibility that Amazonia gave rise to pottery-making cultures in early prehistory; they argued that prehistoric cultures acquired their pottery skills from invaders from non-Amazonian centers of civilization. But the dates accumulated by me and earlier archaeologists are indisputable, showing that pottery appeared in Amazonia 2,000 years before it appeared in the Andes and Mesoamerica. Thus Amazonian cultures could not have derived their pottery from outside cultures; it must have been an indigenous development.

Between 2,000 and 3,000 years ago Amazonians developed elaborate pottery styles as well as cutting tools made of ground stone. And they appear to have begun cultivating tropical staples such as manioc and maize, crops still prominent in economies around the world. The evidence for the early diet comes from the discovery of kinds of griddles commonly used today for preparing manioc and from the chemical analyses of prehistoric human bones showing that by 3,000 years ago settlers in the Monte Alegre area were consuming modest amounts of maize. Judging from the drop in the number of fish and other animal bones in the refuse middens of the period, one can conclude that fish and game no longer formed the centerpiece of the prehistoric diet, though they continued to be the main source of protein.

By 1,000 years ago far-ranging chiefdoms, made up of major settlements that relied on agriculture and the harvesting of natural resources, had arisen in several regions of Amazonia. Today such settlements are covered over by the forest and for the most part are inhabited only by sparse populations of Indians, slash-and-burn farmers or ranchers, if at all. But in their time the complex cultures extended across tens of thousands of square miles, an area far greater in extent than that of the Mycenaean society in Greece, Mohenjo-Daro in contemporary Pakistan, or other major pre-industrial civilizations of the Old World.

One of the most thoroughly studied ancient cultures in the region thrived on Marajó, a large floodplain island at the mouth of the Amazon, where I have been excavating since 1983. The eastern end of the island is made up primarily of broad grassy plains that become flooded during the long rainy season. To adapt to the transient swamps the ancient Marajoarans built their settlements and cemeteries atop earthen platforms between twenty and fifty feet high and from six acres in area (for an individual mound) to fifty acres (for mound clusters). Many mounds contain stacks of adobe hearths and house foundations, built one on top of another, and appear to have been occupied continuously from about A.D. 500 until 1100.

Such mound building was not limited to Marajó. Settlements on the floodplains of the Middle Orinoco River, the Amazon River in Bolivia and Ecuador, and on the coast of the Guianas include extensive ancient mound complexes. Investigators such as the geographer William Deneven of the University of Wisconsin and the archaeologist Clark Erickson of the University of Pennsylvania have discovered that the ancient people of Amazonia built other, equally impressive public works: wide roads and causeways many miles long, drainage canals and, in several regions, hundreds of square miles of large earthworks for raising and draining agricultural fields.

What was grown in the fields and mounds of the chiefdoms? From my studies of food remains and human bones and from paleoecological studies of the pollen buried in ancient lake beds, a fairly comprehensive picture of the diets of the complex cultures has emerged. In the 1,000 years before the arrival of Europeans the chiefdoms intensively cultivated root and seed crops, including maize, and harvested fruit from palms and other trees. Although fish and game continued to contribute protein to the diet, seed crops became the dominant food source in several areas. Pollen analyses conducted by the paleoecologist Mark B. Bush of Duke University indicate that some forests were so densely occupied that mature

stands of trees were replaced with maize fields and secondary growth. Industrial crops also were widely grown in the chiefdoms. Cotton, for example, was woven into long decorated tunics later described by the conquistadors and depicted in prehistoric art.

Without question, then, the scene described by Carvajal in 1541 was no mirage. By his time the banks of the Amazon were lined with towns and villages. Judging from the size and number of mounds, house foundations and hearths, the earlier Marajoaran society may have included as many as 100,000 people at its peak. Later chiefdoms appear to have had even larger populations, according to the historian Ulpiano Bezerra de Meneses of the University of São Paulo and Antonio Porro, an independent researcher also in São Paulo.

According to historical accounts, Amazonian chiefs claimed divine descent and exacted tributes of corn and other goods from faraway villages. Incessant wars were waged between competing chiefs to control land and the people to work it. The chiefdoms produced a huge body of material culture. My excavations on Marajó and at Santarém and Monte Alegre have uncovered a wide range of utilitarian objects, from simply made cooking and water pots to many kinds of stone tool. In caves I have even found corncobs, worked wood and fiber ropes. Excavations by earlier scholars in the Santarém region have yielded elaborate jade carvings and finely painted and sculpted pottery. The

Amazonian cultures produced other hard-to-make objects, including terra cotta statues, nearly as large as life, of chiefs and shamans, and jars three to five feet in diameter; the chronicles of European conquerors speak of canoes capable of holding more than sixty warriors. The ancient societies traded extensively through long-distance networks. The scale and complexity of the economic system in some parts of the lowlands gave rise to exchange currency —typically necklaces strung with shell disk beads, according to early European eyewitnesses.

My studies show that the prehistoric cultures of Amazonia could not have been the imports of their Andean or Mesoamerican neighbors. The elaborate pottery styles of Marajó, for instance, are descended from similar styles of earlier lowland cultures, not from highland cultures. Related pottery styles did not appear in the eastern Andes until 600 years after their appearance in Marajó and could well have derived from the Marajoaran culture.

Thus Amazonia, far from being inimical to human habitation, fostered some of the earliest securely dated settlements in the Americas and was the birthplace of a series of complex cultural innovations. The activities of prehistoric Amazonians no doubt radically altered local environments and caused some deforestation, but the societies did not succumb to ecological damage. Instead, the cultural florescence came to an end only with the arrival of Europeans. Disease, warfare, enslavement and confinement in missions decimated na-tive populations on many of the floodplains and destroyed the political integrity of the complex societies. Historical records indicate that by the end of the seventeenth century independent Indian chiefdoms had disappeared. Within another century of acculturation and intermarriage, Indians of the Lower Amazon floodplains had ceased to exist as distinct populations. To escape interference some tribes turned nomadic, abandoning the rich floodplains for less accessible headwaters, where they survived by hunting and gathering and by practicing a kind of migrant horticulture. Indians who remained near the larger waterways were forced to work on plantations and ranches or to extract rubber from the forests. Skeletons from the period bear pathologies showing that the stress of disease and chronic malnutrition took a heavy toll. Perhaps for similar reasons the average height of Indian men today is some four inches less than that of the men of the ancient floodplain.

Few Indians still live on the major floodplains of Amazonia, which are now occupied primarily by whites and people of mixed ancestry. Of the Indians who do remain, many live in abject poverty at the edges of Euroamerican society. The dominant culture has long tended to discriminate against them, treating them as uncivilized savages fit only for unpaid labor. Modern investigators who present Indians as affluent primitive people well adapted to the tropical forest thus do Indians a disservice. In truth Indians have become a marginal people—biologically, geographically, politically and economically—and they are rapidly losing control of their habitats and traditions. In the past twenty years I have seen Indian tribes all but evaporate from some areas as settlers have expanded from Belem, Santarém and Manaus into native homelands.

The cultural history of Amazonia holds crucial insights for government leaders responsible for charting a future for the region. Some workers argue that the only environmentally sound use for the forests is the commercial extraction of plant products such as Brazil nuts. But the proponents of such plans seem to be unaware that some of what appear to be virgin forests were shaped long ago by the agricultural activities of people and in fact were cultivated in prehistory for longer periods than they have been used for extraction in the modern era.

Indeed, some of the most taxonomically diverse and economically important forests of Amazonia are the ones that grow on the rich black soil of abandoned archaeological sites and ancient earthworks. Such sites are rich in valuable trees that earlier inhabitants introduced to the region or that colonized the disturbed habitats on their own. How ironic, then, that proposals for biodiversity reserves classify such anthropogenic forests as purely natural communities. Committed to an extreme interpretation of "nature" and "natural," some investigators have allowed their theories to obscure the complex causes for biological diversity in Amazonia, and thus are prevented from using the lessons of the past to ensure Amazonia's future.

That some forests of Amazonia were subjected to intensive cultivation in prehistory and have since recovered, however, does not mean that it would be fine to cut down the forest. The forest remains an indispensable refuge for myriad species. Moreover, there is a tremendous difference in scale between the kind of deforestation that took place in prehistory and the kind carried out today near mines and large dams and cities. The timber-cutting activities of prehistoric Indians certainly could have damaged the environment; but communities linked to urban and world markets have a greater potential to cause permanent harm, because they can more easily escape the consequences of ecological destruction. The research of Christopher Uhl, a biologist at Pennsylvania State University, has demonstrated that the intensive harvesting methods of big companies inflict greater damage to the floodplain forests than does the modest, continuing harvesting by small-scale landholders.

If vast areas are deforested for long periods and the animals are hunted out or replaced with cattle, the forest may never grow back. Kent Redford, an ecologist at the University of Florida, has cautioned that the forests may not regenerate without forest animals, which eat and excrete seeds, thereby helping them to germinate. If deforestation is temporary and takes place on a small scale, the animals can seek refuge in neighboring forests and return later, when the forest has regrown. Before timber is cut, then, large reserves should be established nearby to shelter the species that will be needed later for reforestation; such areas could protect valuable biological and human diversity and yield much needed income as parks. People who oppose such conservation efforts often claim that forest resources are too valuable not to be harvested immediately. But if the forests are valuable now, they will become even more so in the future.

What the prehistory of Amazonia reveals is that some land in the region could be used more intensively than it is at present. Doing so would not only help ease the growing pressures of poverty but also serve to protect other, more fragile land from development and ecological degradation. As my archaeological work and that of others has demonstrated, some areas of the Amazonian floodplains, as well as certain upland forests, possess nutrient-rich soils and for long periods in ancient times were intensively cultivated with crops such as corn, manioc and cotton. Why not put the land back into cultivation? The cropping patterns and mound and drainage systems of prehistoric times are obvious models for agricultural development. In fact, similar farming methods have been conducted successfully and without fanfare for years in various parts of Amazonia. As Susan E. Swales, a geographer at the University of Illinois at Chicago, has discovered, nearly all the manioc flour produced in the Lower

Amazon comes from individual family fields and processing facilities; a modest agricultural cooperative in Monte Alegre produces large amounts of maize that are exported to cities in Amazonia. In forests and on floodplains near some big cities, small family-owned companies run successful commercial farms of annual crops, spice shrubs and fruit trees. The ethnic Japanese of Belem have conducted such ventures for decades, providing huge quantities of vegetables and spices for city markets. In the Guianas, on the extensive coastal floodplains that bore maize during prehistory, productive rice farms have long been established.

The greatest obstacle to development clearly is not a lack of arable soil; given the immense area of Amazonia, plenty of that already exists. The critical problem is that much of the land suitable for intensive cultivation and accessible to population centers was appropriated long ago for other uses. Some of the land with the greatest potential for production lies on the extensive floodplains of the lowlands and is devoted to commercial cattle ranching. If that land were put back into cultivation by cooperatives and small holders, it could support many more people than it does. Attempts to convert pastures to subsistence farming will require changes in laws that regulate land tenure and taxation, and they doubtless will be met with great political resistance. Nevertheless, the conversion is inevitable. Amazonia is growing ever more populous and urbanized; the territory is moving inexorably from the ecological frontier into the modern world.

The indigenous peoples of Amazonia can play a crucial role in the future of the region. Descended from a great ancient tradition, theirs is the way of life most compatible with the survival of the forest and its denizens, and they possess indispensable knowledge of a wide range of sustainable land uses. Of all the forest residents, however, the indigenous peoples are also the most fragile, and large areas of Amazonia now bereft of them lie dangerously open to destructive colonization. Making sure that Indians survive in their ancestral territories may be the best thing contemporary investigators can do for the forests. The Indian presence is the insurance policy for the survival of Amazonia.

27

"WHERE'S KOISA?"[1]

Lee Cronk and Beth Leech

Although the rate of cultural change has increased tremendously in recent decades, culture change itself is nothing new. One Kenyan people, the Mukogodo, have been changing for decades, first from hunters and gatherers to herders and, more recently, to wage earners, smal-business owners, teachers, and government workers. As Cronk and Leech report, in the process of changing their subsistence they have also changed their language, religious beliefs, and much of the rest of their culture, and gained a better understanding of the world outside their home.

Koisa ole Lengei was born sometime in the 1920s in the Mukogodo hills of north-central Kenya. For the first few years of his life, he lived with his parents and sister in a cave, surviving on honey, wild plants, and wild animals as his ancestors had done for centuries.

The Mukogodo of Koisa's generation spoke a disappearing Cushitic language called Yaaku. In 1969, a German linguist, Bernd Heine, persuaded Koisa to accompany him to the University of Nairobi to teach him the old language. Koisa never came home. After a couple of weeks in Nairobi, he disappeared. Police searches turned up nothing, and Heine later hypothesized in a linguistics journal that Koisa had been killed by criminals.

Our interest in the Mukogodo began with Heine's article. We studied their history, customs, and beliefs, living among them from late 1985 to early 1987 and returning for a short stay in 1992. We went expecting to find a people in transition from the hunting and gathering way of life of Koisa's childhood to one based on raising livestock. Instead, we found a society that had completed the transition to pastoral ways and was beginning a new transition to the ways of Western technological society.

The first transformation occurred about fifty to sixty years ago, when in a period of about ten years in the 1920s and '30s, the Mukogodo changed their economy, language, and way of life from those of the cave dwellers to those of the neighboring

---

[1]Originally published in *The World & I* (January 1993). Reprinted with permission from the publisher.

Maasai pastoralists. It is interesting and sometimes telling to compare that transition to the one occurring today as Western ideas are brought into Mukogodo by missionaries, the Kenyan government, aid workers, and the Mukogodo themselves.

Bridewealth inflation

Koisa's homeland is a dry forest of cedar and wild olive trees covering a small, rugged range of hills. The area's many riverbeds are dry for all but a few days a year, but small permanent springs of clear water are scattered throughout the forest. On the east and north, the Mukogodo hills drop quickly to a flat, dry plain of thorny, flat-topped acacias and bushy succulents; on the west, they taper off slowly into a series of low, rocky ridges covered with short grass and cactuslike candelabra trees. On the south side, the forest ends at a wide plain of grass and small thorn trees that eventually leads to the foot of Mount Kenya.

In Koisa's childhood, the Mukogodo men, hunters and apiarists, ranged through a territory of more than five hundred square miles. Their many beehives—a man might have had twenty or more—and the hunting of hyraxes, small, woodchuck-like animals, provided most of their food. Other favorite species were buffalo, giraffe, eland, and rhinoceros.

Memories of old Mukogodo religious practices are hazy, but the tribe clearly was monotheistic. The Mukogodo believed that within their territory there were several holy places where they could more easily make contact with God. The most prominent of these was Ol Doinyo Lossos, at almost seven thousand feet the largest mountain in Mukogodo. On its peak, people made offerings of honey and other foods to request rain, fertility, and good health.

Although many Mukogodo now look back nostalgically on the pre-twentieth-century cave period, those who are old enough to remember it well describe a frightening world of enemies, raids, murder, and fear. The Mukogodo were militarily impotent, scattered among scores of far-flung caves in groups barely larger than nuclear families. Although they had little worth stealing, they often were the victims of larger Kenyan tribes, such as the Maasai, Samburu, and Meru. Around the turn of the century, one of their thirteen lineages was nearly wiped out by a single Meru raid.

The Mukogodo of today are Maasai-speaking herders of sheep, goats, and cattle. They almost never hunt, although they still keep a few beehives, and their territory has shrunk to less than two hundred square miles. About one thousand Mukogodo live there, along with a few hundred people from other tribes. They live in loaf-shaped, Maasai-style houses made of dung, sticks, and mud, and their diet, like that of the Maasai, includes cow blood. There are many other similarities between the two peoples: Mukogodo beads and draped clothing mimic those of the Maasai; their naming, circumcision, and marriage ceremonies follow Maasai models; and although rumors persist among neighboring tribes that the Mukogodo still speak Yaaku secretly, in fact they all speak Maa, the Maasai language.

The driving force behind the changes of the 1920s and '30s was the quest for bridewealth, the gifts a man must pay to his bride's father. Until the 1920s, few Mukogodo kept any domesticated animals. Wives were not expensive: A few beehives built from hollowed logs were enough to release a girl from her father. Around the time when Koisa was born, things began to change. Large tracts of land near Mount Kenya were appropriated for white settlement, forcing several small groups of Maasai-speaking herders into Mukogodo territory. The newcomers soon stopped raiding the Mukogodo and instead began to marry their daughters, paying livestock rather than hives for wives. Few Mukogodo fathers would pass up a chance to get such wealth, and hives were no longer accepted as payment. Soon, it became clear that without herds, no Mukogodo man would marry.

And many Mukogodo men of that period, Koisa included, never did marry. Some, like Koisa, were the last males in their lines of patrilineal descent, and the original thirteen Mukogodo lineages were reduced to eleven. Other Mukogodo men were able to obtain stock, either by trading forest prod-

ucts like elephant tusks and rhino horns or from the marriage of a sister. Out went Mukogodo women, in came stock and, eventually, wives from other groups.

The change was rapid and nearly total. Most of the caves were located deep in the forest, far from good pasture, and by the mid-1930s most Mukogodo had moved to nearby grasslands and built Maasai-style houses. Maasai-speaking women from the neighboring groups married into Mukogodo and raised their children to speak Maasai rather than Yaaku. The few fluent Yaaku speakers still living today—by our count, there were twelve in early 1987—express sadness and bewilderment that few Mukogodo now remember more than the old greeting of "Aichee!"

Western impact

The Mukogodo transition to pastoralism took a heavy toll on cultural traditions, but, in one sense at least, it was successful: The Mukogodo increased their number and reestablished their ability to pay for wives. The changes were necessary for their survival as a people, but it was not as a group that they decided to change. The unplanned transition came as individuals and families, one by one, began living differently. Changes taking place today in Mukogodo are a combination of this same sort of spontaneous adjustment to circumstances and a variety of deliberately planned development projects.

For some Mukogodo, the current changes amount to little more than what one aid worker calls "trouserization": Most men today wear pants, at least in town, instead of the traditional wraparound loincloth, and some women wear Western-style dresses and skirts. Many adults dress in a Western fashion but know nothing of the outside world where their clothes came from. For other Mukogodo, the new era has brought education, health care, an improved standard of living, and new ideologies. Just a few decades after new neighbors and bridewealth inflation changed the face of Mukogodo society, schools, churches, and jobs are changing it again.

Today's children will be the first generation of educated Mukogodo taught in government schools—often built and paid for by Catholic missionaries and foreign aid agencies. Six primary schools and one secondary operate in Mukogodo Division, which includes areas now dominated by non-Mukogodo people. Mukogodo children attend two of the primary institutions, and a few older boys and young men take classes at the secondary school, which opened in 1986. Many families send at least one son to primary school, and those who live close by often send most or all of their children, including daughters.

Motivational and attendance problems plague both students and staff. Parents rarely take an interest in their children's education, and even the best students may be absent as much as half the time. Many teachers consider Mukogodo a miserable assignment, and some are sent there as punishment for misconduct or incompetency in other, less remote parts of Kenya. Yet a growing number of Mukogodo are being trained as teachers and returning home to work. The headmaster of one of the primary schools is a Mukogodo. Two of his relatives teach at other institutions in the division and a third is attending a two-year teachers college.

Most Mukogodo no longer look for God atop Ol Doinyo Lossos. Four churches hold services in the Mukogodo area, though only three are attended by Mukogodo. The Catholics run the largest mission, with a church, a boarding school, and a clinic. The Anglicans also have a complex of buildings, and their services often are conducted by Mukogodo church officials. American Baptist missionaries have been active as well, setting up a church in town and training a Mukogodo lay preacher. So far, Mukogodo church attendance is dominated by a handful of families, but the ideological influence of the churches is felt even in very traditional households. One man enthusiastically recounted the "Mukogodo" myth of origin, complete with the story of Adam's rib and the fall from grace.

For the most part, foreign aid donors in Mukogodo have avoided large, capital-intensive projects, which have long been out of style in development circles, in favor of smaller, simpler projects. Some of the projects have benefitted the Mukogodo. During the drought of 1985, cornmeal from the United States helped feed many who otherwise might have starved. The Catholic mission in Don Dol runs a clinic that provides free health care to the indigent and next-to-free health care for those who can afford to pay a few cents per visit. The Catholics also have provided dormitories so that some children who live too far from a government school to walk home can receive an education.

Plagued projects

Other projects that may seem small and simple to an outsider become hopelessly complicated in a place like Mukogodo, especially when the aid workers and the local people they are helping have conflicting goals, little communication, and almost no knowledge of each other. Take the examples of the gardening classes and the rain tanks.

In 1986, Action Aid (a British non-governmental organization), the Child Welfare Society of Kenya, and the Norwegian aid agency (NORAD) sponsored the introduction of gardening classes to Mukogodo primary schools. In the words of the local NORAD worker in charge of the project, "We must teach these Maasai something about keeping a garden." What they were taught, it seems clear, is that keeping a garden in Mukogodo makes little sense. Despite the construction of heavy brush fences by project employees, the gardens were regularly ravaged

by livestock and wild animals, and natural rainfall had to be supplemented by huge quantities of water hauled by donkeys. A small garden of potatoes, spinach, onions, and carrots—about ten yards in diameter—required ten gallons of water a day after the seasonal rains had stopped. That may sound like little water, but a typical Mukogodo woman with five children hauls as little as six or seven gallons (about fifty to sixty pounds) of water a day for up to several miles on her back for all her family's cooking and washing needs. NORAD and Action Aid gave the schools donkeys and plastic jerricans to haul water for the gardens, but owning a donkey is too expensive for most Mukogodo families.

In another local project, Action Aid, the Child Welfare Society, NORAD, and the Peace Corps built concrete rainwater storage tanks at several primary schools in 1985 and 1986. The goal was to provide the schools with water for cooking hot lunches and for the use of the teachers, who usually live at the schools. Although the technology and goals of the project were simple, the water tanks did not function as planned. In some cases, the gutters were mounted incorrectly, so that in a heavy rain, most of the water shot past them and onto the ground. At one school, everyone for up to a mile around came to use the water. In a few weeks, the supply that was meant to last the school several months had been depleted. The heavy use and misuse of the new tank finally wore out the faucet, rendering the entire tank useless. A replacement faucet had not been purchased when we left Mukogodo in February 1987, and the situation remained unchanged upon a return visit last year.

The construction of the new tanks also encouraged the schools to be lazy about maintenance of older, smaller tanks they already had, and at least one school ended up with no working water tanks. To make up for the water loss, the school had to obtain further funds from donors to buy another donkey, a cart, a yoke, and several more plastic jerricans to haul even more water two miles from a well.

Simple, small, and apparently promising projects can fail for reasons other than complexity or inappropriateness. In 1985, World Vision, a Christian donating agency, gave a honey refinery to the Anglican Church in Mukogodo. Given the traditional Mukogodo expertise in beekeeping, nothing could seem better suited to the area, yet the refinery never has been used. When Mukogodo have tried to sell honey to the church, they have been turned away. The reason seems to involve tribalism and religious prejudice rather than simple ineptitude. Most of the people involved with the church are Kikuyu, members of Kenya's largest tribe. The Kikuyu privately refer to the Mukogodo and other Maasai-speakers by the biblical pejorative "dogs and evildoers" because these peoples circumcise their sons and daughters. They have refused to accept the honey because they want to

have as little to do with the Mukogodo beekeepers as possible.

Modern Mukogodo

Development aid projects sometimes have helped the Mukogodo in times of need, but they seldom have sparked indigenous efforts to raise the standard of living. In that regard, the Mukogodo themselves are the best development workers of all. Kelasinga LeSakui, the lay minister of the local Baptist Church, has almost singlehandedly started two cooperative businesses. The first, a small cafe that offers tea, doughnut-like *mandazis*, and, on good days, maize and beans, is doing a good business. The other, newer venture is a cooperative chicken coop. Each member contributes a few chickens, and the profits from the sale of eggs and chickens are shared. Most Mukogodo follow Maasai food taboos and find the mere idea of eating a chicken disgusting, so their sales are all to people of other tribes in the nearby town of Don Dol. But a few Mukogodo have begun to feed eggs to their children, and tastes may change within the next few decades.

Both of Kelasinga's businesses were begun without outside funds. Start-up money was supplied by the participants, a disproportionate share from Kelasinga's own pocket (he has a job with the forestry service, which administers parts of Mukogodo territory). The local Baptist missionary, Jerry Daniels, donated a couple hundred dollars for a new chicken coop several months after the cooperative was started, but he insists the original idea was Kelasinga's.

Fifty years after the transition to pastoralism and almost twenty years after Koisa's disappearance, the quest for bridewealth continues to contribute to cultural change and economic development among the Mukogodo. Young men now routinely venture beyond Don Dol to Nairobi and other Kenyan cities and towns for temporary jobs to earn money to pay for wives. Wages are low —most are employed as night watchmen at sixty to seventy-five dollars a month—and wives are expensive. A girl might cost as much as ten cows and other gifts totaling as much as two thousand dollars.

The work trips are taken in order to continue the Maasai marriage customs and social patterns, but what the men see outside Mukogodo and bring home is one of the greatest sources of new ideas and knowledge. A city offers the first glimpse of tall buildings, masses of people, electricity, unfamiliar tribes and races, telephones, movies, businesses more complex than a general store, global politics, and different social customs. Men who have seen the outside world are more likely to allow their children to attend school, and some have gotten ideas from the city that helped them start their own small businesses.

The people of Koisa ole Lengei's generation have seen the Mukogodo way of life change twice. The second of the changes is still occurring, and most of Koisa's contemporaries do not yet understand the new world of which they are now part. Those who still remember the old language rattled on in it hopefully to us in the belief that Koisa went with the linguist to the land of the white people and taught them all to speak Yaaku. Slightly younger people made demands based on that belief. "Write your father," instructed one man in his fifties. "Write your father in America and tell him to find Koisa. Tell him to come home."

Younger Mukogodo, many of whom have worked in Nairobi and are well aware of its dangers, know better. One young father in his mid-twenties, Menye Sapukian LeLeitiko, took charge when an older woman accosted us with questions and accusations about Koisa's disappearance. LeLeitiko did not try to explain that Koisa was dead but merely that Europe, where the linguist was from, is very far from our home in America, and that Koisa clearly is not in America. The geographical knowledge was new to the woman, and it seemed to satisfy her.

LeLeitiko has high hopes for his children, two girls ages one and three. He hopes they get more education than their mother, who did not attend school, and more than the five years of school he attended. Perhaps they will get jobs as teachers and, unlike the women of today, go beyond their homes in the hills. They already know more about the world beyond Mukogodo than their forefathers ever thought possible. They know that Koisa ole Lengei is not coming home.

28

RETURN OF THE KAYAK[1]

Phil Hossack

At the same time that Western culture is sweeping the globe, people around the world are finding ways to rediscover their lost traditions. The Inuit, formerly known as the Eskimo, of the newly autonomous region of Nunavut in the Canadian Arctic, are a case in point. As Phil Hossack explains, the small boat known as a kayak was an Inuit invention and one of the essential elements of their traditional way of life. At the same time that the kayak was gaining enormous popularity among non-Inuit as a form of transportation and recreation, it was largely abandoned by the Inuit themselves. The irony is that it is now being reintroduced to the Inuit community of Pelly Bay, not by an Inuit, but by a woman from Manitoba.

Guy Kakkianiun stands in the living room of his two-storey house, his six grandchildren sprinkled through various rooms, and pauses to consider his thoughts. As a young man, says the 64-year-old in Inuktitut, his only exposure to the kayak was the broken, wooden frames scattered and rotting throughout the community. It was the "old people" who made and used kayaks, he says.

Kakkianiun is a respected elder in the hamlet of Pelly Bay, a fisherman who, like his ancestors, survives by fishing the arctic char that swim from the rivers to the ocean and then back here—220 kilometres above the Arctic Circle. Today, powerboats and nets are the tools of his commercial fishing enterprise and those of his neighbours in this village of 520, mostly Inuit, residents.

As we leave Kakkianiun's home, he notes that the kayak is not the only tradition that has all but disappeared here. Gesturing toward a pair of grandchildren watching television, he shrugs. "I don't know how to speak English," he says, struggling to use the few words he knows. "And my grandsons don't know how to speak Inuktitut."

The tide is rising in the harbour a short hike from Kakkianiun's house. Children are racing along the beachfront

---

[1]Originally published in *Canadian Geographic* 119(1): 58-64 (January/February 1999). Reprinted with permission from the author.

toward a grandmother from Winnipeg who is in Pelly Bay on a mission akin to the proverbial salesman trying to sell iceboxes to the "Eskimos": Victoria Jason, an experienced long-distance kayaker, is here as part of an effort to reintroduce the kayak to Pelly Bay.

Jason's buoyancy, warmth and unwavering patience draws the young. The crowd of kids on the beach grows rapidly from six to almost 20, each jostling for a chance to try the small yellow kayak that is tethered to her wrist. The 30-metre length of rope allows the students just enough freedom to explore new-found skills as Jason wades knee-deep in the numbing cold of the ocean, sometimes for hours.

The kayak was a vital tool in this community about two generations before the children on the beach were born. Martha Ittimangnak, 80, remembers the painful labour of stretching and stitching a skin covering over the spruce frames her husband had created. "We used caribou skin, wet it first to make the hair come off easier," she says through her son-in-law, Vincent Ningark. Sinew from the neck and back of the caribou was used for thread. "It's a lot of work sewing the skins together. When it's wet, it's much harder." The skins and sinew shrank as they dried, making a watertight seam.

Kayak design varied slightly from region to region, but the goal remained the same—to provide a fast, manoeuvrable hunting platform at sea. Its design also allowed tools to be lashed to the deck, including harpoons, sealskin floats, bird spears, lances for dispatching

wounded animals and, in later years, a rifle. Kayaks supported the semi-nomadic Inuit as they moved from one hunting camp to the next, a lifestyle common to coastal arctic peoples from Siberia, Greenland and Canada.

Motorboats began to replace kayaks as southern technology encroached in the 1950s and 1960s. For a time, some hunters still made *umiaks*— open, flat-bottomed skin boats—to check fishing nets or retrieve seals shot from the shore. But it wasn't long before modern aluminum boats with powerful outboard motors prevailed. Today, outboards rule the waterways.

"Back in the old days, the kayaks were quiet, the animals weren't afraid. Now with the boat and motor, the animals are afraid," says Ittimangnak. "The young will not want to use a kayak to hunt; it is slow and time-consuming compared to modern boats." Still, Ittimangnak believes kayaking should be taught to the young people "not for hunting or sports, but to keep the tradition alive."

At the beach, social worker Robert Mathieson happens by and joins in the kayak lesson by keeping track of who is next, adding names to the list as more arrive. Until the mid-1960s, he explains, the stone church and priests' houses were the only permanent structures. The seasons and the movement of animals dictated where the Inuit lived and camped. The people here have "gone from the Stone Age to the computer age in 30 years," he says.

Behind him, Jason shows another child how to grasp the double-bladed paddle and move the kayak in a straight line. She teaches in English with translation needed only when she is communicating with an elder. But sometimes words are not needed. People here often learn by watching, says Mathieson, and when new skills are acquired, they are passed on to someone else.

Great skill was once required to manoeuvre the narrow, tippy, sealskin kayak, particularly while aiming a harpoon or firing a rifle in a rocking ocean swell. Moves like the "Eskimo roll"—righting an overturned kayak without leaving it, or flipping the craft upside down to avoid an oncoming wave, all with a sweep of the paddle—were essential. Modern, fibreglass kayaks are more stable than their traditional counterparts, so Jason can quickly focus beginners on paddling skills. "The kayak knows what to do" is perhaps her most repeated lesson.

To paddle with Jason is to understand why she is in the Arctic. Sweeping across St. Peter Bay, an inlet ringed with islands that shape the hamlet's harbour, we land on a rocky isthmus. All the way there and back, Jason's resonant voice drifts across the bay in song (her kayak is aptly named *Windsong*). Today she explores her way through the chorus of "You are My Sunshine."

Another day, another paddle. The sea is calm. A gentle swell, a gift from the afternoon winds, lifts the kayaks. Marvelling at a mushroom-shaped ice floe, we sit wide-eyed as the "stem," formed by sea water eroding its base, explodes. The cap, tonnes of ice, collapses into the ocean with the rumble of an earthquake. Behind us, red granite cliffs reflect light from the sun as it rises on the northern horizon on its continuous circuit across the July sky. We hug the shore returning to Pelly Bay as Tom Kayaitok, one of the hamlet's tour guides, hunts caribou from his kayak alongside us.

It is a long way from Jason's Winnipeg home and her former life as a Canadian National Railway employee. Jason accepted a buyout when the railway downsized in 1995. "After 28 years of office work, I traded my high heels for neoprene booties," she says. A self-confessed claustrophobic, Jason speaks of freedom and open space, of "arctic beauty." "There's such a liveliness in the wind; the long days," she says.

Jason says she first found peace in the Arctic's solitude on a multi-year paddle that took her and *Windsong* through the Northwest Passage during the summers of 1991 through 1994. Returning to Pelly Bay in 1996, she was intent on a solo paddle around Simpson Peninsula to Repulse Bay. Despite warnings from Pelly Bay residents of "too much ice and too many polar bears," she left for Repulse Bay in the company of Martin Leonard, a kayak designer and adventurer from Valdez, Alaska.

Paddling from Pelly Bay at the start of their adventure, she remembers seeing children waving goodbye from the shoreline. The image stayed. "I stewed about it all winter." All this stewing led to an idea: why not bring a few kayaks to some northern communities and see how the children respond? Back home, she approached Nunavut Tourism and Pelly Bay's recreation coordinator. Neither replied.

In the spring of 1997, Jason called Michael Hart, then Pelly Bay's Koomiut Co-op manager, to check the weather in advance of another trip. During the conversation, Jason stirred Hart's imagination by asking: "How come the kids are playing basketball instead of kayaking in the summertime?" His response was immediate. "Order what you need and I'll look after it."

"By the time she arrived I'd gone farther than she'd anticipated," says Hart. He applied for and received funding under the Northwest Territories Brighter Futures Program and purchased four boats. Then he approached the principal of the hamlet's school. "That way every single student got a chance in the water."

Hart's mind whirled in new directions. He asked Jason to invite adults to her sessions as part of the co-op's mandate to create employment. Kayaking guides might help draw tourists to Pelly Bay, he thought.

Hart prefers to say that Jason "reacquaints people with kayaks," not wanting to offend anyone by saying that she is "teaching or instructing" the very people whose ancestors gave the world the kayak. At the same time, he is not afraid to boast, "instead of hearing stories or watching films (about it), every kid here has had an opportunity to try a kayak!"

Elders too have embraced the modern boats. Hart had to "walk lightly," he says, "because I didn't want to jeopardize anything, particularly because we were bringing up southern kayaks." But the elders accepted the programs, as well as the new fibreglass boats. "Seeing that, the entire community came aboard."

In 1997, the first year, more than 330 residents, half of them school-age children, paddled the boats. There are now 20 kayaks—two 10-footers for the children and the rest between 17 and 18 feet—for tourists and the four guides. Jason says she is committed to at least two more years with the program. "I never intended to start a tourist business," says Jason. But she now sees the children as "the next generation of guides."

While students are developing kayaking skills, few expect them to hunt from the boats. "Kayaking today is to make money," says Kayaitok, whose last name, ironically, means "no kayak." "Especially with the tourists. If we have them every year, it will be good for the community."

Last year Pelly Bay saw its first tourists—11 people from Winnipeg, Toronto, Wyoming and Michigan—who responded to a special promotional offer to kayak in the region with the co-op's Inuit guides. By all accounts, the trips were well received, leaving Hart enthusiastic about the venture's potential for success.

Still, Hart's enthusiasm has some limits: Jason has been unable to turn him into a paddler. When he does venture out he says he feels "overpowered" by the ocean's open expanse. "You realize how small you are out there."

Pelly Bay residents used to complain to Hart about job shortages and suggest ways to bring in tourism.

He remembers joking that if he ever saw a tourist here, he would "stuff and mount him in the hotel coffee shop for everyone to see." In three to five years, he says hopefully, there will be 15 guides running tours, and the handful of Pelly Bay artists will be selling their work to visitors. "And," says Hart, "the whole idea started with one kayak coming north . . . *Windsong*."

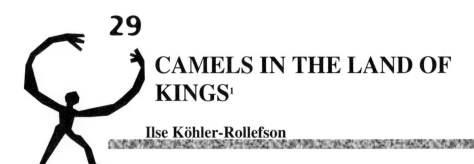

29

CAMELS IN THE LAND OF KINGS[1]

Ilse Köhler-Rollefson

Applied anthropologists work with people around the world to use anthropological methods and knowledge to solve practical problems. One group that may be in need of such help is the Raikas, a Hindu caste of camel breeders in India. Because of changes that have taken place in their area in recent years, the Raikas now face some tough choices between maintaining traditions that may eventually result in the end of their way of life, and maintaining some aspects of their traditions by losing others. As Köhler-Rollefson reports, at the center of both their way of life and their current conundrum is their relationship with their camels.

In February, against a backdrop of several hundred camels spread out to graze, five turbaned men huddle beside an impromptu campfire. Passing around a clay pipe, they discuss the outcome of the previous fair in Pushkar, the west Indian town where each November they sell their annual crop of young male camels. Even the batch of fluffy baby camels playfully darting around does not distract the men from their gloomy thoughts. One, a younger man named Gautamji, finally summarizes their predicament for me:

Look at us. Only fifty years ago we had 10,000 camels—so many that we never even cared when we lost one in the jungle. Twenty years ago, there were 5,000. Now, only about 1,000 camels belong to our village. Ten years from now, or even sooner, we will have no more camels.

The men are Raikas, members of a Hindu caste that specializes in breeding livestock. While they also keep sheep, goats, and cattle, the Raikas are renowned as experts in camel breeding. Inhabitants of the state of

Rajasthan, "the land of kings," many of them take pride in their centuries-old heritage as caretakers of the camel breeding herds that the local maharajahs once maintained to insure a supply of the animals for warfare.

Rajasthan's bleak landscape is dotted with forts and palaces that testify to past glory and heroism. Before independence, the region, which includes the harsh Thar Desert in the west, comprised several kingdoms. The rulers, who belonged to the Rajput warrior caste, were known for their courage, preferring death to defeat. Perpetually involved in internecine battles between their desert kingdoms or in repelling invading Muslim forces, the maharajahs used camel corps and relied on batteries of pack camels to provide logistical support in their arid territories.

The Raikas were one of many castes that provided specialized services to the Rajputs in exchange for their protection. When India gained independence in 1947, the feudal system was dissolved, and most of the royal camels became the property of the Raikas. The military uses for camels have dwindled over the years, but India's security forces still use them to patrol the boundary with Pakistan. Fortunately for the Raikas, however, a new purpose for camels developed: they came to play a crucial economic role as draft power.

In the past forty years, the camel cart has quietly revolutionized transportation in many parts of western India, notably in the states of Rajasthan and Gujarat. Modeled on the oxcart, the camel cart is considerably larger and equipped with used airplane tires that enable it to go anywhere, regardless of the condition, or even the presence, of roads. Ownership of a camel and cart for hauling loads provides a decent livelihood for thousands of people. In India's arid west, camels represent an indispensable source of energy that saves the cost of imported fuel.

The market for camels is still going strong, but the Raikas, who are the main suppliers of camels to farmers and small-scale transport entrepreneurs, are pessimistic about the future. The reason is simple. As traditionally practiced, camel breeding relies on access to large expanses of open, often communally owned land—once amply available for grazing under the formal control of village councils. Within the span of this century, however, Rajasthan has witnessed phenomenal population growth, with the Thar Desert now deemed the most densely populated desert in the world. The consequent expansion and intensification of crop cultivation is one of the factors responsible for eliminating pastureland. Furthermore, some of the Raikas' traditional summer pastures in the Aravalli Hills, east of the desert, have been listed as nature reserves, and access to them has been drastically curbed. Although partly denuded of its dense vegetation, this ancient range still harbors considerable wildlife, including wolves, jackals, and a few tigers.

With grazing land scarce, the majority of the Raika camels are now teetering on the brink of starvation, and their chronic hunger has resulted in a drop in their fertility. Under optimal circumstances, camels are slow reproducers, a female giving birth to one calf every two years. The Raikas traditionally sell off only the male calves, keeping the female calves to replenish the breeding stock, which they regard as an ancestral legacy. At best, therefore, they can hope to have one male calf to sell per year for every four breeding females. But now the situation is far worse, for many of the females experience a delay in sexual maturity, suffer abortions, or die. Reluctantly departing from custom, the Raikas are now also selling off some of the females. These factors, combined with the loss of animals due to disease, have led to a drastic drop in camel holdings. In addition to their economic woes, the Raikas complain that while they were once respected members of the larger community, they are now harassed whenever they show up with their herds. They are bullied by forest officials and even driven away by landowners, who once welcomed them with gifts of food and tea for the fertilizing manure the camels left on the fields.

Having studied camel pastoralists in other countries, I have always been struck by the limited way in which the Raikas use their camels. These self-imposed restrictions make it difficult for them to see a way of solving their current dilemma. To begin with, they follow an absolute taboo against the slaughtering of camels and the consumption of their meat, something that, to my knowledge, does not exist among any other camel pastoralists. When, at a recent conference that dealt with their problems, the Raikas learned that camels are a popular source of meat in parts of the Arab world, they sought, unsuccessfully, an immediate ban on the export of camels to those countries.

This uncompromising attitude may have rubbed off from the taboo regarding cows in the Raikas' Hindu religion. The local Muslim groups take the same stance, however, although they may be less adamant about it. "The camel is our best friend—why should we kill it?" one Muslim commented. Since most of India's Muslims converted to Islam only in recent centuries, this attitude may be a holdover from their Hindu heritage.

In addition, the Raikas are nowhere near exploiting their herds' potentials for milk production. For African camel pastoralists, camel milk is often a staple. But the Raikas milk their camels only sporadically. This has to do partly with the social organization of herding. Unlike other camel pastoralists, who travel as a group, following a nomadic lifestyle and living in tents or other mobile dwellings, the Raikas reside in colonies at the outskirts of villages. Women, children, and older men stay year-round in permanent houses. Only some of the able-bodied men accompany the herds on migration, when they need to search for pasture.

Often traveling more than 100 miles, the herdsmen take no cooking equipment with them—their entire gear consists of a blanket, a rope, and a clay container used as a milking vessel. Often they subsist almost exclusively on camel milk for weeks. But because a herd of 100 animals can be managed by about four men, only a few of the camels need to be milked.

While it is common practice among other camel-oriented cultures to sour camel milk, the Raikas maintain that milk must be drunk fresh without heating, and they refer to various gods and saints who prohibited the manufacture of curd from camel milk. Thus they take no advantage of the possibilities for processing camel milk into longer-lasting products such as cheese or ghee (clarified butter). Occasionally, however, they make kir (rice pudding) or condense the milk of newly lactating camels into an invigorating tonic.

Milking, other than for immediate consumption, is also discouraged by a Raika caste rule that the milk of their animals should not be sold. The feeling is that one should not profit from milk, and that excess milk should be given to the needy. "Selling milk is like selling your children," I was once told by a Raika elder.

Utilization of the products of the dead animal, such as leather and bones, is also taboo for the Raikas and left to members of lower castes. The Raikas do shear their camels for wool on the occasion of the annual festival that marks the transition from the cold to the hot season. The wool is spun by the men and then handed over to a caste of weavers and leatherworkers, who weave it into blankets.

The restrictions the Raikas place on their use of camels should not be regarded as inherently irrational. The taboos once served the Raikas well, given that the herders' express purpose was producing the maximum number of transport animals. Exploiting camels for milk would probably have resulted in longer birth intervals and a higher mortality rate in the young camels. But the traditional taboos may now prevent the Raikas from adapting to changing circumstances.

Shedding old views will be difficult, however. For the Raikas, camels represent more than utilitarian objects. The group's association with this animal is an essential part of Raika identity. According to their mythology, Lord Shiva, one of the three principal manifestations of God in the Hindu pantheon, created the Raikas expressly to look after camels. I have many times listened to renderings of the touching story in which Parvati, Lord Shiva's wife, playfully shaped the first camel from a lump of clay. She then beseeched Shiva to breathe life into her toy, but the living camel proceeded to cause a lot of trouble. Implored by Parvati to stop the nuisance, Shiva then created the first Raika from a piece of his own skin and his sweat.

The camel is also an essential component of a Raika wedding. The bride's dowry includes a number of female camels given to the groom's family. And the bridegroom sits on a camel during critical parts of the marriage ceremony and, from the animal's back, touches the wooden arch erected for the occasion.

The strong emotional attachment of the Raikas to their camels is matched by the depth of their traditional knowledge about all aspects of camel breeding and management. As is the prerequisite for all pastoralists, the Raikas are intimately familiar with the terrain, the seasonal availability of pasture, and the properties of forage plants. Although the herdsmen are illiterate, they keep careful mental notes of their camels' pedigrees and can recite the ancestry and life history of each individual animal they own. They conceptualize their breeding stock as representatives of certain female bloodlines known for particular qualities. Stud camels are carefully selected for desired traits, including the performance of their female relatives. To avoid inbreeding, the stud camels are changed every four years.

For observers from a Western culture, in which farm animals are often regarded as unpredictable and are restrained accordingly, the way the Raikas supervise and control the movements of hundreds of camels without any visible effort is particularly impressive. Much is done by voice, and a simple command can suffice to separate mothers and young into two different groups. The Raikas distinguish their female animals less in terms of milk yield and more in terms of easy milking. In the case of some camels, anybody can just walk up and milk them, while others have a close relationship to a particular herder and can be easily milked only by him. Many will not yield their milk unless their young are nearby, but some will comply when talked to in a sweet voice.

Another important component of the Raikas' indigenous knowledge is animal health maintenance. The Raikas distinguish a long list of diseases for which they have an array of treatments. The scourge of camel breeding is trypanosomiasis, a parasitic blood disease that resembles human malaria. Transmitted by biting flies, it is prevalent especially in years with above-average rainfall. The Raikas can diagnose it from the smell of the camel's urine—a method that has been deemed equivalent in accuracy to examining a blood smear under the microscope. Unfortunately, while the Raikas have several treatments for this disease, none of them cure it, and modem therapeutics are beyond their financial means.

For camel pox, which afflicts mainly young animals, the Raikas have developed a simple, effective vaccination. They take a sample of the blistered skin from an infected animal, mix it with water, and then rub it into shallow incisions in the nose of the animal to be protected. For chronic diseases, Raika animal healers resort to "firing"—they apply a heated iron to prescribed or affected areas. Firing is an accepted practice in Western veterinary medicine, especially with horses, because it is thought to increase blood circulation and thus promote healing.

The Raikas' large body of traditional knowledge and their aptitude in handling and managing camels are invaluable assets, yet these will be doomed to oblivion if camel breeding becomes an obsolete occupation. How can the Raikas adapt to the decrease in pastureland? With more investment, particularly in terms of better veterinary care and provision of fodder, the productivity of the herds could be increased. But such inputs are expensive and seem beyond the relatively meager incomes that can be made from selling male camels.

Because the Raikas have placed so many cultural restrictions on camel utilization, I was not particularly optimistic that they would find a solution to their quandary. I could not expect them to break with their traditions and slaughter unproductive animals or commercialize milk production. Yet sometimes—and especially in India—extraordinary things happen. Not long ago, my field assistant, Ruparam Raika, heard rumors about camel milk being sold in some remote areas of southern Rajasthan and the adjoining state of Madhya Pradesh. Soon after, Ruparam and I, along with my long-time interpreter and adopted brother, Hanwant Singh, made a trip to the area in question and discovered a thriving camel milk market.

The market had its beginnings about twenty years ago when some Rebaris—members of a caste closely related to the Raikas—started selling milk from a few of their camels to the owners of tea stalls. Their desperate attempt to break out of poverty paid off. They established extensive customer networks and expanded their herds accordingly and still could not supply enough milk to fulfill the demand.

In India, milk is an essential ingredient of tea, but also in the Rebaris' favor were the advantages of their product over the competition. The numerous tea shops generally have no refrigeration, and because camel milk can be kept longer without going sour, it wins out over cow and buffalo milk. It is also cheaper. Fear for their market share even induced some cow and buffalo milk sellers to stage a protest and strike against camel milk, charging that it was a human health hazard. In line with scientific findings, however, a number of local authorities supported camel milk as being of good nutritional value.

As news filtered back to the Raikas of the handsome profits being made from camel milk sales, they did not take long to reconsider their staunch resistance to such ventures. They have already submitted a list of camel breeders willing to break with tradition and have requested support in making the economic transition. Two nongovernmental organizations with which I am involved have taken up their proposal and have launched the Camel Husbandry Improvement Project, or CHIP, to investigate how camel breeding can once again become economically rewarding.

Whether camel milk can now do for the Raikas what the camel cart did earlier remains to be seen. A prerequisite for milk production is a better fodder supply. The options that need to be explored are purchasing supplementary feed, rehabilitating communal grazing grounds, and reopening some of the forest areas in the Aravalli Hills to grazing.

For the sake of the economic health of the Raikas, the survival of their camels, and the perpetuation of their traditional knowledge, I hope solutions can be found.

30

OF MUSCLES AND MEN[1]

Alan M. Klein

Although cultural anthropology developed as the study of exotic cultures, more and more anthropologists are working closer to home, often in the United States. In this article, Alan M. Klein describes his experiences studying the subculture that surrounds the sport of bodybuilding. Despite the short distance between his home and his field site, Klein had to deal with many of the same challenges and problems that are faced by virtually all anthropological fieldworkers.

On this night at Olympic Gym—names have been changed to protect people's privacy—the manager, Dave Bigalow, was getting irked by requests for the latest copy of *Flex*. No one had purchased a copy of the magazine, but bodybuilders draped over the glass counters were staring at the photographs of themselves and others in the issues for sale, making snide comments or passing compliments about their compatriots' photos, depending on who was or was not in the gym: "Look at his calves, man. Dude has polio legs."

Sales of gym paraphernalia were brisk, but Dave was tired of it all and was fighting to keep his patience. Standing a few feet away, a middle-aged woman from Tucson shouted shrilly, "Wait'll the girls see these shirts! Oh,

they'll just roar!" Dave winced, then caught my eye. Voyeurs are part of the regular scene at Olympic, but because they often buy items, the management's orders are to deal with them politely. Dave smiled his handsome smile and answered patiently, as the woman's husband pumped the hand of Tracy Pram, one of the elite pros at the gym. Their gangly son snapped a picture of the couple with Pram, who indulged them even though he was visibly tired after a taxing workout.

At the far wall high-powered lighting signaled a shoot—a photographic session. A leading bodybuilding publication was doing an article on a young rising star, and Olympic Gym is a favored location for such features. A small circle had formed around the subject, Ben Fletchworth, who held a forty-five-pound dumbbell in each hand. The audience marveled quietly at Ben's enormous arms. The gleam in his eyes told all that he was perfectly aware of their admiration.

Surrounding this pastiche was the ceaseless flow of bodybuilders as they moved from one machine or rack of weights to another. However haphazard the movements may appear to the untrained eye, they are governed by an absolute order. Each body is the result of a quest for the most effective form of training. Strength is not frittered away, as it might be in a health spa, but economized and calculated. Woe to him who violates the subtle rules of space and time.

For all the seriousness of the gym—posing, training, preparations for contests—there is still time for purely social encounters. Old friends may drop by just to talk about personal matters. Often a bodybuilder will come to the gym to look at the job postings on the bulletin board, or, having just been bumped from a job, one may come looking for some quick money or a place to stay. People often argue publicly in the gym as well, though tonight all was peaceful.

Clearly Olympic Gym is more than an aggregate of bodies. Many people will spend their best years here, their youth consumed with this life. In a world often short of meaning, each of us might appreciate this niche carved out of Los Angeles, one of America's most alienating cities. Some 2,000 people pay annual dues to Olympic Gym,

ranging from the occasional to the twice-daily devotee. And there are thousands of walk-ins, who pay to train for a day, a week or a month. Indeed, after languishing for decades in obscurity, bodybuilding has risen to mass appeal. The award-winning film *Pumping Iron,* released in the mid-1970s and starring a then unknown Arnold Schwarzenegger, sparked national interest, and the subculture began to gain wider visibility. A survey conducted by a Dallas-based firm, Sports Marketing Group, ranked bodybuilding thirty-fifth in a list of the most popular sports in the country, behind tractor pulling but ahead of Professional Golf Association golf, Olympic hockey, men's bowling, and harness racing.

Aside from its popular appeal, what makes bodybuilding and its culture a suitable topic for serious anthropological research? Four years before this night at Olympic Gym, in 1979, I had embarked on what would be a seven-year field study of elite bodybuilding. Why would I devote seven years of observations—and, more pointedly, why would my colleagues support my work with grants, leave time, their own time as manuscript referees—when the subject of study is such a seemingly familiar, and to some, trivial, aspect of contemporary American life?

Traditional anthropology has focused on the exotic, deriving insight about the human condition by exploring what seem to be the cultural extremes. Such boundary conditions define and locate contemporary Western culture in a broader context, and in some cases the new perspectives even help us reconceptualize the familiar features and transactions of our own society. Anthropology has frequently offered exotic perspectives on such topics as the criteria for membership in a group, the distinctions between insider and outsider and the language and symbols for preserving those distinctions, the sacred and the profane, and the major roles that people play within a community. Recognizing that a penis sheath in one society is functionally similar to a powerful motorcycle in another is hardly profound, but it does confer a kind of deepened understanding of the home culture as well as the foreign one. And, in a large sense, that is just what cultural anthropology seeks to accomplish.

When the tribe under scrutiny is a part of the home culture, a further step is needed before the study can make its traditional contribution as anthropology. The anthropologist must make the familiar exotic. In their 1986 book, *Anthropology as Cultural Critique,* George E. Marcus and Michael J. Fischer, both of Rice University, refer to the process whereby one can look at one's own culture as "defamiliarizing." They write: "Disruptions of common sense, doing the unexpected, placing familiar subjects in unfamiliar, or even shocking, contexts are the aims of this strategy to make the reader conscious of difference." Defamiliarization is initially carried out only to reintroduce the subject later as familiar. In my ethnographic description of bodybuilding I decided to emphasize the

foreignness of the subculture. Thus a typical night at the gym takes on a slightly carnivalesque aspect.

Although my project was a social and psychological study of bodybuilding, it was at the same time a study of masculinity. Masculinity as it is seen in the bodybuilding world stands in stark contrast to the view of masculinity of the average American or even the average weight-training enthusiast. And yet, despite the foreign, even bizarre picture of masculinity that bodybuilding affords, the constellation of traits swirling at its core is startlingly familiar. Men view their bodies as instruments or in forceful and space occupying ways. Without sinking into essentialism, I would argue that every man determines his sense of self through some sort of response to the biological emblems of masculinity: possessing a penis and male musculature. Bragging about the size of grants won or the numbers of publications one has is the same thing, in this respect, as showcasing a massive chest with a skin-tight T-shirt. Nevertheless, the male body can be a chimera, a psychologically defensive construct that looks invulnerable but really only compensates for self-perceived weakness. Olympic Gym is home to many who, like the Wizard of Oz, labor day in and day out to construct an imposing exterior that will convince others of what one is not convinced of oneself. Whereas typical men are different from the bodybuilders I describe and analyze, bodybuilders are, without a doubt, like all men. And although I may seem critically oriented in my interpretation of this subculture, I am at the same time critical in my analysis of mankind—all men, including, perhaps particularly, me.

Primates long ago learned not to stare at unfamiliar or threatening creatures. Most people glance quickly, then look away, when a troop of bikers cruises the streets—unless they are willing to face a confrontation. But people do enjoy staring unnoticed; Americans are a nation of voyeurs, who take a perverse delight in almost anything outside everyday experience. I am fortunate that my own voyeuristic impulses are professionalized. I am an anthropologist, and my job is to stare, or as we in the field prefer to think of it, to observe.

I had prepared myself for the subculture of bodybuilders, much as one would prepare for a visit to an uncharted human population along the upper reaches of the Amazon, and I was perfectly ready to sit and stare blatantly at a group of unfamiliar, large men. I am trained in techniques of observation, experienced in imposing myself on others (anthropologists are seemingly a presence to be tolerated), and I was convinced there was no behavior so grotesque or outlandish that I had not seen, read or heard about it.

Still, when I crossed the threshold of Olympic Gym, I froze, utterly confounded by the scene before me. Here was a room full of people pulsating with what seemed like some mysterious, erotic force. The collective grunting and

swaying, the seminudity and the hyper-intimate preoccupation with the body proved disconcerting. Where was the public face of Olympic? Why were its inhabitants not self-consciously monitoring their behavior in accordance with modesty? It later became apparent that there is a highly ritualized set of behaviors in which everyone is expected to engage. But to me the whole place seemed caught up in one large orgasm, and in that first encounter I dreaded interrupting the erotic encounter between human, mirrors and metal.

"Can I help you?" The voice of a man behind the desk filtered through my concealed terror. I turned, frantically trying to think of something to say, some reason for being there, for standing like an idiot, looking at this scene. How embarrassing. Had I been gawking for an eternity?

I'm safe if I buy something. "Uhm, I'll take one of those T-shirts in medium—make that large." *Consume a bit of their culture: tribute to the brigands.*

"What color?" The voice came back.

Damn, I don't know what color. I don't even want one.

"Blue," I said.

It was not until I had paid him that I remembered why I was here. I was to meet with Swede, the general manager of the gym, and thus the gatekeeper of this society. Such is the power of ethnographic gatekeepers that they can—within seconds—unhinge a project that took months to put together.

If Swede did not give me permission, my study would be over before it began.

"What kind of study do you want to do?" Swede asked, looking over the letter I had sent him a few weeks before. Having expected just such a question, I decried the second-rate position of the sport, the erroneous myths, the need to address whether or not the subculture was in fact compensation for shortcomings. On and on I went in a torrent of reasons and rationalizations that were clearly excessive. But Swede calmed my concerns by saying it would be just fine, and he even would personally introduce me around. I slumped back in my chair while Swede answered a knock at the door: I relaxed for the first time in weeks.

Two young men, Sam Behrouze and Ken Jefferson, entered the office. Ken closed the door and greeted Swede warmly. I recall thinking that their affability was not what I expected from bodybuilding superstars. In my preparation for the field study I had, against my better professional judgment, anticipated some conclusions—many of which, with a fine poetic justice, turned out to be nonsense. Bodybuilders, I had imagined, all suffer from Clint Eastwood disease, a disorder that constricts the facial muscles and jaw and makes everyone speak in short, choppy sentences. The malaise induces quick tempers and subsequent violent deaths.

The upcoming Mr. Universe contest had prompted Sam's visit. Reflecting the hyped atmosphere at Olympic Gym, Swede chided his brawny companion about whether he had done anything to get ready for the contest, now a scant two weeks away. All three laughed, since it was common knowledge that few trained harder than Sam, who was favored to win his weight class. Before the hilarity subsided, however, and before the grin left his deeply tanned face, Sam reached for the waistband of his sweatpants and pulled them down to his knees. Replay: Man One asks a seemingly legitimate question about training, and Man Two pulls down his pants. What was going on?

All eyes, minus mine (I winced), focused on Sam's massive thighs covered by skin so devoid of fat that, like parchment, it was almost transparent. I did not know whether to excuse myself, for fear that some very private thing was about to take place, or to lean in for a closer look. I began rummaging through my briefcase. Swede and Ken, however, looked attentively at Sam's thighs and nodded appreciatively. They were impressed, which, it finally occurred to me, was some sort of answer to Swede's question.

Sam, still smiling, turned fully to face me. His pants somewhat restricted his movement, but he shuffled over to me and waited for my comment. I think I said something clever like, "Piece of cake. You've got the contest in the bag," but I had not the slightest idea of what was good or bad, just that bigger was probably better. Sam still did not pull his pants up; instead he flexed his thighs, looking at them the way someone would watch a prize German shepherd go through its repertoire of tricks. As his veins strained to break through his skin, it dawned on me that he was merely making a visual report of his condition. Nothing sordid or questionable, just an athlete asking for confirmation of his readiness. I had been at Olympic Gym less than half an hour and already had twice been forced to come to grips with my biases and preconceived notions of the subculture. This was all the more alarming, because for years I had been working out in gyms. I was, nonetheless, unprepared for Olympic Gym.

The study was supposed to be easy and familiar, but my complacency was shaken by several disturbing revelations about myself. I vowed vigilance. Each day I would patiently watch as the members of the gym came and went, talking to people as their time permitted. Each interview was logged and its high points noted, and after a month I grew more confident that things were at last beginning to take shape. The old sense of successfully anticipating my conclusions came over me again.

Such a dangerous state of mind can, if undetected, lead a fieldworker to miss data or misconstrue them. For example, one subject that came up often—though indirectly—was the generalized and militant homophobia at Olympic Gym. The bodybuilders mocked one another by imitating gay men, accused one another of homosexuality and generally behaved in ways insulting to homosexuals. And although such joking is standard locker-room humor, it was particularly vicious at Olympic Gym. On one occasion, after an effeminate-acting man had walked into the gym to work out, the man I was speaking with said in a voice loud enough for everyone to hear, "Alan, if there's one thing I can't stand, it's seein' queers work out here." Other members chimed in, and the man in question hurriedly left.

Shortly afterward, I was working out in a gym near my apartment when I realized that that gym was primarily gay. I decided to interview people around me informally to determine how they felt about being involved in a sport whose upper echelons so roundly condemned them. Some members introduced me to the two gay owners of the gym, who laughed when I told them what people at the top thought of gays. "Almost everyone over there at Olympic Gym has been 'made' by us 'fags,'" said one facetiously. "Come to our party in a few weeks and you'll see them [the top bodybuilders] all there," said the other.

They went on to chronicle the long-standing and widespread incidence of relations between gay men and bodybuilders, casually listing name after prestigious name and connecting anecdotes with them. I left sensing that, confirmed or not, those views represented serious contradictions within the subculture, and I had again erred in forgetting to avoid preconception and the face value of my data.

Back at Olympic Gym people denied any systematic involvement with gays. "Look, there are as many gay plumbers as gay bodybuilders," was the way one put it. But now I was alerted to denial and wondered whether a core issue in the bodybuilders' self-identity was involved. By the time I learned to read the signs, people would become more open with me about that subject.

Two weeks later I was again forced to encounter my naïveté. A highly respected and widely recognized bodybuilder told me that he had at one time taken steroids—synthetic male hormones condemned by the sport's establishment—but that he no longer used them. He claimed he had mastered the intricacies of diet and training, and he earnestly gave me a detailed account of his diet and regimen.

A few days later I noticed a group of bodybuilders huddled over the latest issue of *Muscle and Fitness.* The bodybuilder in question, flanked by his friends, was poring over the magazine and commenting on each picture. When he reached the advice column he writes, he read—in the high-pitched voice of an adolescent—a question sent in by a teenager from Pontiac, Michigan, concerning what steroids were best to take. Laughter all around. He then read his reply: "Don't destroy yourself. If you want a physique like mine, don't take shortcuts." Convulsing laughter. "I didn't win my titles by taking drugs. Chemicals are no substitute for hard work." He would have continued, except that he was wiping tears from his eyes, and his friends were on the floor.

I concluded that being gullible is, oddly, an integral part of the anthro-pological field experience. Initial data pose a threat if one takes them at face value. Cultural understanding comes in direct proportion to the anthropologist's ability to discern and play with—that is, interpret—behavioral contradictions. To assume people are telling the truth is naïve. There is no reason to think that toying with the fieldworker out of playfulness or boredom, or leading him away from potentially damaging information, is not in the "native's" mind. And since anthropologists are rarely in a position to determine the accuracy of their data, they often rationalize its validity or lay a thick smoke screen around it to prevent questions from arising.

Doing fieldwork in one's own society, where one presumably shares the language and (partly) comprehends most of the behavior, is a blessing—at least, compared with working in cultures in which one is a complete stranger and totally ignorant. But it is also a curse. If the validity of my data in a "home" subculture was now a legitimate concern, I had to question all fieldwork done by all anthropologists for all time. Was it really reasonable to assume that such people, or any others, would, at the sight of an anthropologist, spill their secrets, revealing their deepest contradictions? Why would they not have some fun with an outsider? At last, I hoped, I was coming of age at Olympic.

The Charles Atlas advertisements of two generations ago continue to encompass the psychological and mythical appeal of bodybuilding. Recall how a bully kicks sand in the face of a ninety-seven-pound weakling, who then buys the Atlas secret, develops a physique in his bedroom and two weeks later avenges himself on the bully. The attraction of that ancient ad lies in the promise of change, in the transformation of self from unimpressive and vulnerable to heroic and imposing, with psyche following form. The dancing mirage of a better life worked out in the privacy of one's bedroom is hard to squelch, making the lure of such a promise, such a transformation, seductive. Bodybuilding is an acceptable means of doing something about yourself. The dead-end job, the unfulfilled relationship or the generalized angst may continue, but you can control the last vestige of your ever shrinking empire: your body.

All too often, however, even bodybuilding and weight training do not bring about the desired transformation. Narcissus fell completely in love with his own reflection. The bodybuilder longs to but cannot. Inside his head is a mind that harbors a past: a scrawny adolescent or a stuttering child who forever says, "I knew you when. . . ." The metamorphosis is doomed to remain incomplete.

But becoming a bodybuilder at Olympic Gym masks more than a generalized insecurity. The path taken by those wishing to accrue flesh has much more to do with gender insecurities. To be male has, in our culture, been linked with dangerous and demanding occupations and roles, such as frontiersman, soldier, policeman and doctor. But the

golden era when "men were men" has passed, and the powerful roles traditionally the exclusive province of men have vanished, weakened or are no longer gender specific. Accordingly, many bodybuilding men have clutched to themselves the only trait that gives them hegemony over women: their size.

The tragic irony is that for all the elements of hypermasculinity the bodybuilder has gathered around himself, he is still left with the gnawing, unclear sense of being no closer to a genuine understanding of his place in society or of what it is to be a man. Thus bodybuilding, as a response to gender insecurity, can prop up some of the most reprehensible male characteristics—misogyny, homophobia, hypermasculinity—in particularly dramatic fashion.

One of the most insightful and critically self-reflective accounts of the life of a bodybuilder written to date is Sam Fussell's *Muscle: Confessions of an Unlikely Bodybuilder*. The educated son of academics, Fussell felt vulnerable and physically threatened growing up in New York City, and so to him, finding Schwarzenegger's autobiography in a local bookstore came as a revelation:

A glimpse of the cover told me all I needed to know. There he stood on a mountain top in Southern California, every muscle bulging to the world.... As for his body, why, here was protection, and loads of it.... He had ... used the weight room as his smithy. A human fortress . . . to keep the enemy host at bay.

One can readily understand the association in Fussell's mind between the muscled body and safety; but one has to ask, Why this response to a threatening environment? Why not learning a deadly martial art, carrying a weapon, or taking part in community activism? Fussell gives an indirect answer a paragraph later, when he mentions that the reason he did not practice tae kwon do was that "one had to actually engage in street combat to use it." Muscles were preferable because "I would never be called upon actually *to use* these muscles. I could remain a coward and no one would ever know."

Fussell's refusal to take on something that might make him inflict physical harm or risk it himself provides an insight into his own masculine identity. Such a refusal could constitute a critical stand on male aggression and reflect a softer side that would prefer not to bully. But Fussell uses the word *coward* to describe that state; thus a masculine linguistic form transforms gentleness into cowardice. Yet Fussell has unwittingly uncovered the ambiguous perhaps even progressive role that bodybuilding plays in gender construction: mediating between the desires to be gentle yet not to be seen as a coward.

As bodybuilders and anthropologists struggle valiantly with conflicting images of masculinity, mainstream America looks on but only from afar. I remember a day at the gym when I saw a young mother in tennis whites pedal up on her ten-speed with her two-year-old child strapped into a seat on the back of the bicycle. She stopped and looked into the gym while still seated on her bike.

I noticed that she seemed attracted to the sights and sounds of Olympic, and I casually made my way to the chain-link fence that serves as a back wall while the gym is open. "I honestly don't know why I came down here, except that I've heard so many things about Olympic Gym and muscle men. And, since we were on the beach . . . well, I decided to have a look. Josh is enjoying it, too." She declined my invitation to come in and have a closer look, obviously feeling more comfortable on the "safe" side of the fence. Her tentative manner, controlled smile and slightly uptight eyes told me all I needed to know. But she stayed, riveted by the shadowy world she had only heard about and seen on television.

A bit later I noticed one of the gym's larger men move toward her as if to strike up a conversation. She saw him and flitted away, poise intact. Part of her wanted to stay, to talk with this alien; and he had overcome his awkwardness around women enough to approach her. But the mother was too threatened and the bodybuilder too self-conscious to make it happen. The bear of a man who had gone to the fence to say hello or perhaps play with the child leaned against the chain-link, staring at the spot made vacant just a few seconds before.　Mainstream and marginal had just missed . . . again.